Recovering American Catholic Inculturation

Recovering American Catholic Inculturation

John England's Jacksonian Populism and Romanticist Adaptation

Lou F. McNeil

LEXINGTON BOOKS

A division of
ROWMAN & LITTLEFIELD PUBLISHERS, INC.
Lanham • Boulder • New York • Toronto • Plymouth, UK

LEXINGTON BOOKS

A division of Rowman & Littlefield Publishers, Inc.
A wholly owned subsidiary of The Rowman & Littlefield Publishing Group, Inc.
4501 Forbes Boulevard, Suite 200
Lanham, MD 20706

Estover Road
Plymouth PL6 7PY
United Kingdom

Copyright © 2008 by Lexington Books

All rights reserved. No part of this publication may be reproduced, stored in a retrieval system, or transmitted in any form or by any means, electronic, mechanical, photocopying, recording, or otherwise, without the prior permission of the publisher.

British Library Cataloguing in Publication Information Available

Library of Congress Cataloging-in-Publication Data

McNeil, Lou F., 1939–
  Recovering American Catholic Inculturation : *John England's Jacksonian Populism and Romanticist Adaptation* / Lou F. McNeil.
    p. cm.
  Includes bibliographical references and index.
  ISBN-13: 978-0-7391-2453-6 (hardcover : alk. paper)
  ISBN-10: 0-7391-2453-6 (pbk. : alk. paper)
  1. Catholic Church—United States—History. 2. England, John, 1786-1842. 3. Christianity and culture—United States. 4. United States—Church history. I. Title.
  BX1406.3.M39 2008
  282'.73—dc22   2008022046

  eISBN-13: 978-0-7391-3049-0
  eISBN-10: 0-7391-3049-8

Printed in the United States of America

∞™ The paper used in this publication meets the minimum requirements of American National Standard for Information Sciences—Permanence of Paper for Printed Library Materials, ANSI/NISO Z39.48–1992.

Table of Contents

Preface	vii
1. *Introduction*	1
2. *Life, Vision and Response at the Margins*	19
3. *Living and Leading within a Minority*	55
4. *A Vision from the Margins*	89
5. *Dimensions and Directions in the Ecclesial Response*	157
6. *Conclusion*	217
Appendix: *The Constitution of the Diocese of Charleston, 1839.*	235
Bibliography	249
Index of Names	257
About the Author	261

Preface

Every book is the work of many people. This volume only attempts to convey the vision and soul of John England's creativity. To the degree it accomplishes that it is because of John England's clarity and persistence in the thought he left recorded. There are other specific people to whom much is owed. I cannot name them all. Most importantly is Jeanne Evans, my wife, who read and reread the manuscript, but whose questions were even more helpful for the clarification of my own thought. Christopher Kauffman of the Catholic University of America read the original and rough manuscript and made a number of helpful suggestions. Judy Jones, a Religious Studies major, patiently typed a considerable part of the original draft and Brian Fahey, the archivist for the Diocese of Charleston generously and readily assisted me. I also am indebted to colleagues, who through the years have corrected, stimulated and supported me in my interests in religion in the American context, particularly in the cases of Bishop England's ecclesiological contributions and C.S. Peirce's pragmatism. One of those has been Clifford Grammich of the Rand Corporation, who earlier was an associate with me at the Glenmary Research Center. Their insights and objections have driven and forced me to be clearer and more convicted as regards the importance for American religion of C.S. Peirce's semiotics and theory of inquiry. Elements of Peirce's thought are certainly seen in John England's practical thought and leadership. It is with John England as a case study that I find deeper commitment to both Peirce's philosophy and England's inculturating impulses. Another factor behind this study was my experience in Mississippi from 1966-1976. It taught me that we can find much insight and wisdom at the margins of society's mainstream. Finally, several years on the board of the U. S. Catholic Mission Association followed by two years as associate, and then director, exposed me to an array of missiological thinkers whose scope and vision of life greatly expanded mine. While they were usually among the marginal in the Catholic ecclesiastical world, it was among them the gospel seemed most clear. Finally, thanks to the graduate and ministerial students who have expanded my knowledge during the past ten years.

Chapter One

Introduction

When I first began the study of theology in the 1960s my generation's interests were in the development of a "North American" Catholic theology. It was to be a theology self-consciously cognizant of and a proponent of the traditions developed in North America subsequent to its colonization by the Europeans. It was firmly believed that this tradition would enrich and enliven the Catholic tradition. While a similar thrust was also to be found among Protestant theologians at the time, the Catholic focus often centered on a retrieval of the "Americanist" Catholics and their predecessors, Bishops John Carroll and John England. Mid-twentieth century developments in the United States, especially the Kennedy era and the experience that Catholicism was on the precipice of mainstream influence in the socio-political American tradition generated excitement and ambitions unlike those earlier in the Catholic community. These factors, along with the emergence of lay Catholics 'doing' theology and the recent conclusion of Vatican II and its reforms were the background to those who embarked on graduate studies in theology at the time.

Among those working and leading the efforts in this direction in the latter 1960s and early 1970s were Dr. Harry McSorley and Dr. Gregory Baum, whose work in ecumenism and the social sciences was groundbreaking for North American Catholics at the time. Dr. Baum and Dr.

McSorley's work and their institution, the Institute for Christian Theology (ICT) at the University of St. Michael's College in the University of Toronto, directed their efforts at the preparation of lay people for theological leadership in Catholicism. These were the magnets that attracted and shaped many of us as we sought our voice as both Catholic and North American. Yet, what I discovered there was far more than I expected. Classroom exchanges in courses offered on the University's campus by Marshall McLuhan, Bernard Lonergan, Northrop Frye, Emil Fackenheim, Walter Principe, Oliver O'Donovan, Richard Longenecker and Paul Ricoeur, among others, swept up the students and focused the issues and agenda for a theology that could engage a "new" generation of young Catholics, who sought to integrate their faith and the cultures of North America.

My early reading, nonetheless, was quite flatfooted—being too literal, too rationalistic and too theological—and consequently quite thin and superficial. While the "American theologians," Jonathan Edwards and the New England divines, articulated the religious experience and imprinted it on the theological character of the North American churches, there had been a tendency to overlook other less explicitly theological dimensions in American religiosity. The American philosophical and political traditions, most particularly C.S. Peirce, A.N. Whitehead and Thomas Jefferson, became more and more pertinent, it seemed, to an understanding of how Catholicism was capable of being American. Along with these remarkable people I discovered various American Catholic thinkers of the nineteenth century that led to strains of thought and activity that were not easily sorted out or well organized. Theology alone could hardly explain what was "going on" when people such as Jefferson, Peirce, Bishop Carroll or Bishop John England of Charleston, South Carolina, were studied solely from a philosophical, political or theological perspective.

In this study, John England will be the person on whom we will dwell at length. The reason is that he is a revealing case study. In what follows we will see in John England a series of extraordinary initiatives. Theology and ministry alone cannot explain them. Nor is biography a sufficient explanation. While we will examine John England's biography, and in such a case Karl Marx's insight about the role of our biographies as a large factor in understanding our activity, the social, economic, and political influences must be given far greater place than often is the case. There are organizational and managerial factors, demography, economic populism, ethnic, class and inter-personal dynamics that also come into play. In this study, the focus is a case study that will allow us to observe clearly such a confluence of events and their centrality. The case of Bishop John England illustrates the interplay of chance and orderliness and their role in the emergence of creative leadership.

History done "from below" may often overlook the glaring reality that individual leaders are often and unquestionably the ones who set social agenda. Surely they participate in their culture and contexts, but culture and contexts are inextricably linked to the actions of individuals. What I suggest in this study is the leader is indeed nurtured by social factors but that "from below" studies ironically mirror a macro-study approach insofar as they can offer largely generalized and sweeping glimpses of the historical forces at play. In the end, such studies *suggest* a myriad of valid conclusions to the reader that, in their own turn, may be far from compelling evidence. An illustration of this was my experience in Mississippi during the latter half of the 1960s. The significantly different patterns that existed in the housing, educational opportunities, health standards (availability of clean water and a sewage system), work demands placed upon laborers, and general living conditions of African-Americans that was evident from plantation to plantation led to stunningly different living and social conditions. Such differences could often as not be traced to the remarkably different circumstances from plantation to plantation. The owner of each plantation bore surprisingly large responsibility for the very development of individual tenants and their lives. A collection of such data itself can lead only to tentative and general conclusions. In short, "from below" history confronts the same issue as that "from above." In what valid way can we suggest our evidence supports substantially the conclusions that have been drawn? My claims here are modest. John England leads and influences people and events. In a case study of John England, we will see personal traits, institutional proclivities, historical circumstances, social location, political and economic dynamics that yield a few insights about the dynamics of leadership and the major impact it can have on the thought and actions of others. The final suggestion found in our case study will be a picture that will have been drawn that sheds light on the manner in which leadership is chosen both to lead and to be followed, the vetting processes that can undermine genuine leadership and the community formation that follows upon leadership, and the strategic role leadership plays in the establishment of a direction in the public's agenda.

Inculturation

Since Vatican II Catholicism has given much more mature thought to the issues of religion and culture. The ferment of the last number of decades has crystallized the realization that theology cannot simply be statements of universal, a-cultural truths. Catholic theology prior to Vatican II had become almost exclusively identified with *Roman* theology—that is the officially proscribed theological methods and expressions. Such a narrow range in theological research and expression had not, of course, been the long tradition of Catholicism. Nevertheless, during the papacies of Pius IX (1846-1878) and Pius X (1903-1914), the theology of Thomas Aquinas was assigned the role as the norm. (Although theological expression was not absolutely restricted to Thomism, it was nevertheless offered as the norm, yet allowing for concomitant scholastic thought in the Franciscan and Jesuit traditions.) Prior to these later nineteenth century efforts at a normative philosophy for Catholic theology, Rome had entertained somewhat diverse theological visions. The most notable was the theological explanation of sacramental causality offered by the Thomistic School, instrumental efficient causality and the Franciscan occasional causality. Nonetheless, the Thomism and neo-scholasticism urged during the papacies of Pius IX and Pius X *largely* prevailed until the years leading up to Vatican II.

The momentum during those years leading up to Vatican II was breathtaking and by the conclusion of Vatican II in 1965, the Catholic Church swirled with new theological and pastoral initiatives. The work in the fifty or so years that had led to the Council by scholars such as P. LaGrange in biblical scholarship, Y. Congar in historical research, M. Blondel, J. Marechal, J. Maritain and G. Marcel in philosophy, H. DeLubac in overcoming the dualism of the natural and the supernatural, and J.H. Newman in the awareness of development was critical.[1] Each provided significant support to the new paradigm that emerged at the Council.

Often overlooked, however, were those leaders and theologians who had operated at the margins of the theological and institutional mainstream, the missiologists. They were equally as important, if less credited. There was Joseph Schmidlin, the German missiologist, who in 1931 emphasized Catholic evangelization was to proclaim the "word of God" in contradistinction to "planting the church" (whose proponents could rally around the Frenchman, A. Semois). This latter missiology, for all its validity and communal and ecclesial focus, nonetheless too often rested satisfied with establishment of the institution. There was the American, Louis Luzbetak, who in the 1950s and early 1960s introduced American Catholicism to the cultural and anthropological dimensions of ministry and theology. In more recent years, the Catholic Theological Union missiologist, Robert Schreiter, has produced a corpus that spans an impressive expanse of cognate fields and whose method brings better focus to the nature of the way theology, as local theology, requires great sensitivity, not simply to cultural differences, but to *praxis*, semiotics, folk wisdom and ritual activity. In other words, theology and ministry must have diverse disciplinary methodologies.[2] The work of creative contemporary missiologists and the leadership of Pedro Arrupe set the patterns for reflection on the issues of communication of the Gospel and ministry for our time.

Pedro Arrupe, S.J., the Superior General of the Society of Jesus, wrote to the Jesuits throughout the world in 1978, and introduced the notion of *inculturation*. It clarifies and focuses the issues of a global church in a way hitherto not recognized. In the letter Arupe writes,

> Inculturation is the incarnation of Christian life and the Christian message in a particular cultural context, in such a way that this experience not only finds expression through elements proper to the culture in question, but becomes a principle that animates, directs and unifies the culture, transforming and remaking it so as to bring about "a new creation."[3]

American Catholicism's reluctance and hesitancy, prior to Vatican II, to embrace the notion embodied in the concept of inculturation was reflected in the frequently stated understanding that American divergences from the classical Euro-Catholic expression were due to "American exceptionalism." This would fall by the wayside following the Council. Until Arrupe's suggestion of *inculturation* as a theological category, American Catholic acceptance of the separation of church and state, religious liberty and ecumenism were all attributed by the Roman theologians to a pragmatics that as a minority such acceptance was strategically, not theologically, permissible. Now it had become clear that a universal, abstract theology above or transcending culture would never do. Arrupe had both affirmed the traditional approach to Catholic theology as eminently *sacramental*—that is, mediated in and only in the cultural and personal contexts in which it operated—and that the gospel could be carried by any number of cultural expressions. Neither culture nor an individual community could validly be permitted to capture and possess as its own the Christian message. Not even the ancient European Catholic expression—that is Roman, could any more than any other single church in the *communio* privilege its expression of the Christian experience. While the gospel message was *always and necessarily* communicated culturally, specifically and personally, it was not restricted to a singular expression. This will be the paradox of which Cardinal Dulles was so aware when he warned that even the good systematician must at times be willing to depart from the system.[4] Logic cannot imprison the revelation. Anything less would be to presume the wisdom of God.

In the chapters that follow, we will recognize that the principle of *inculturation* operated long before it was given expression by Arrupe. The usefulness of the concept is that it clarifies experiences and expressions that we encounter when we gaze backward into the Church's history. John England practiced inculturation, even if the term had not been coined.

The key point of *inculturation*, of course, is that something "new" necessarily emerges in every cultural context when the Christian message is encountered. The principle behind *inculturation* was present in various ways during every period of history, even if canonical proscription, talent or temperament often marginalized or obfuscated its theological or ministerial expression and implementation. An American theology had been present unavoidably at the very arrival of Catholicism and the establishment of the colony of Maryland. The leadership of Archbishop John Carroll in the early years of the republic, Bishop John England and Gabriel Richard, S.S., pre-date the so-called "Americanists" of the later half of the nineteenth century, but they represent the same impetus to communicate *effectively* the message of the gospel to a given historical and cultural context. Throughout the nineteenth century others, with little doubt, obfuscated their instincts as they walked the thin line between creative, effective pastoral responses and the constrictive mandates placed on their ministry by institutional leadership far removed from the *communio fidei* and the *sensus fideles* of the new republic. The much broader energy directed by so many during the nineteenth century to

Catholic schools, support of the wage worker, and acceptance of the separation of Church and State characterized even the most cautious of American Catholics.

What this book addresses is the authentic, but creatively faithful response of American Catholic theology when a hierarchical church and the democratic tradition meet face to face. The currency of this question rests in objections made by some Catholic historians and theologians that an uncritical enthusiasm for Enlightenment values permeated the accommodations of the "Americanist" strains in nineteenth century Catholicism.[5] These critics suggest that these accommodations were, in fact, a process of assimilation that represent the failure of religious conviction in the face of secularism and rationalism. The thesis of this case study is that such an assertion misconstrues what occurred.

Bishop England: Case Study for Inculturation

Bishop John England, of Charleston, South Carolina, 1822-1842 is our case study of inculturation of Catholicism in American society. We will set out to demonstrate that he was *not* uncritically motivated by Enlightenment values, but that he opposed, as any contemporary critic of the Enlightenment would, its presuppositions regarding individualism, rationalism and secularism. Instead we will observe that his temperament, talent, and consistent situation as a member of a minority in one manner or another throughout his life energized Bishop England's efforts. Because of these factors he was especially alert to his surroundings. Firstly, this awareness made him much more cognizant of opportunities for new responses to old situations since, as someone at one or another cultural-political margin he personally had, and as a leader within the minority offered, a different perspective. His social and geographical locations and the perspectives he gained as a consequence prompted a native impulse for him to see and understand things differently.

As a Catholic in Ireland, he was different certainly from the colonial occupiers, the English, but every bit as importantly his family and he differed in education and background from the typical Irish of the time. His exposure to Protestantism and a broader culture was significantly different. As a bishop in Charleston, South Carolina, he was an outsider both as a Catholic and as a bishop. As the bishop of Charleston he was an outsider to the bishops of larger, affluent and more prestigious dioceses. Finally, as a bishop in the slave-holding South, he lived during years of increasing polarization that led to the Civil War. In each instance, his social location is a major consideration in the views and insights that directed his actions.

A second consideration is that his motivation was neither that of a revolutionary nor an Enlightenment thinker. His attitude was never that of someone eager to attack the principle of authority as such, secular or religious. He was critical of the Archbishops of Baltimore because of substance and policy differences, never because of the office and its authority. Catholicism never represented an authoritarian, undemocratic, anti-modern or institutionally insensitive faith for John England. Rather in the classical theological manner, his *Works* demonstrate a retrieval from the church's own resources, the very seeds of the modern world that he found around himself in the nascent American democracy and for which he argued. He allowed that modern European democracy was birthed in the monastic tradition and in the Catholic city-states such as Venice and San Marino.

A third consideration in our use of John England as a case study for inculturation is that he was never proscribed, censured or forbidden by the papacy for the serious and effective actions he took to inculturate Catholicism in the American republic. On the contrary, his skills were both recognized and used by the Vatican as attested by his appointment as the Nuncio to the Dominican Republic, while serving as the innovative bishop of Charleston. This is particularly notable since the Vatican at the time had full knowledge of his administration of the Charleston diocese through the use of a constitution about which several of his brother bishops in the American hierarchy had not hesitated to complain and condemn in letters to the Vatican.

This study of John England will examine 1) the character traits of a gifted individual and the manner in which those traits were shaped by a minority experience that may well be repeated frequently in persons with similar or analogous backgrounds *and* 2) the pragmatic and practical theological expression that we will also associate with a pastoral or theological esthetics that reflects effective ministry and leadership situated within a scale of community that is face to face. The bureaucratic ability at good organization, insofar as it is necessary to any and all organizations, was exemplified in John England very well. However, the bureaucratic insofar as it may mean "living slavishly or largely by the book" was not. Our interests in John England will not be simply in what he accomplished but more importantly in what he represents. We will argue as we move through the book that even if his diocesan constitution did not survive his death, nevertheless, he illustrated the characteristics and directions that we should expect to find among creative leaders today in similar circumstances. Similar temperament and talent exists today in potential leaders. Therein rests his continuity. It may be that the Church is less capable to draw on such talents today. Theologically, sociologically and individually the grace or charism that existed in John England exists now in our pool of leadership resources. No more than any individual in history was John England God's unique and sole gift. God's love for his community and people is not so restricted. The confluence of social location, human scale, talent and temperament creates leadership that grace builds upon. We see that in John England. Our conclusion, among others, will be "Why is this less so today unless it has to do with a process that either culturally or ecclesiastically vets out God's Spirit that "blows where it will" in favor of more comfortable candidates.

Earlier research and work by Patrick W. Carey, *An Immigrant Bishop: John England's Adaptation of Irish Catholicism to American Republicanism*,[6] highlighted many points upon which I am dependent. This study, however, will address more fully the ways in which John England's thought moves beyond his Irish Catholicism and will trace more fully his development in relationship to Jacksonian democracy and the significance of his position as the bishop in a small diocese spread across three states and among a Catholic minority in a sea of Protestants. From another perspective, we will also see that John England did not simply represent Irish Catholicism, since a position most characteristic of him, his Anti-Veto stance, was at variance with much of the Irish hierarchy and people.[7] Yet, it is quite important to recall that his Anti-Vetoist position arose from his personal and familial character and were given their particular form during his Irish years.

This study, however, will observe the theological issues surrounding some ideas that found their maturity in his American years. These are the pastoral and theological issues during his episcopacy in the United States. that will be central to our concern as they were to his. This concern hones in on England's efforts that we will attempt to tease out and use to clarify the notion of inculturation and the creative and pragmatic dimensions of his ministry. An urgency exists to this task because of recent and increasing critiques of positions like John England's as "modernist" and passive accommodation to Enlightenment rationalism and individualism that were virtually non-existent when Carey's dissertation and book were published. These critiques will receive attention here since they represent an understanding of ministry and church that inhibits reasonable pastoral pragmaticism that could issue in a joyous spontaneity many come to hope for in ministry. Among the issues criticized have been that England's 1) republicanism lends too much support to American individualism, 2) support of the separation of Church and State vacates Catholic or Christian influence on the development of the nation's public agenda, and 3) promotion of religious liberty severely hinders a proper concept of legitimate religious authority and integrity of truth as objective. Whereas others would understand the *subjectivity* of truth to mean truth is found and verified by the knowing subject while the *relativity* of truth would mean that truth is whatever the knower's mind or thought believes it to be, on the other hand, objective truth would be static or in the words of Vincent of Lerins, "The same always, everywhere and among all." Such truth, some would suggest, is to make pretense to "know as God knows," that is, perfectly.

In the chapters that follow we will see that Bishop England recognized the nature of the religious, anthropological, social, political and esthetical dimensions that required his attention if he were to communicate effectively the gospel message in his world and context. Our thesis is that he genuinely and reflectively *inculturated* (even if he would not have known the term) the gospel message and was not simply assimilated into the secular rationalism or its attendant individualism that characterize our era more than his. He was adamant as regards the seamless nature of faith and reason and he reflected a vigorous commitment to a republicanism that acknowledged the primacy of the republic itself, and not a vague and ideological heralding of individual liberty.

During the period 1822-1842, and even to the present, several points were clearly a challenge to the Catholic tradition in the United States: 1) American Christianity was stringently *christo-centric and Bible-centered*. It was intensely personal and stressed an immediate encounter between the individual and God without need of the mediation either of sacraments or priest. Catholic notions of tradition, community, mariology, the communion of saints and ritual would require attention. 2) Anthropologically religion and the ground of the Spirit's authority were understood to some extent as *egalitarian*. Consultation would be necessary if one were to lead effectively in the American context. 3) Religion was socially localized in the congregation, just as decision making was. The inclusion of *congregational* elements along with the connectional ones had to be acknowledged and incorporated in the structure of the church. 4) Politically religion required some degree of reconciliation between the larger democratic-republican experience as egalitarian and simple, populist and non-aristocratic in expression in both liturgical style, substance and *polity*. 5) Finally, American religion celebrated, particularly as it underwent changes as a consequence of the two Great Awakenings, affective and expressive dimensions of the conversion experience and worship. Preaching and worship services themselves would require a firm foundation on *personal experience and affect*. Grand rituals might have their place in New York, Boston, Charleston or Philadelphia, but the aristocratic overtones suggestive in Catholic and Episcopal churches' liturgy, clerical dress and prescribed etiquette toward leadership were alien to the religious demeanor that found expression in the United States.

We will see in this study how John England responded throughout his lifetime to his environment in his attempts to address these and similar religious expectations of his people. He made every effort to bring the people into active leadership roles during public worship. He established consultative structures with his diocesan constitution. He set decision making at both the parish and diocesan level with procedures for representative meetings of lay leadership in both forums. Unfortunately, in the instance of the American characteristic of significant affective expression in worship, Bishop England did not particularly distinguish himself by any effort to bring such qualities to bear in Catholic worship. No doubt this may have a great deal to do with not only his Irish background, but also his family's and his own social location.

What I consider central to creative leadership, but certainly not a universal law or rule, is the paradox that such leadership often encompasses an experience at the margins (in some manner or another), but at the same time arises from some personal or familial role that affords leadership training *within that community of marginality*. Such a paradox is not unfamiliar within the religious community. Sociologically, leadership, even rebellion, seldom emerges from the desperately poor. Some aspiration and/or opportunity needs to awaken vision. Both opportunity and aspiration are found, if you will, at the margin as well of the marginal community. The prophets of the Hebrew Scriptures often exemplify precisely this and the Synoptics certainly make precisely this point about Jesus of Nazareth. Jesus, as some biblical scholars attest, was not utterly impoverished. He was gifted and experienced to the degree that he could inspire with his words and had the freedom and time to do so. This study presumes that an insightful and talented person at the margins has often a much wider perspective (both intellectually and emotionally) than does one at the center and closely involved with the policies of the center. In John England we will recognize that such a situation and personal temperament will play a strategic role. One of our conclusions, then, will be that *should we look for creative leadership today, our focus should be primarily, but certainly not solely, upon talented individuals who in one way or another have experienced life and its difficulties at the margins.*

Chapter two, therefore, deals with Bishop England's background and the circumstances of his appointment to be bishop of Charleston. In Ireland, he was a Catholic child educated in Protestant schools. Particularly interesting will be the less prestigious seminary he chose to attend, Carlow, rather than a more prestigious alternative, Maynooth. Personal traits seen in his predispositions in the selection of friends, ecclesiastical and political will be observed. The Irish cultural and personal experiences and traits will be followed and discussed as they appear in his early career. They will be seen to be significant factors that shape his mind and spirit in preparation for the emergent world of republican enthusiasm and the adaptation to a new culture he will undertake in the United States. Most importantly for our understanding of his Irish period will be to realize that he was a colonial in an English-occupied Ireland. As a diocesan priest and editor, furthermore, he was in a Catholic minority with his opposition to the Irish bishops' support of the Vatican's political accommodation with the British Crown's desire for a veto over episcopal appointments in Ireland. When he arrived in the United States as the Catholic bishop of Charleston, he shepherded a population spread over three states (North and South Carolina as well as Georgia) that hardly constituted a large sized Protestant congregation in Charleston at the time. If the man had time on his hands, after an extremely active life in Cork, it was be because the appointment offered him the luxury to visit and know people face to face. It was a time when the administrative office of being bishop would not burden him. Instead, he was free to mingle beyond the circles of his own church's membership and consequently learn a great deal from and make an impact upon the larger world.

In Chapter three we will see the challenges the young bishop faces in his sparse and far-flung diocese. These challenges prepare him for a ministry and vision much larger than the membership of his own ecclesial community. He will become a public figure far beyond the boundaries of his church constituency. At the same time, he will address quickly the obstreperous lay trustees at parishes within the diocese, successfully managing to balance the interests of a democratic lay leadership and his church's sensitivity to keep in check the principle that "he who pays the piper calls the tune" so as to protect the church's proper vocation to prophetically challenge its members. His first Pastoral Letter adroitly addresses ecclesial authority with sensitivity and clarity. He asks for obedience on the basis of the common good even as he assures and insures the people that his leadership will be consultative and leadership roles will be provided them in the development of the new diocese. He will almost immediately embark on writing, therefore, a constitution for the administration of the diocese. The intellectual acumen of the bishop will be recognized in the defense and rationale offered for the government of a Catholic diocese under a constitution. In this his political and interpersonal skills sparkle. An institutional scale that allowed continual personal contact on matters of practical concern, without a doubt, played an important role in his leadership development and success.

Chapter four will address in detail the process of approval, the principles involved and the specific articles of the constitution under which the Diocese of Charleston operated. It is in the close observation of the bishop's actual, not imputed beliefs, which we find in rich detail the leaven of inculturation that he introduced into the American Catholic tradition. He moved beyond Archbishop John Carroll's American republican vision in that he was both a populist and an intellectual. (John Carroll was certainly no lightweight intellectually, but we can be certain he was not in the least bit likely to be a populist or in the company of the "popular man.") England will delineate Catholicism as the source and fountain of Western republicanism. He will confound the pamphleteers with his "common man" approach and style, even as he relishes the company and principles of a tradition that at the time directed many caveats at the very egalitarian values he espoused and promoted.

Chapter five addresses the pastoral (programmatic), practical (interdisciplinary grounded application) and ecclesiological dimensions found in Bishop England's ministry and theology. We will see that any system given to his thought must bend to the pastoral and practical without abandonment of core principles. We will suggest this follows the Aristotelian and Thomistic appreciation for the theoretical and the practical modes of reasoning. The former constitutes the principles while the latter constitutes specific application of principle to specific case. The theoretical, therefore, is the basis without which practical judgments cannot be made. It is the same dynamic as motivated canon law through the centuries. Equity in law serves as a principle by which law is appropriately applied in concrete situations giving due respect to the law, the lawgiver and just application or imposition of the law. Interpretation or hermeneutics is key to the just administration of law. As examined in this chapter, for John England much of this is explicitly realized, although much of it remained implicit in his understanding and application of authority and law. The chapter will also review the way in which his pastoral approach comes to bear on topics as diverse as religious liberty, republicanism and individualism. We will see a marked similarity between the pragmaticism of C.S. Peirce and John England. The similarity is that their pragmaticism is neither organizationally, functionally or programmatically oriented (all rather short-term goals), if by that we understand that accomplishment or closure drive their actions. Rather they both essentially place the common good, community and equity (embracing both short-term and long-term goals or final causes) at the center. Both hold positions of pragmatic realism encompassing an approach that understands the health of the community must be rooted in a holistic understanding of the factors that compose our social and individual lives. For both, the "really real" surpasses things or that which has individual existence and embraces the reality and importance of reality of individuality found in its context or community, its esthetics. Religious belief is in "real things," but England, as Peirce, recognized the somewhat fragile nature in our ability to demonstrate the validity and stability of such knowledge of the "real" if it was not rooted firmly in a community's experience over time. For C.S. Peirce knowledge was discovered in the community's endless inquiry after truth. For England it was the Catholic Christian community's tradition: that is, articulations, activities and arts that were bequeathed to the present generation. Both emphasized a pursuit of rationality must be *in a communal context*. Both emphasized the roles of faith and reason in the search. Finally, as we see in the fourth chapter, both appreciated the importance of esthetics and affectivity in the pursuit of truth. What the fourth chapter suggests is that within the elements of the American tradition there has been an extraordinary confluence of Enlightenment rationality with the communal world of the popular arts and religious affect that recalls the medieval appropriation of Aristotle in a grand synthesis.

Louis Hartz in his perceptive analysis of the American socio-political scene, *The Liberal Tradition in America*,[8] suggested that the U.S. experience struggled because of the absence of a significant political-philosophical influence from either the social or communal vision of the Middle Ages or the radical social critiques of the second half of the 19th century. He believed the United States was founded and endured almost solely in the liberal Enlightenment tradition of individual liberties and rights. While Hartz saw the social dimension absent and dismissed as being formative the anti-liberal Tory influences that remained but a remnant in the American tradition, he did not sufficiently highlight the social vision of the Whigs who also played their role in the development of the American Republic. Recent renewed interest in C.S. Peirce as well as a look at the often forgotten Catholic intellectual tradition in the United States may have helped Hartz discover more than a pertinent libertarianism in the American Republic. Chapter five is indebted, therefore, to the work of Philip Pettit and a school of political philosophers who have re-examined the roots of American republicanism that they contend cannot be dismissively assigned as simply an expression of liberal Enlightenment individualism and rationalism. Such clichés can no longer be sustained in light of scholarship and research that clearly underscores the common good among the republican responsibilities that grounded American republicanism.

The final chapter will review what can be learned from the life and practice of Bishop John England and highlights the value found in John England as a case study for an apologetics of inculturation. In that review we come to appreciate the relationship between theology's theoretical and practical dimensions. John England's Catholic principle and pastoral practice will be recognized as the reasoned risks that issue in a Catholic *esthetics* that characterize his theology of ministry. He creates the beautiful and the good by threading together the theoretical and the practical. His diocesan constitution, leadership style, missiology, ecumenism and, most importantly, nascent views on Catholicism and the separation of Church and State represent a virtual symphony of elements that together make for a newer and different Catholicism, but Catholicism nonetheless. From his storehouse he wove together both the old and the new. The final chapter assesses, therefore, the importance of the bishop's efforts at American Catholic inculturation from the standpoint that those efforts mirror well the manner in which church and culture interact to the benefit of both. Putting aside a dualist understanding of religion and modernity that would be in some manner or another intrinsically at odds, England's thought and practice, along with Peirce's more nuanced thought later in the century, suggest more properly that inculturation rejects a sectarian response to modern science, personal freedom, democracy and pluralism. Inculturation is driven by a principle of esthetics: *The pastoral artist paints an image in the beloved community that is one of the beautiful and the good because pastoral sensitivity creates order, peace, and equity.* Sewing principle and practice together yields such a community, beautiful relationships, good science, a pacific democracy and a happily (if relatively) content society that is participative.

Bishop John England wed together well an inherent tension between the individual and the community. Practical wisdom and a thorough grounding in the reality of pastoral experience assured him that an individual is neither free nor morally accountable until that individual is assured "freedom from coercion." This was the eminently republican value that underwrote John England's constitutionalism and his support for the separation of Church and State. This study refers to critics who suggest that such republicanism was merely the assimilation of secular, privatized, rationalist values of Enlightenment individualism. Relying on John England's writings and recent scholarship on the actual nature of 18th and 19th century republicanism, the position taken in the study is that, to the contrary, Bishop England successfully models inculturation and that inculturation is a successful model of evangelization. The bishop engaged the culture and chose not to flee it. This is relevant to any critic who suggests the processes and efforts at the inculturation of the Christian gospel simply hands the religious agenda over to secular interests. Non-engagement, the bishop believed, would more likely vacate the process of agenda setting. It may be, on the other hand, that history often appears to teach us that not to dialog with the larger society may simply be an unconscious ruse to cover triumphalist or imperialist designs to dominant culture.[9]

Notes

1. P. LaGrange. *Evangile selon saint Jean.* (Paris: Etudes Bibliques, 3rd ed., 1927). Y. M. Congar. *Divided Christendom: Principles of Catholic Ecumenism* (London: G. Bles, 1939). M. Blondel. *L'Action* (Paris: Alcan, 1893). H. De-Lubac. *Surnaturel,*(Paris: Aubier, 1946). J. Marechal. *Le Pointde la depart de la*

metaphysique (Paris, Alcan, 1922-1926) and J.H. Newman. *Essay on the Development of Doctrine* (1845 ed. J.M. Cameron ed. London: Penquin, 1967).

2. Joseph Schmidlin, *Catholic Mission Theory* (Techny, IL: Missions Press, 1931). Louis Luzbeak, *The Church and Cultures* (Maryknoll, NY: Orbis Books, 1988). Robert Schreiter. *Constructing Local Theologies*, (Maryknoll, NY: Orbis Books, 1985).

3. Cited in Peter Schniller, S.J. *A Handbook on Inculturation* (Mahwah, NJ: Paulist Press, 1990), 6.

4. Avery Dulles. *The Craft of Theology* (NY: Crossroad, 1992) on the problem of method, 41-52 and 69-104.

5. "Americanism" was condemned by Pope Leo XIII in *Testem Benevolentiae* in 1899. The condemnation was not directed to any specific person or persons but to certain "modern" ideas, such as those condemned by Pius IX in the *Syllabus of Errors*. The particularly 'American qualities' concerned were 'individual freedoms' such as associated with religious liberty and democratic notions in the face of authority, particularly in the areas of religious beliefs and practices.

6. Patrick W. Carey. *An Immigrant Bishop: John England's Adaptation of Irish Catholicism to American Republicanism* (NY: United States Catholic Historical Society, 1982).

7. The Anti-Vetoist movement in Ireland, of which John England was a major leader, opposed an accommodation by the Vatican that would have permitted the English Crown to veto the appointment of Catholic bishops in Ireland. Most of the Irish hierarchy, for practical, political reasons, supported the proposal.

8. Louis Hartz. *The Liberal Tradition in America.* (NY: Harvest/Harcourt Brace Jovanovich, 1955).

9. Brian Stone. *Evangelism After Christendom.* 111ff.; Michael J. Baxter. "Catholicism and Liberalism: Kudos and Questions for *Communio* Ecclesiology," *Review of Politics*, 60(1998) 4, 760. John Witte, Jr. *God's Joust, God's Justice: Law and Religion in the Western Tradition.* Grand Rapids: Eerdmans, 2006, 10. Stone and other theologians have suggested that Christianity was in some manner or another subverted in a substantial way during the Constantinian period and having accepted the agenda of the "secular" world the gospel message had no room in the public exchange. This subversion, for Stone, is highlighted in the American tradition of the separation of Church and State much as it is for the Catholic priest Michael Baxter, "Catholicism and Liberalism," because the public agenda "excludes the Christian understanding of freedom . . . [that individual's purpose and society's obligation is to act] in accord with one's destiny and final purpose—to see God." 746. Such a teleology and its consequent agenda is "left at the door" when secular society sets the agenda. The Constantinian narrative Stone suggests (and Baxter presupposes) has resulted in a merging of the church and the world and with it the triumph of secularism (Stone, 17). Such a thesis must, in some manner, be understood to suggest an

expansion of a well-worn Pietist lament, if not self-congratulatory assumption, that Christianity had lost its way and effectiveness for more than the thousand years preceeding the Reformation. In Baxter's case a primitive radicalism or pietism along the order alternately of Dorothy Day and of the Radical Reformation searches for a restoration of "original purity," perhaps associated with the primitive church in *Acts 2*, although certainly not in the following chapters in *Acts*. Such pessimism about Christian history is difficult to reconcile with the biblical assurance that "another Paraclete" (Jn. 16:7) shall abide always with the church "against which the netherworld shall not prevail." (Mt. 16:18) John England and untold numbers of other laborers in the vineyard appreciated and availed themselves fully of the surfeit of grace a generous God has showered throughout the ages on individual believers, their communities and the general public, secular and religious.

Chapter Two

Life, Vision and Response at the Margins

> Christianity, with its doctrine of humility,
> of forgiveness, of love, is incompatible with
> the state, with its haughtiness, its violence
> its punishment, its wars.
>
> Tolstoi.

Appointment to an American See.

Ambrose Marechal, the Archbishop of Baltimore, was overtaken with frustration when news arrived from Rome of the division of his diocese. His request that the Vatican create a diocese to the south of Baltimore, preferably at Charleston, had developed quite differently than he had hoped. As early as June 1819 Cardinal Fontana of the Congregation for the Propagation of the Faith (The proper title for the Congregation in the period after Vatican II became the *Congregatio de Evangelizatione Gentium*, The Congregation for the Evangelization of Peoples. Hereafter it will be referred to as the Propagation Office.) had indicated Rome's interest in creating two sees: one at Richmond, Virginia and the other at Charleston, South Carolina. The entire situation had arisen because Marechal, with his suffragans concurring, had suggested to the Propagation Office that the tumultuous disorder caused by the trustee controversies in the churches at Norfolk, Virginia and Charleston could best be solved with the ready presence in each region of a bishop. However, it was one, not two dioceses that they saw as feasible.[1]

Marechal's jolt at the news on that Monday morning in July 1820 had been further compounded when the worst suspicions of the past months were confirmed. Two Irishmen who had never set foot upon the soil of the United States were to be the bishops.

The Archbishop had done everything possible to avert this turn of events. When news first reached him of the possibility of two Irishmen being appointed to the sees, he decided immediately to make an effort to prevent the appointments. He appointed Benedict Fenwick, an American priest, as his vicar-general for the Carolinas and Georgia. With deftness Marechal then wrote Cardinal Fontana at the Propagation Office that the horrendous schism had been brought under control by Fr. Fenwick. He added that should Fenwick not be named the bishop of the new diocese it was feared that "great difficulties and even schism [would] break out in a serious way."[2] Yet for all his efforts, it came to this: On Monday morning, July 8, 1820, Rome buoyantly notified Archbishop Marechal that he was to have two new suffragans: in the diocese of Charleston, John England of Brandon, Ireland, and in the new diocese of Richmond, Patrick Kelly of Kilkenny, Ireland. Patrick Kelly remained in Richmond for approximately a year before apparently giving up and requesting appointment elsewhere. He was subsequently appointed to the Diocese of Waterford and Lismore in his native Ireland. His efforts in Virginia are generally accounted as insignificant. In this respect his episcopate served to underscore Ambrose Marechal's fears that an Irishman would be ineffective in dealing with the trustee problems. The trustees were frequently Irish immigrants or of Irish extraction. Just as frequently the pastors in the trustee controversies were themselves also Irish and supportive of the trustees.[3]

The flawed relationship between John England and Archbishop Marechal clearly existed long before England even had an opportunity to meet his metropolitan, Marechal. The archbishop had made clear in his own mind several principles that prevented his extension of a warm welcome to the two new bishops. He believed, first of all, that persons appointed to the episcopacy in the United States should have been born there, or at least have served in the country for several years. He also believed that Rome should have consulted the American bishops before making new appointments to the U.S. hierarchy. Charles Hebermann gives a sympathetic appraisal of Marechal's motives in objecting to Roman appointments to U.S. dioceses without consulting the American hierarchy. He overstates his argument, however, when he suggests "in some cases, the prelates sent had proved to be unacceptable to the government of the United States, because they were subjects of the power with which the U.S. had recently been at war."[4] This was precisely the concern dealt with in the initial appointment of a Catholic bishop to the United States. At the time Benjamin Franklin clearly stated the U.S. government's mind when he reported that the Congress stoutly refused to make a suggestion to the Vatican who would be or would not be acceptable. Guilday saw this as a bid by Marechal for power in his request to Rome that episcopal appointments be checked with the American bishops. Guilday believed Rome wished to deny Marechal the right to exercise such power over ecclesiastical appointments in his province.[5]

A more sympathetic interpretation is that Marechal merely wanted the right for the American bishops to make presentments on future episcopal appointments. Congress, Marechal reported to Rome, felt that such advice and concern was beyond their competence. Moreover, since a significant proportion of the difficulties encountered with clerical discipline in the United States, and in particular with regard to the trustee controversies, involved Irishmen, Irish appointments to the American episcopate appeared to him as both untimely and impolitic.[6] Marechal's judgment in each instance is generally unassailable. John England himself would eventually espouse each of these same views. Certainly in Marechal's mind, the dismal efforts of previous Irish-born bishops in the United States indicated a lack of firmness in dealing with diocesan administration. Furthermore the appointment of Irishmen in Richmond and Charleston where the trustees were baiting French-born pastors would have appeared to be a concession to the rebellious trustees—and of course a defeat for the Archbishop.[7] However, in 1820 before he had any indication of the reception awaiting him from his brothers in the American episcopate, John England (and Patrick Kelly) was already the object of a cool and aloof response over which he would have little control. He unwittingly symbolized foreign intrusion into American Catholic Church concerns.

An Irishman with a Difference

Had Marechal been able to foresee, however, the directions that one of these disappointing new episcopal appointments would take, he would have appreciated the irony in his initial reaction. In time many of the reservations of Marechal's first response to the appointments of England and Kelly would be directed by Bishop England at the Archbishop himself. England eventually saw the Archbishop as a Frenchman out of tune with the American spirit and, indeed, attempting to "gallicanize" the American Church—that is., to fashion it in the image of the pre-revolutionary (1791) French Church. For his part, the Archbishop's objections to John England would ironically be clarified around the theme of "democratization" of the Catholic Church. Marechal eventually came to believe that the Charleston prelate was going much too far in the "Americanization" of Catholicism. At the 13th convention of South Carolina, 1837, England would turn full circle on Marechal and his Franco-American successors. The Charleston bishop explained to his people that he refused to send men to the seminary in Baltimore, run by the French Sulpicians, because it was not under the rule of the American episcopate. Indeed, England was even to accuse some of the Franco-American clergy of being unfriendly to republican institutions.

Bishop England's appreciation of the American republic and what was to be learned from it has drawn some criticism. In more recent years a current of historical analysis among American Catholic Church historians has suggested that many of the nineteenth century leaders in the American Catholic hierarchy were much too disposed to accommodate what the critics believe were the Enlightenment and liberal thought of the times. This assessment both of the period and the leaders, among them John England, is more often an anachronistic projection of current views. The best current analysis of England's vision would be that it was neither simply liberal nor Enlightenment-driven as outlined by Daniel F. Kearns, "Bishop John England and the Possibilities of Catholic Republicanism," in *South Carolina Historical Magazine.*[8] We will return to England's republican principles and perspective when we treat of his Diocesan Constitution. It is sufficient here simply to note that he was an 18th and 19th century Catholic bishop. His work and efforts clearly underscore his rejection both of rationalism and rugged, liberal individualism. The critique that recently has been offered fails to grasp the nineteenth century realities of those who attempted to bring Catholic experience and expression to bear in the American context. England, the foreigner, eventually was effective in preempting Marechal and his successors at Baltimore, as well as many of the native American clergy, by calling for even greater adaptation to American society than they could possibly endorse. It is the failure of some critical observers of this effort to appreciate the fact that the inculturation of the Gospel into new situations, whether it was the Judaic and Christian expressions of the earliest layer of Christian faith on meeting the Greco-Roman world or the hierarchically structured European and medieval church on meeting modernity, addresses the fundamental thrust underscored in a properly apprehended and utterly transcendent God. No single language or culture is sufficient to God's revelation. Most assuredly no single cultural expression can encapsulate either God or God's revelation. The turn to reason and the liberation of the individual did not inherently constitute either a rejection of divine revelation or the priority of the common good. Nineteenth century republican liberation for the individual was viewed as liberation from authoritarianism. It was not a rejection of the belief that the individual in the natural state of things was a social being and accountable to the common good.

John England also remained squarely within the Catholic tradition as he walked the line that ran abreast of faith and reason. He was, and remains it appears, a forerunner among those who articulate clearly that a healthy individualism is not identical to privatism or privatization. For England, as we will see in his constitution for the Diocese of Charleston, the process of discernment need not be narrowly restricted to a strict hierarchical structure. In fact, he is quite clear that faith and reason urge us to the recognition that wisdom resides with God's people and the gifts and charisms they possess in baptism. Further, he had experienced in his Irish years the colonial and class systems imposed by Britain and was quite convinced from experience consequently that consultation may even be God's chosen path. In this context, then, he sought to inculturate the Catholic experience into the modern world in which God's gifts were not associated simply either with the aristocrats, the bourgeoisie or the hierarchy. This becomes clearer when we come upon Bishop England's sympathies during the tumultuous years of Jacksonian democracy's ascendancy in the mid-1820s. The American experience clearly coincided with and solidified John England's appreciation that hierarchical structures, while playing an important role, hold no exclusive claim to divine preference in the discernment of policy and priorities in pursuit of the common good. Power-sharing in the determination of community goals was the republican goal and John England saw no intrinsic contradiction between that and his role as a hierarch and a leader. John T. McGreevy highlights this struggle well in his recent book, *Catholicism and American Freedom*.[9] Much of the remainder of this study is devoted to this dialectic.

Struggles within the American Hierarchy

Marichal's disappointment, however, with the two appointments was quite understandable at the time. It would, in ways quite ironic, remain a source of profound disappointment to many in the hierarchy long after Marechal. From the time of John Carroll, the first bishop appointed in the United States, the American Catholic hierarchy had been suspicious of the Propagation Office's motives in episcopal appointments. In addition to motivation, the Americans had also been hesitant initially to receive a bishop appointed by the Propagation Office because such an appointment might be perceived by others in the country as an intrusion of foreign jurisdiction into American affairs. Papal authority would be best received by their fellow Americans if it were clearly and solely spiritual in scope. The American priests of early Maryland, themselves, had argued that the Curial Offices would be and were, in fact, perceived as secular and temporal bureaus or extensions of the Papal States. The Propagation Office would, therefore, be seen not as an office of the spiritual order but, as it was argued, an office of the temporal state, namely the Papal States.[10] An additional fear on the part of the earlier generation of American clergy (i.e., before the appointment of the first U.S. bishop) had been that the Propagation Office was eager to gain control of both the Jesuit property held in trust during the period of the Society's disestablishment and to control the process of episcopal appointments. The Americans knew that control of such appointments meant control of the Catholic Church in the United States together with all its resources. This suspicion regarding the Propagation Office continued for years. Many could not reconcile themselves to the fact that the American Catholic Church had been placed and remained under the direction of the Propagation Office as a "missionary" church rather than as an established national church. They saw such a condition on their self-determination as a church as quite unusual. Though they were small and insignificant as a church body in the United States, they saw themselves as quite distinct from the "missionary" church in a "non-Christian" nation. Whatever their particular reasons, the Americans generally believed, therefore, that the Propagation Office made episcopal appointments for reasons quite other than those that were most directly in the interests of the American Church. Those reasons, many of them believed, were to insure the centralization of authority and power in the Vatican. The apparent permanence of this "missionary" status chafed the American bishops, who often thought that Rome was too eager to sustain its control over American church matters. The Archbishop's expectations of Irish episcopal appointments were also based upon the unhappy experiences of two earlier appointments. Michael Eagan and his successor, Henry Conwell, had both proven to be quite inept in their administration of the Church at Philadelphia. A similar incompetence was evident in John Connolly's short tenure at New York. The Archbishop's pessimism therefore was understandable. A history, short though it was, of administrative incompetence on the part of Irish appointees, a lingering suspicion of the Propagation Office's motives and the experience of Irish feistiness in the trustee controversies would have given most people pause when the two new sees and their Irish-born bishops were announced. Marechal's pessimistic expectations of the two appointments were quite understandable. Writing to the Propagation Office, Marechal reported, "Neither Americans nor Englishmen, nor any persons coming from other European countries have disturbed and continue to disturb the peace of Charleston, Norfolk, Philadelphia etc., but Irish priests are given to intemperance or ambition."[11]

Yet John England would prove a striking exception in the series of appointments of Irish priests to the United States hierarchy. The particularity of his personality and talents are surely the explanation. He had been taught and educated as many of his contemporaries were taught and educated, but he saw and reacted quite differently than they. Nonetheless, John England's Irish and American contexts were highly significant in leading him in the directions he took. These same contexts did not always lead to the similar responses from others. His personal history, gifts and temperament play key roles. They evoked the leadership and responses that will come to characterize the future bishop. The democratic and collaborative instincts we discover in him flourished, at least in part, because of the hospitable context that adduced them. These same circumstances, I suggest, have called forth similar responses from many others who have followed. The central factor at play, perhaps, in John England's leadership was his experience at the margins as an Irish national in Ireland under British rule, a Catholic youth educated in Protestant schools and as a Catholic bishop in Charleston, South

Carolina. From this, all of us have much to learn of what emerges in such a talent situated at the periphery.

Ireland and the Irish Context

Introduction

An examination of John England's background and family offers nothing that extraordinarily unique to him, given the context into which he was born and reared. Nonetheless, each of these factors cumulatively contributed to a history that he carried with him throughout his life. It is a history of preferment within the Irish-born context of his family's class and background, combined with the marginalization such an Irish family would have likewise experienced in the English-governed society that was Ireland at the time. Dissent and innovative propensities would not have been unique either to John England. He found broad support among the people of Cork and its surroundings. The support emanated, no doubt, from the same experiences among a wide swath of peoples in Ireland at the time. What I suggest is that as we read and examine his background, we recognize a confluence of experiences and talent, drive and ambition within John England that makes him both unique and, at the same time, a lens through which we can recognize the vigor and creativity that emerges in circumstances that offer similarity even in their dissimilarity. The citizens of Cork, in part for sure, offered support to this somewhat maverick of a priest. But it must be granted that this man, John England, acted on what so many others did not. The power of his faith and of his convictions attest to a personality, while not unique, not common either. The accumulation of a multiple of factors created the person who was ready to lead dynamically. The circumstances of the times permitted the Church to call upon such talents and because of that, the Church flourished in ways that a more cautious and fearful church does not.

Family and Seminary Training

Born September 23, 1786, in Cork, John's father, Thomas, was known as a man of strength and integrity. His father was jailed once for teaching the rudiments of reading, writing and mathematics to a Catholic child. The legal pressures exerted on Thomas England, as well as many Irish Catholics, to deny their faith were great.[12] Thomas England, like most Irish Catholics, refused to submit to these pressures. It was the example of his father, as well as those of many others of that generation, that gave life to the future bishop's own social and religious convictions.

Though a series of laws was progressively enacted mitigating the penalties associated with being Catholic, the lessons of religious and social bigotry were burnt deeply into young England's psyche. This was summarized when he wrote years later that the history of Ireland was a mirror for the American nativist movement.[13] His early education, somewhat surprisingly, was in Protestant schools. In fact, it is quite possible he may have been the only Catholic in his class during these early years. After finishing his basic education, he turned to the study of the law, after which he spent two years in the service of a Cork barrister before deciding that he was called to the ministry.

John England's experience was that of his generation with the exception, of course, of his early schooling, which was both unusual and usual. Hedgerow schools were a minimal experience of education in the Ireland of the time. Those who were educated more formally were likely to receive that education in established, and therefore, Protestant contexts. This will be one difference that may explain England's larger horizon or view as regards ecclesial questions and structures. It may help explain his ability to design later a diocesan constitution modeled as it was on the Anglican or Protestant Episcopal model he observed both in Ireland and South Carolina. The central factor that distinguishes England's formative background may have been that he chose, particularly interesting given his educational and social advantages growing up, the ministry— and that he was promoted to the episcopacy.

The shape and nature of his episcopal ministry reflected the years that he spent as a priest in Ireland (1808-1820). Yet questions have been raised by several of his biographers that may give some greater insight into the man. Many people walk the same paths in life, yet there is no accounting for the personal stamp each places upon shared life experiences. Motivation, drive, ambition or altruistic zeal is fostered uniquely in each. Something within John England, something of his temperament, personality and faith began to emerge in several ways with his decision to enter the seminary. The obvious choice of a seminary, for example, would have been Maynooth. It was closer to Cork and was also, by far, the more prestigious of the two Irish seminaries. With the revolution in France the Irish saw the dissolution of their continental seminary system. As a result, beginning in 1793 they developed their own seminaries, first the Carlow and then the Maynooth, both faculties heavily influenced by the French. Yet, Maynooth, unlike Carlow at this period, received financial assistance from the British Crown.[14] Given his early educational advantages such a choice, as we have said, should have been obvious, yet for some unknown, personal reasons, it was at Carlow, St. Patrick's that he enrolled in 1802. Whether as a young man of sixteen years he would have made such a decision on the basis of socio-politico-theological considerations can be doubted. Yet as early as 1799 the Maynooth faculty, the Royal Faculty, had demonstrated interest in some accommodation with the Crown on church-state relations. The accommodations of Maynooth developed into the controversial Veto question. The Veto would have ceded to the Crown the right to exercise a veto over Irish Catholic episcopal nominations in return for certain rights and financial assistance granted to the Catholic Church in Ireland. The Carlow Seminary faculty had taken a position in opposition to such accommodations with the state.

Shortly following John England's death, Bishop F.P. Kenrick of Philadelphia wrote that the seminary training England received at Carlow was "not favorable to a just estimate of the pontifical prerogatives."[15] The causes for this, he reasoned, were that the Anti-Vetoists unfairly and too severely criticized Rome as too favorable to the British government throughout the Vetoist controversy. As implied in Kenrick's remarks, England's exposure to theology at Carlow was marked with a spirit of independence *vis-à-vis* Rome. Though little is known of the Carlow faculty, we do know that three French seminary professors, refugees of the French Revolution, were on the faculty at Carlow. Fr. Doyle, who likewise held a chair in the faculty, was known to have used the manuals of Professor Louis Delahogue, who at the time was himself teaching at Maynooth. It is generally presumed that the textbooks used at Carlow were the same as those used at Maynooth.[16] Among the textbooks used at Maynooth were Bailly's *De Ecclesia,* which argued strongly the separation of ecclesiastical and temporal powers and Hooke's *Naturalis et Revelatae Principia*. This latter work argued that the political power (the State) was supreme within its own competency. Hooke addressed the enflamed issue of the times and concluded that the pope possessed neither the power to depose kings nor dispense people from their obligations to civil authority.[17]

In light of John England's approach regarding papal authority in "Letters 'On the Roman Chancery'," Louis Delahogue's treatment of church authority appears to have been a likely source of his thought. The index, *Questionum de ecclesia* of Delahogue's tract, *De Ecclesia,* reads like the skeletal outline of England's own apologetics. This is particularly evident in some of the chapter headings of the tract: *De unanimitate inter episcopos necessaria ut alique definitio censeatur esse corporis Episcopalis, et infallible Judicium.*[18] Again, a similar treatment found later in John England was presented in Delahogue's appendix to the same tract, *De tacitio episcorporum consensus.* It treated of the manner in which episcopal consent was tacitly given to an apparently unilateral papal definition.[19] Finally, there was the clear restriction of the divine commission given to Peter and his successors: "Christ granted neither direct nor indirect authority in the secular realm to Peter, his successors or the church."[20] This argument that the church has no authority in the secular realm (temporalities) appeared frequently in England's own apologetics and defense of his Diocesan Constitution, as we will see. These and other quite similar arguments were also presented by Bailly in the same manner England did in the "Letters 'On The Roman Chancery'." Both men argued, England apparently dependent upon Bailly, that the Fourth Lateran Council was a "double council" at which civil and ecclesiastical leaders gathered together and enacted legislation pertinent to both competencies. The papal prerogative to dispense citizens from civil obedience was a concession granted by the Christian princes in the hope that harmony could be maintained between principalities because of the moral authority granted to such an arbiter. The pope alone was believed by these princes to be capable to stand above national and regional interests.[21] Such a decision was a political and practical one, not one of divine institution.

The theological thought to which the Irish seminary students were exposed during the first quarter of the nineteenth century could be seen even more clearly in the testimony received by the Irish Commission of Education in its eighth report of 1826. The purpose of the Commission was to ascertain the nature and quality of the training received by those being educated for the Catholic priesthood. To do this the Commission interviewed various members of the faculty and student body at Maynooth. The testimony received by the Commission appears to have been consistent and nearly unanimous. Among the theological propositions attested to were the following. The pope, the interviewees maintained, had no temporal power in virtue of his spiritual authority. There was also a clear distinction to be made between civil and spiritual authority. Papal power to dispense from oaths given or owed civil government was clearly attained by human concession, not divine. Papal infallibility was simply a theological opinion. The penal canons of the IV Lantern Council were civil, not ecclesial decrees. And finally, regarding the question of the "conciliar" decrees of the Council of Constance, with one exception, the interviewees held to the "Declaration of the Gallican Clergy." [22] From this evidence Richard Rousseau concluded that: "it is clear from these interviews that the spirit and even the letter of the Gallican articles pervaded the Irish seminaries at this period."[23] Rousseau's conclusion is a bit overdrawn, however, when he adds, "The spirit and even the letter of the Gallican articles." In their fight for Catholic emancipation, the Irish frequently played the government against the Vatican and vice versa. The motivation in Ireland, while it certainly included some degree of ecclesiastical independence from Rome, was essentially a drive for emancipation of the faith's practice in Ireland, not particularly a Hibernian church or even a conciliarist theology. For a historical analysis of the Gallican notions in Ireland see James Brennan, "A Gallican Interlude in Ireland."[24] Although treating of Gallicanism in an earlier period, Brennan notes that it appeared too Protestant on the question of papal authority insofar as the Irish were concerned. Whether or not this conclusion is fully accurate, the sense of independence noted was indicative of the spirit found in the future bishop of Charleston. But this independence may have been founded more firmly on German romanticism exemplified by Drey and Schelling than upon the characteristics of the Enlightenment.

Drey's major works more fittingly offer an insight into England's episcopal style, particularly his stress upon consultation and his identification of the people as the "church." Patrick Carey quotes Bishop Doyle (a former seminary professor and bishop during England's priestly ministry in Ireland) that the Irish seminarians were more influenced by Locke and Paley than either Bellarmine or Bussuet, the Gallicans. Carey also notes a distancing of some of the faculty at Maynooth from Delahogue on questions regarding the divine right of government. But in any case, as we will see in the leadership style and political sympathies that will characterize Bishop England during his episcopate, one would have solid grounds to suggest that the ideas of the German romantic theologians, particularly J.S. Drey at Tubingen, may have shaped John England's reflections, actions and thoughts more than either Gallicanism or Enlightenment rationalism would have.[25] As we will come to see, England's Jacksonian sympathies and behavior, as well as the Diocesan Constitution he will develop, mirror well German philosophical *Zeitgeist.*

It is essential to recall that John England and many others of his period should hardly be cast as Enlightenment rationalists. Gerald McCool details this quite well for us. If the theologian Drey may serve as an example, we find in his thought, McCool notes a theological approach that is anti-Enlightenment, communal and ecclesial. Drey challenged Kantian and post-Kantian assumptions. My position is not that John England read and appropriated Drey—we cannot know that. But similar theological responses to similar (religious diversity, romanticism and nationalism) contexts can be recognized in John England's outlook and practice, especially his views on the cultural and structural dimensions of the church.[26] We will need to return to this question in chapter four.

Irish Emancipation and the Vetoist Controversy

Nonetheless, the influence of the theology taught in the Irish seminaries during the student days of John England cannot explain entirely the striking differences between him and others who were similarly taught. It should be noted that this argument about England's theological dispositions, while found inchoate in England's training, is nonetheless circumstantial since the textbooks and testimony referred to can be dated only to a period immediately or shortly *after* England's ordination in 1808, and at Maynooth not at his own school of Carlow. One should not assume, however, that England's theological reading had ended with ordination. If one can assume such, since he was an obviously literate journalist as a young priest, much of his pastoral behavior and thought is consistent with the theological *Zeitgeist* (certainly at Tubingen) and the notion of the kingdom of God as a metaphor for church developed by Drey.[27] It appears that England's temperament, personal background and bent must be taken into account as factors that played a determinant role that led to the verve and tenacity that took him down less traveled routes as a churchman. Few of his contemporaries reflect the same ecclesiological perspectives we find in the bishop at Charleston.

Some of these personal traits can be recognized as early as his ordination in 1808 by Bishop Moylan. Perhaps not the major factor, but interestingly Bishop Moylan of Cork and the patron of John England was a brother to General Stephen Moylan of George Washington's Continental Army.[28] Personal exposure and acquaintance with a general of a republican army in that era cannot be simply overlooked. Nevertheless, other factors serve to suggest that John England's early education outside the Catholic tradition, his intense interest in the Vetoist and republican issues alive at the time in Ireland, as well as his role as an editor of some controversy set him apart from the average priest or hierarch in the Irish Church of the time. Soon after his ordination he became very actively involved in the Vetoist controversy. The question of the Veto had arisen with the first petition for emancipation in Ireland presented by the Irish Catholic bishops to the British Parliament in 1799. In exchange for emancipation the Crown wished a veto over episcopal nominations. The controversy surrounding this concession raged from 1799 until 1829 when emancipation became a reality. In 1799 the ten bishops who were the trustees of Maynooth had agreed to the government's proposal, much to the dismay of their many Catholics. Each time the issue came up for discussion through the years, an enflamed series of attacks resulted. John England did not jump into the battle until 1812. Yet, the confluence of temperament and talents that were John England even at this early period testify to the combustibility *and* creativity we will see emerge later as well.

While editing *The Religious Repertory* from 1808 to1810, England had written only occasionally against the Veto. However, as Cork became increasingly polarized over the issue, *The Cork Mercantile-Chronicle* became the organ of the Anti-Vetoist movement. When *The Mercantile-Chronicle* faced financial ruin, the Diocese of Cork stepped in and bought 50 percent of its assets. The bishop immediately had Fr. England appointed the newspaper's trustee. To this point England's involvement had been slowly but steadily escalating in the Anti-Vetoist movement. His appointment as a trustee of the principal Anti-Vetoist newspaper clearly committed him to the cause.

There were also other early indications of John England's direction in political affairs. In the election of 1812 when a pro-Catholic Minister of Parliament had been defeated for reelection in a heavily Catholic district, John England was determined not to have that ever happen again. He recognized the vital importance to Irish Catholic interests of the elections to Parliament. He launched therefore a voter-registration drive hoping to make certain that in the next election pro-Catholic sentiments would be clearly and emphatically expressed at the ballot box. And on February 16, 1814, when news arrived in Ireland of the famous *Quarantotti* rescript granting Great Britain the Veto in exchange for emancipation, the reaction was swift and unambiguous in its opposition. (By this time the Anti-Vetoists had increased their strength within Ireland to near unanimity among the Catholics.) Writing in *The Religious Repertory* England called the rescript "an abominable anti-Irish document."[29] The shrillness of the entire affair and John England's personal commitment to the movement culminated in his appearance in court because of the Anti-Vetoist articles in *The Repertory*. In the opinion handed down by the court, he was guilty of "republican disorderliness" unbecoming a clergyman. The future bishop's words were to become a *shibboleth* of the republicans of Ireland: "The only way to preserve peace and unanimity among us is for all persons to support the desire of the majority, even though you (the majority) should decide against me, I shall acquiesce in your determination." [30]

So deeply involved had the young priest become in this Church-State question that by 1818 he actively undertook a role as speaker and campaign manager for Christopher Hutchinson, a M.P. candidate in the election of that year. The denouement of his activity had probably occurred several years earlier when *The Cork Mercantile-Chronicle* had commented favorably upon a speech of Daniel O'Connell attacking the Holy See for its support of the Veto. A copy of the article is no longer available, but whatever it said stirred Bishop Coppinger of Clone to write to England's new ordinary, Bishop Murphy, that "I should be surprised if a general call for his [John England's] suspension were forthwith to arise from all quarters."[31]

Given his personal history and the republican and political commitments that seem so apparent in it, as well as the ecclesiological implications of his positions for Roman theology, clothed as it appeared to be in the diplomatic interests of the Holy See, John England's thought may easily be supposed (not decisively demonstrated) to fit well with the *zeitgeist* found in the Tubingen theology then emerging. The *volk zeitgiest*, a type of folk romanticism that easily allied itself with the new republicanism of the era, clearly characterizes John England's stance with the people or folk of Ireland and against their British overlords. This populism, we would hope not to be accused of a certain antiquarianism here, can easily be understood to lead one to stress an ecclesiology modeled far differently than the enlightened despots that some, like John England, may have seen as the unfortunate cultural model of his era for the Church. While his personal library was destroyed in a fire years later at Charleston, the bishop's trait as a reader cannot be doubted. His temperamental dispositions seemed quite likely, given his behavior and activism, to be responsive to the new thoughts sweeping the intelligentsia of the time. As we noted, however, his thought was quite explicitly still rooted in the communal and religious faith that impelled a string of ecclesiastical leaders in republicanism that was quite distinct from the stereotypical rationalist, individualist persona projected onto the era by some contemporary historians. We will return to this question again.

His activity in the political arena had made England a steadily greater embarrassment and nuisance to some in the Irish hierarchy. The tradition that he was promoted to a diocese in "the republican United States" because of this cannot be documented. On the other hand, the logic of such an appointment seems evident.[32] LeBuffe asserts that it was England's involvement in the Anti-Vetoist movement that as much as anything confirmed him as a republican and a democrat.[33] It should be added that it was also grounded in his family and education. John England was not the average priest, hierarch or Irish person of the time. He was a leader and schooled in leadership in his family's household. We will look into the question of what it meant, or possibly meant, to John England and his contemporaries when one used the term republican. What does become clear about Fr. England and his involvement in the Anti-Vetoist controversy is that while he was an American bishop different in thought and tone from the remainder of the American hierarchy, he had also been an Irish priest largely different in thought and tone from his brothers in the Irish clergy. He stood beside the great civil leader Daniel O'Connell as the churchman leading the fight for Irish rights.

There were other intellectual influences abroad in Ireland during England's formative years. One such influence was Fr. Arthur O'Leary, O.F.M. A man of some intellectual complexity, he defended the Oath of Allegiance to the Crown as compatible with the faith. It was, however, an oath that John England strenuously opposed. While their positions differed in this regard, their arguments were similar in their denial of the deposing power of the pope. O'Leary was a loyalist, which England was not, yet he was also (paradoxically) a staunch champion of Irish nationalism. His loyalty to the Crown rested upon very similar grounds to England's loyalty to American institutions. For O'Leary loyalty was "an opportunity for the Catholics of Ireland to prove the staunchness of their loyalty to their legitimate rulers and break down once and for all the "No Popery" charge of doubtful allegiance."[34] O'Leary's work in this area of Catholicism and its relation to a Protestant society and government is duplicated in England's apologetics at a later date. Issues of loyalty and freedom of conscience were central to the thought of both men. O'Leary ironically turned to the Quakers and William Penn as models of civil and religious toleration. Fr. O'Leary, as Bishop Doyle (the same who had been at Carlow teaching while young England was there), relied heavily upon Montesquieu and Locke in his writings and lectures. In fact, the social compact theory of Locke, to which England also referred later in his writings, was widely popular in Ireland at the time and was in no way restricted just to lecturers like O'Leary and Doyle. England's own republican and progressive thought is starkly clear with his adherence to a Lockean vision that the social compact is between persons and not founded upon the notion that secular rulers are directly designated by the divinity, as was dominant in Catholic thought at the time.[35]

It was in the context of the social compact that England began to see the Veto question in terms of an overall relationship between Church and State. As a result he alluded more and more frequently to the American republic's experiment in the separation of the two authorities. Of course, the relatively novel idea received from Locke is that rights and duties emerge from a *decision of the citizens* [emphasis mine] in a compact with one another, not as a result of governmental coercion. This republicanism reflects England's own examples of religious orders as we will see in chapter three. In making this argument for the social compact, John England effectively sidesteps the objections Roman theology at the time would have offered to a republican notion of government. What is important was that the analogue of religious orders underscored the *responsibilities and obligations* of the republican to the community. This was a classic argument found in the republican apologists, religious or secular, of the time. Locke in the "First Treatise of Government" stresses the social responsibility of citizens and the common good they are to pursue.[36] John England was not a privatist in his understanding of faith, reason or the public good. His republicanism, as Daniel Kearns points out, stressed the communal that emerged from the classical impulse "to preserve virtue by serving the republic unselfishly." De Tocqueville had it correctly when he observed "Catholicism is like an absolute monarchy; if the sovereign is removed, all the other classes of society are more equal than they are in republics."[37] If anything, as John England claimed, his republicanism emerged from his Catholicism and its classical (Greco-Roman) heritage, medieval monasticism and the Franciscan tradition that followed. His republican view of government was not one that was individualistic in the least. Rather, the individual was understood and acknowledged best when the community guaranteed a "freedom from coercion." Such "freedom from" is a necessary substratum for a genuine act of religious faith. The contemporary republican view was not that the individual was self-directed, but was free within a theory of natural law that understood the person as dependent upon and rooted within a community. The natural law basis of the republican tradition in nineteenth century America reflected the republican conceptions of Locke, Montesquieu and Catholicism, but particularly and most explicitly the latter two. The confluence of natural law and republican theories can be seen analogously parallel to Thomas Aquinas's "grace builds upon nature."[38] It was an era that still wrestled with classical concerns such as "the one and the many" and recognized the dialectic that made each experience not a stranger to the other, but realities to be held in their proper tension.

If the community does not honor the individual, the community risks its own life. We will leave until later the discussion of the public role of religion in a modern pluralistic republic. The concomitant question about the use of law to promote or support either a religiously articulated vision of humankind's purpose or teleology will also need further clarification that may be found in our case study of John England. It will require some reflection on the manner by which such support would either constitute some establishment or some degree of coercion, whether physical, legal or psychological, by which the individual is subsumed into the will of an oligarchy or majority. To equate republicanism, the Lockean tradition, and the separation of church and state, on the other hand, simply with Enlightenment rationalism, libertarian capitalism, or as an instrument that denies the individual a religiously teleological "freedom for" in the public realm will also need to be returned to later in our analysis of John England's contributions.

Issues of the Irish Catholic Church in John England's Ministry

The situation in Ireland during Fr. England's training and early ministry played a large part in shaping his vision. Because Catholic emancipation was still a matter of hope, several formative questions had confronted the future bishop as they did the entire Irish Catholic community. One of these was the question of the proper relationship of Church and State. Was voluntarism or State support best? What was the theological foundation for religious liberty? And finally, the larger ecclesiological question pushed itself forward—what really was the role and mission of the church in society?[39] The situation in Ireland surely shaped the views the future bishop would espouse in his ministry while in Ireland as well as later in the United States. As regards the Church-State question he was led to a position that distinguished and defined the scope of both spiritual and civil jurisdictions. He took the position that not to place the clergy in the pay of the State was a distinct advantage. He preferred a Church voluntarism that might lead to a genuine practice of evangelical counsel (virtue) of poverty as opposed to personal and institutional security. Such a church, to his mind, was more in accord with the religion of Jesus. He embraced religious liberty on principle, not as an expedient. This was attested in a resolution he promoted in April 1816 to support toleration for Protestant practice in Catholic France. He was a forceful advocate of the long tradition of the freedom of conscience. He understood this freedom not only as a *post factum* reality, but a principle to be respected even in the process of the formation of conscience.

During this Irish period of his life, he also viewed the church as a constitutional monarchy, though later in the Diocesan Constitution of Charleston his conception of the Church changed to a republic in which the pope and bishop *by divine right* possessed power and authority that was limited constitutionally. Patrick Carey offers a fine ecclesiological analysis of the church in light of Bishop England's reflections. Carey himself, however, in a later work demonstrates a less sympathetic view of the role of lay trustees when he diverges somewhat from his earlier position and suggests that the nature of the church is such that its mission would be difficult to maintain within a democratic or republican discernment process.[40] Such an assessment would bear reexamination in light of a greater appreciation for the role of the Spirit in the church. John England's instincts and experience may well be better understood today in light of contemporary pneumatology and trinitarian theology. Earlier ecclesial outlooks were frequently taken up with a relatively static and traditionalist conception of theology and divine revelation. Such a focus arose from an understanding of divine commerce between God and humans that largely limited the action of the Spirit and divine revelation to the Sacred Scriptures. If, however, the long tradition of the faith and Spirit led community is understood also to be a witness of and to divine revelation, then we will need to deal seriously with the notions of change and development as John Henry Newman taught us. Had the Catholic Church been better equipped to espouse the emergence of the change and development reflected in the republican vision retrieved by Pettit, Kearns and others, perhaps the field would not have been yielded to the secular world. Instead a religious faith with a deeper appreciation for equitable social relationships might have emerged as a greater presence and determinant in the modern world. The failure to inculturate has been a double-edged sword. While the Church played it safely in the trustee conflicts protecting its interests against the intrusion of lay interests that could have been negative, it also lost an opportunity to influence society more effectively. The distance between the Church and the laity represents the same dialectic as Robert Frost refers to in the "Mending Wall." This is certainly not to suggest that the trustee movement was without need for significant refinements or adjustments, but simply that it possessed an instinct that had troubled ecclesial leadership through the centuries: Is the monarchical expression and structure of ecclesial authority *de jure divino*? If so, would the theology of grace and the sacraments need refinement as well? John England's confrontation with the English monarchy sowed seeds of doubt that "by divine right" was genuinely *de jure divino.*

John England's reflections might often lead one to believe that he espoused an unrestricted freedom of conscience—that is, a type of libertarianism. Yet, when faced with the trustee crisis, Bishop England was not hesitant to stress leadership and the Christian notion of obedience in pastoral matters. The longer Catholic tradition appreciates and values the tension to be maintained between authority and obedience within the community. It is the foundation of personal and individual identity. Obedience to the community allows for the flourishing of the individual, but the community's appreciation of its composition as the children of God underscores the fact that individuals cannot be reduced to mere cogs in the machinery of the community. Hauerwas and Pinches sum it up well in their discussion of the Christian virtue of obedience. They highlight the point that obedience is a virtue that moves us beyond reason alone to a recognition that 1) community is the source of our very selves and 2) reason alone cannot assure us in most instances of a "factual" or final answer on a broad range of issues. Rational knowledge is valued, but there are times that being "rationally correct" is not the "right" thing, particularly within relationships, for either individuals or community.[41]

An earlier lesson from history, of course, was learned during the struggle with the Lay Investiture in the first millennium when evangelical values (gospel and ecclesial) were subordinated to secular (political, ethnic and economic) ones. Yet, the lesson from the Lay Investiture controversy plagues the memory of the Catholic tradition with the fear that secular values or the State will impose itself onto the affairs of the Church. Nonetheless, the trustee question, at least in our context, must also reflect on questions surrounding clerical and personal accountability structures *within* the believing community. It will be the genius of John England to recognize that such accountability could be introduced into the Church through a constitution that allocated responsibilities among the whole of the Church's members. He would never have suggested that such structures were beyond abuse. Any system of accountability or process of discernment from the very nature of a Catholic understanding of sin and the need for divine redemption precludes any claim that they could be perfect, but that is no argument in opposition to such.

England held to the principal of individual liberty within a context of social responsibility founded upon the Christian virtues. *All* authority necessarily was to be limited in any society that upheld individual rights rooted in the concept of the freedom of conscience, because of the precedence owed the commonweal. At the time, John England's Catholic heritage found a comfortable alliance with the Southern republicans (Democratic Party) of the Jacksonian party that explicitly situated individual liberty in the context of social obligations. He and they were opposed to the Whig tradition that represented both the more classically rationalist and liberal proposition that favored the minimally restricted entrepreneurial freedom of an emergent capitalism. The American Jacksonian republicans, in general, were focused more on government's "non-domination" of its people, which they viewed as consistent with regulation or the responsibility of government to interfere or intervene in the interests of the commonweal. In the nineteenth century American context, such republicanism focused, not on a question of libertarian opposition to government and power, but on the fact that the American colonists had been rendered "unfree" by their British colonial masters.

The political scientist, Philip Pettit, argues that interference by a republican government, as conceived by earlier generations of Americans, was not arbitrary and simply in the interests of individuals, but rather early American republican thought allowed for the more optimistic notion that the community and its leaders needed to intrude or insert themselves into individuals' lives in the common interest. Such a political perspective is readily recognized as coherent with the Catholic tradition, certainly, but with the Western political tradition generally. It follows that the priority of the common good is grounded in personal freedom that flows from freedom of conscience. Without the assurance of such personal freedom from coercion, moral accountability becomes virtually unintelligible.

The tension, nonetheless, between some proponents of republicanism in this period and Catholic theology can be seen in the anthropology supporting each position. Catholic theology would, perhaps, take exception to too great an optimism about humankind's innate goodness and offer caution about humankind's propensity to sin. Nevertheless, Catholic moral theology stressed, even as it did during the Reformation, the essential goodness of humankind. It is this optimism about the nature of humanity and the moral accountability of the individual that John England's republicanism reflected. From the ground of grace found in individuals arose the freedom to act justly or unjustly, but always the power of God's freely given grace outweighed during the course of history that of evil. Thus, England could look to the people as a source of God's revelation, certainly not infallibly graced, but freely and ordinarily. If this was not the case, John England would have wondered how people could be held to account. Such was not libertarianism, rationalism nor secularism. It was a traditional understanding of grace and the Spirit as concretely present in history. It was from the time of Bentham and Hobbes that "non-interference" or a kind of libertarianism arose, but neither of these thinkers' ideas directed the American republican tradition and certainly not that of the radical Jacksonian tradition of the "common man." John England's source for republicanism came, therefore, from neither Bentham nor Hobbes, but rather from a position quite consistent with Pettit's clarification about the nature of the republican tradition in the United States.[42]

The criticism that progressives, such as John England, made too great an accommodation of the Gospel to a culture of individualism and rationalism rests on a superficial reading of history that projects contemporary libertarian and rationalist influences onto republican thought of the eighteenth and nineteenth centuries. The republicans of the time would normally have been surprised and shocked by arguments for privatization of individual interests and rights. They may have favored small government, but for them that would have largely mirrored their interests that government be local and at hand. Given the communications and travel possibilities of the time, such made great sense. It did not reflect an ideology that the government was not to protect and promote the common good, let alone promote the interests of plutocrats. Such a critique fails to credit, as well, the explicit appeals to the common good we often encounter in John England's writings (as those of most republicans of his era), and the assumption, at times explicitated by many people—including Adam Smith, that the institutions of society were natural counter-balances to one another as a result of the face-to-face relationships that characterized the smaller communities and tighter neighborhoods of the time. Smith wrote that he expected that the great capitalists need not be regulated by the government because they would be restricted by local religious institutions and their communities and neighbors. It was they, in a demographically different world than ours that would counter-balance and control individual greed. Thus, early republican thought was motivated not on the basis of "non-interference" (a libertarian expression of republicanism) but on "non-domination" of the individual citizen. The interplay of the language of citizen or individual rights and the government certainly did reflect in several trajectories, one of which would issue in a type of libertarianism exemplified by Thoreau, perhaps as well as by many pioneers of the American West.[43] Yet a certain anti-intellectualism has driven a critique that suggests that this was the major, let alone sole dynamic in understanding the founding tradition of American republicanism. It is a thin evaluation that renders history and generations as relatively homogenous. It is difficult to believe that Jefferson, Madison, Hamilton, Adams, the Whigs, and the Democrats, however, so easily coalesced on the questions of individual and governmental prerogatives so uniformly.

A better understanding of England's vision of social responsibility in both the secular and religious realms is seen in his Irish context. While we have referred largely to intellectual and socio-political contexts to help us understand the shape given the outlook and responses of John England in his Irish context, we should emphasize again that very personal factors also came into play. The most evident of these was his mentor Bishop Moylan, whose brother, we mentioned earlier, was a general in the Continental Army of George Washington. Another factor in the experience of Irish Catholicism prior to emancipation, and far more important, was the strong ecclesial congregationalism in Ireland where the structures of a national church endured under close British oversight and limitations. This was the case because strong organization at either the diocesan and national levels had long been restricted by law for obvious reasons. The Catholic Church could easily rally the populace around itself as a symbol of opposition to British Protestant presence. This was the context for the direction much of the Irish leadership—lay and clerical—took in the early trustee battles in the United States. Failing to recognize this dimension of the Irish experience is to wreak an injustice upon the trustee question that plagued or shaped, depending upon one's disposition toward its values, the early American Catholic experience. Some of the Irish were quite comfortable and experienced with local and lay leadership in the parish. The parish, at times, varied little from the hedgerow schools that had developed in Ireland. A revisionist historical appraisal of nineteenth century American Catholicism is hamstrung by its own ecclesiological sectarianism and its failure to grasp the possibilities of discernment processes or decision-making structures possible within the Catholic tradition. Too easily such a thin grasp of Catholic experiences facilely permits accusations that adaptation of unfamiliar structures in the government of the church are without precedence. Yet as we have seen, some bishops, such as John England, and theologians such as Drey and the Tubingen School (as early as 1817)—even before J.H. Cardinal Newman—understood that the Church had adapted and developed both its teaching and its structures throughout history. Historical consciousness helped them to realize that the Church in so many cases adapted itself to the needs of the people and the times in a manner fully coherent with its mission to be a light that shined and brought clarity to the ever newly emergent questions in history.

It is precisely the breadth of John England's understanding of the tradition as regards the discernment of legitimate authority that best captures his importance to the Catholic heritage. The Irish context from which he emerged called the people to oppose British colonial attitudes by rallying them together as a community which included among its accomplishments freeing the Church from interference by the Crown. The American context as well represented a Catholic community that also sought freedom from a government that would restrict its practice of Catholicism. The very same context, however, also reflected the interests of a Catholic membership that assumed the right to hold the Church's bishops, who were their brothers, accountable for the restrictions placed on the assignment of priests and parochial development within a prescribed radius of the see city (seat of the diocese) because of concerns focused primarily on the oversight and management of a celibate clergy. Finally, John England came to appreciate that his credibility in the new democratic world required that he consult and inform the Church's members more appropriately, given the circumstances of the new nation. We shall see more of this in his implementation of a Constitution for the Diocese of Charleston.

Because of his Irish experience of strong pastoral leadership at the congregational level and the degree of congregational autonomy in Ireland, it should come as no surprise that the frequent trait in Irish-dominated parishes was the presence of the trustee controversies.[44] England would have had no burning desire to extinguish local autonomy and we do not find, for example, among his pressing concerns the need to deny canonical assignment to pastors, a situation that permitted greater autonomy to a local pastor. Such canonical assignments bestowed on the pastor/priest an "irremovable" status that resulted in the pastor's ability to yield great authority locally, while effectively being beyond the reach of the bishop on many scores. England's response was to assure that the local pastor (as he in turn) would be held accountable in some manner to the people of the parish. Like the founding fathers of the United States, he was equally clear that sheer popular government could lead to abuse. Some balance or distribution of authority is necessary.[45] A dispersal of responsibility was paramount, but the loss of equitably distributed authority was also to be avoided. The opposite thrust was highlighted in most of the Irish-born bishops in the United States, who reflected the episcopal efforts in Ireland to organize and give direction to the national and diocesan churches under the difficult circumstances they continued to experience prior to emancipation. When John England was appointed to the United States. He was pressed by conditions in the United States to meld these differences into both local and national structures in a way that seemed demanded by and more consistent with what he found in his new environment: in the first instance, republican balance of powers in both the parish and the diocese and in the latter, a national conference or council of bishops to coordinate supra-diocesan needs for a very undeveloped and small church.

Quite obviously, most of the bishops, whether in Ireland or the United States, placed much greater priority on the connectional and hierarchical and less on the congregational aspects of the Church than would the laity. John England, on the other hand, was concerned to address both priorities, the bishops' and the people's. In Ireland, emancipation was an opportunity for Rome and its appointees to reaffirm their own episcopal prerogatives and to guarantee that political opposition to the British government not subvert the larger and more pressing mission and role of the Church. On the other hand, Great Britain had its own interests itself in seeing that episcopal leadership was strong. Such a concentration of authority and accountability within Irish Catholicism made the task of "ruling over" Ireland much easier for the British. John England reflected both his own temperament and Irish history. He followed neither the weaknesses seen in his Irish-born predecessors, Bishops Eagan, Conwell, Connolly, and Kelly who provided little supra-parochial leadership, nor by the strong-willed episcopal style of most of his Irish-born successors such as John Hughes, McQuaid and so on. Some of the latter, while they partook of much of the same historical, cultural and theological milieu, both in Ireland and the United States as did John England, their experience was not to issue in the same synthesis we find in England. Quite obviously each also shaped his times and life very differently as well. What explanation can be offered for this seeming dichotomy? A factor that seems to illustrate the difference dramatically is England's penchant to analyze the Church in the light of political theory and practice. While each of the others, whether predecessors or successors, tended to be ecclesio-centric and their interest was to establish and shepherd the local church, John England had an added and more public interest as well. He understood his role to evangelize included the larger community in which the Church found itself. In part, the difference may be seen also in the locale of each one's episcopacy. John England worked with a small, scattered community of immigrant Catholics in an overwhelmingly Protestant environment and so it consumed his energy and thought to a lesser degree. The others, particularly his successors in the hierarchy, represented more closely a leadership developed and exercised within a teeming and growing Catholic population, not infrequently best served by developing parallel structures and institutions to those of the larger community. David O'Brien notes this difference well in his typologies of immigrant and public Catholicism.

The clearly ecumenical and public nature of John England's episcopal imperative accounts for a major perspectival divergence that led to a very different outcome in his appraisal of how one could be both Catholic and republican. To someone keenly aware of the larger world that constituted the country, episcopal authority needed to be handled in a more consultative and American manner. His understanding of leadership was not so exclusively defined by theological or ecclesiastical language and cultures. In addition, John England was more predisposed to place himself in the larger world than that of the Church alone because of his Irish context and opposition to the Veto question and the episcopal propensity in Ireland at the time to assuage the British Crown by serving as the conduits of British authority on a range of public issues not explicitly religious. It was not difficult for Bishop England to see that the "leadership classes" could gravitate to one another quite readily since they paradoxically shared a similar interest in governing. If we see in John England a quick response to republican ideas in how he demonstrates "congregational" sympathies, it is in his decision to disperse authority, both real and moral, *less intensely* in the episcopal office he exercised. Such a decision also can be traced, in part at least, to the Anti-Vetoist controversy and the Irish bishops' role in it. On the other hand, he was certainly not an assimilationist since, as his Diocesan Constitution indicates, authority within the community was invested *first and fundamentally* in the Gospel message that stands above the community and to which all members owe their obedience. Secondly, authority within the community, one to another, rested upon the moral obligation, as he understood it, to *exercise* a collaborative authority that spanned both the hierarchy and the parishioners—that is, all members.

The Preface to the Constitution makes clear his distinction between the nature of the Church's government that is inextricably both divinely and humanly derived. Title one of the Diocesan Constitution offers the bishop's theology of divine revelation. It was a quite sophisticated theological statement, given the period. It recognizes the communitarian foundation for the discernment about what is *de jure divino* (from God) when we speak of divine revelation and then sets what is understood as *de jure humano* (of human origin) in the tradition that passes on the received revelation from God. What is *de jure divino* can be discovered as only humans can, through structures and processes that are *de jure humano:* language, reason, experience, witness. But the two, the divine and human dimensions, cannot be divorced. Simply put we must obey (revelation) reasonably, with plausibility, because the alternative would be to enter ceaselessly on negotiations within relationships devoid of affect and reduced to logic, reason and law. John England remained steadfastly in a tradition of divine revelation that accepted the vision of a shared, communal governance wherein the "ways of the world" were not necessarily either democratic chaos, individual assertion, nor aristocratic or oligarchic authority but rather the pursuit of the common interests of the community of God's people, since God's grace provided just such a hope for this world.[46]

There had been other influences in addition to the intellectual, socio-cultural and political ones that account for the development of John England. There was, for example, the priestly and pastoral ministry of John England during his earlier years. From his ordination in 1808 to his departure in 1820, he had served in various pastoral and diocesan capacities. Initially he was assigned as chaplain to the nuns of the North Presentation Convent in Cork. Shortly afterward he was named the "first lecturer" of the Cork Cathedral, which was, according to unsubstantiated tradition, endowed by the ex-bishop of Cork, Lord Dunboyne, in reparation for his laicization. It entailed delivering "a well-developed sermon" each Sunday at the Cathedral. As a young priest he also served as chaplain to the jail at Cork; founded the monthly, *The Religious Repertory,* became president of St. Mary's Seminary, Cork; served as trustee of *The Cork Mercantile-Chronicle*; and published several textbooks.[47] Eventually he was assigned to a pastorate in the Protestant town of Brandon, not far from Cork. It was from Brandon, three years later, that he was appointed bishop of Charleston. In other words, England's ministry continued to be a public one in contradistinction to a more narrowly parochial or congregationally anchored one. Even his pastoral flock at Brandon was distinctive in as much as he served a small Catholic minority in a larger Protestant community. Some had seen his assignment to Brandon as an exile imposed upon him for his political activism.[48] A sidelight to this period is that just several months prior to his being sent to Brandon (May 1817), Fr. England had written the Propagation Office in Rome requesting permission to be incardinated into the Diocese of New York.[49] The Propagation Office asked Bishop Murphy of Cork to provide England with an *exeat* (permission to transfer) to New York. Perhaps, for political reasons—that is, fearing a negative popular reaction if so popular a figure went off to another country as a missionary—Bishop Murphy refused. There has been a good bit of speculation regarding the circumstances of this request and Bishop Murphy's refusal to honor it.[50] Eventually, however, John England was sent to the United States as a member of its hierarchy. Bishop Murphy may well have reached the point that John England's presence in Cork was a nuisance or irritant in the relationship of the Irish Episcopacy and the British government. To rid himself of the young England was best accomplished through promotion to a land, as in *Fiddler on the Roof* Tevye sings, "A blessing for the Tsar? May God bless him and protect him and . . . keep him far, far away." At the same time, of course, the Irish episcopacy could claim it had bestowed a favor upon this popular son of the Irish people. The decision earlier to deny England's initiative to be sent to New York was likely related to the negative impression such a transfer elicited. Murphy and the Irish episcopacy would have been suspected of caving in to the British. The appointment as a bishop, however, to the United States was something else and Bishop Murphy's mind may be seen in his later letter of recommendation of the promotion to the episcopacy for Fr. England. On September 23, 1819, he wrote the Propagation Office that "no one boldly immerses himself advising about certain political affairs, as about Catholic affairs, than he [John England] does, and so, governance in this realm is difficult. It is better, I think, that he be given care of Catholics souls where his contribution in the political or religious-political would be received."[51] The Propagation Office described him in a list of clerics it was considering for the American episcopacy as "he is the more attractive, more eloquent of all these clerics."[52]

There are a couple of interesting stories about England that may offer insight into his character. One recalls an experience while he was prison chaplain. It is said that once while attending to the spiritual need of a condemned man, he accompanied the prisoner to the gallows. When the moment of execution came, the hangman botched the job, and the poor prisoner dangled above the platform alternately strangling and finding relief by making foot contact with the platform. England, seeing the inhumane situation, dove for the man's feet, putting the agony to an end.[53] Another relates to an election in Cork. It was suspected that the anti-Catholic segments of the population were not above fraud in their desire to win. Since the Orangemen had two candidates in the field, England drew them aside and warned them that he would watch each closely on the day of election. If the supporters of either would intimidate or otherwise defraud a Catholic (and a Liberal) at the polls, he would have ten men ready to vote for the Orangeman's Tory opponent. In telling the story William Read concluded, "The result was natural. Men respect the rights of those whom they see able and willing to maintain them." [54]

At his episcopal consecration he again departed from the expected. Whereas Patrick Kelly, who had been named at the same time to the See of Richmond, took the Oath of Allegiance to the Crown, John England refused. He made his stand on the grounds that he was shortly to leave for the United States where he intended to become a citizen. This action is particularly pertinent to an understanding of the temperament of the man when we recall that his friend, William Read, wrote that the bishop (John England) had said to him on one occasion that "he would never wear a mitre in any country where the British government exercised any control." [55]

John England, shaped in his childhood home and family, was likely bent to a sympathetic posture toward the marginalized (then viewed by many as the democratic mob). He had possibly chosen Carlow for reasons of its plucky opposition to British domination of Ireland. At Carlow, he was exposed in a moderate manner to the pre-revolutionary Catholic theology of Gallicanism associated with France. Again, his sympathies leaned against the centralization of power and authority that mirrors the general attitude of people at the margins of an empire rather than those at its center. He was promoted to the See of Charleston to remove the embarrassment his bluntness and popularity caused the Irish bishops. Having championed the "little person," it would be of little surprise that he found the wave of Jacksonian democracy appealing when he arrived in the United States. Finally, his battles, if that is what we can term the tensions that characterized his relationships with the remainder of the American hierarchy, reflected not only the sympathies already mentioned, but also the personalities of himself and the other bishops. Often the men appointed following England's own episcopal appointment were reflections of Gregory XVI's interests and theology, quite conservative to reactionary. The men appointed before him had developed in very different cultural and social contexts. They refrained from appointing permanent canonical pastors and held all "real" decisions to themselves, as we noted earlier. However, bishops in that earlier period may have had an argument since they could easily point to the difficulties at the recruitment of accountable and reliable priests for the scattered and lonely missions of the American Catholic Church at the time. This, they maintained, forced them to much closer supervision over these "less suitable" recruits for pastoral ministry. Furthermore, the bishops and people experienced a far greater sense of isolation as Catholics in the early federal years than their Protestant neighbors and had become accustomed to a more reticent style in the public realm. Thus England reflected a daring found among some individual leaders, but he also reflected a confluence of events and context that were a window of opportunity in the development of the American Catholic experience to introduce new patterns and thought. His "Americanist" inculturation was not that of John Carroll, who reflected much more the oligarchic and mercantile republicanism of the revolutionaries. Nor was his 'Americanist' vision that of Cardinal Gibbons or Archbishop Ireland who acted on behalf on the industrial workers and their interests. Yet while he stands as a signal figure in terms of the socio-political culture of the young republic he brought to the consciousness of Catholicism, he also reflects a coherent leadership thrust upon the American Catholic hierarchy that spanned from the 1790s to the 1980s. It was a crew of leaders who inculturated Catholicism and the American experience in varying ways. In John England's instance, it is his republican contribution that brought both praise for his insight and creativity for his ability to demonstrate its compatibility with what is historically "catholic" and Catholic. As Kearns notes,

> Accusations of Catholic anti-republicanism were not new in John England's time. Such charges extended back to the earliest English settlement of North America. They coalesced in well-written form when John Adams portrayed Catholicism as a feudal and despotic religion in his 1765 "Dissertation on Canon and Federal Law." Indeed, a communitarian cultural ideal, an extreme emphasis on "virtue" and "sacrifice," and a fear of corruption and tyranny all link republicanism to Puritan and

English antecedents. Republican thinking emerged in Catholic milieus too, like France and Ireland, and its proponents ranged widely in their views from Enlightenment-style republicans who valued hierarchy to evangelical republicans who valued egalitarianism. . . . Bishop England, like republicans since the days of Rome, declared that ordered liberty and equality could only survive in a virtuous people.[56]

Inculturation has for many in recent years seemingly run its course theologically. Yet, one cannot believe that the Gospel is unable to be served validly by the cultures of all peoples. The insight of the late Superior General of the Jesuits, Pedro Arupe, is one we need to treasure. To inculturate the Gospel properly into every culture requires that we understand that as the Gospel becomes one with a culture it becomes new, without being, at the same time, assimilated. Does the Church ever really accomplish inculturation properly? If by properly we mean perfectly and without risk, the answer is likely no. But a theological anthropology, faithful to the Christian Catholic tradition, insists on the fact that reasonable risk finds its plausibility in the grace that overcomes sin. Risk and failure is never the end of the Christian's story. Hope prevails where faith is present. In this also, Bishop John England serves as a singularly important case study. As his missionary's efforts to inculturate Catholicism with the American experience produced great fruit, we must also remember the genuine tragedy that clouds the reputation and contribution of John England. His identity with those at the margins was specific and particular. As with all humans, hope is mixed with disappointment, success with failure and vision with myopia. Much of the bishop's vision and hope was honed in the Anti-Vetoist controversy. As a result his *ideas* were exceedingly progressive and both republican and populist in tenor, but these virtues were later placed into and developed within a social setting unlike Ireland. It was a setting in which, consciously or not, never led him to rub elbows with *all* the people as he had done in Ireland. His intellectual approach, temperament, responsibilities and office distanced him from the most pressing issue of his day, slavery and the plethora of attendant horrors: the destruction of families, the perversion of the explicit meaning of the Gospel used in defense of slavery, the economic aberrations and, of course, the violence wreaked upon uncounted thousands and hundreds of thousands. If the political measure of periphery/center is an apt metaphor to understand

John England in his Irish years, it serves equally well to understand the years in Charleston, South Carolina. Where he was at the margins, he was salt that gave savor to the ministry, but he was not at the margins *vis-à-vis* slavery and as a consequence his vision, creativity and response failed to be what we would have hoped. Yet, he was a visionary in other ways. As Paul Ricoeur and C.S. Peirce remind us, signs (verbal, visual, esthetical and oral) both reveal and hide at the same time.[57] Such was the soil of his human situatedness, his personal and historical specificity both freed him and imprisoned him. But that is what Paul wrote to the Romans: "I do what I do not wish to do, and I do not what I wish." Humanity's glory is not perfection or perfect strength, but the vulnerability that forces us to discover just how much we need one another.

Notes

1. Cf. Peter K. Guilday, *The Life and Times of John England* (N.Y.: America Press, 1927): vol. I, 283.

2. Cited by Guilday, *Life*, 289.

3. P.K. Guilday, *The Catholic Church in Virginia:1815-1822* (N.Y., United States Catholic Historical Society) and P.K. Guilday, "Trusteeism," *Historical Records and Studies*, XVIII (1928):7-73; and Guilday, *Life*, I, 12.

4. Charles G. Hebermann, *The Sulpicians in the United States* (N.Y.: Encyclopedia Press, 1916):184-185. In this regard see also Jules A. Baisnee. *France and the Establishment of the American Catholic Hierarchy* (Baltimore, Johns Hopkins, 1934); Guilday, *Life*, I, 15. Hebermann and Guilday, unlike Baisnee, make this charge regarding the unacceptability of certain episcopal appointments but they provide neither data nor any suggestive evidence for their case.

5. Guilday, Life, I 15f.; II, 82.

6. Guilday, Life, I, 10. John England did not, in general, dispute this appraisal, cf. *The Works of John England: 1786-1842* (Baltimore, John Murphy, 1849) 5 vols., III,.252.

7. Guilday, *Life,* I, 12, 31.

8. *South Carolina Historical Magazine* 102 (2001): 47-67.

9. John T. McGreevy, *Catholicism and American Freedom* (NY: Norton, 2003), 192-204.

10. Baisnee, 138; James Hennessey, "Papacy and Epsicopacy in 18th and 19th c. American Catholic Thought," *Records*, 77 (1966): 175-189, esp. 180. The

Papal States constituted a significant political entity across the central part of the Italian peninsula until 1870.

11. Guilday, *Life*, I, 10. *"Non Americani, non Angli, non aliarum Europeanarum gentium advenae, pacem perturbarunt aut perturbant , Caropoli, Norfolki, Philadelphiae etc., etc., etc. sed sacerdotes Hiberni intemperantiae aut ambitioni dediti...."* The Latin, of course, reflects the familiarity of the archbishop with the language.

12. William George Read, "Memoir of Bishop England," in *Works*, I, 4.

13. *Works*, V, 54.

14. Guilday, *Life*, I, chapter two, esp. 65. Guilday also discusses the surprise that most biographers express at England's choice of Carlow.

15. Francis P. Kenrick. "Review Article: Reynolds' Edition of the Works of John England," *Brownson Quarterly Review*, 7(1850):142f. This unsigned article is now generally attributed to Bishop Francis Kenrick rather than Brownson. See in this regard Thomas Ryan, "Bishop England and the Laity," *American Ecclesiastical Review*, 155 (1966) 103, n.2; Leon LeBuffe. *Tensions in American Catholicism, 1820-1870: An Intellectual History* [unpublished thesis] (Wash., DC: CUA, 1973), 25 and Sr. Virginia Lee Kaib. *The Ecclesiology of John England, the First Bishop of Charleston, South Carolina* [unpublished thesis] (Milwaukee: Marquette Univ., 1968), 71.

16. Richard W. Rousseau, *Bishop John England and American Church-State Theory* [unpublished thesis] (Ottawa, St. Paul Univ., 1969), 37; Guilday, *Life*, I,67. John England's personal library that may have told us a great deal about the influences brought to bear upon him was destroyed by the burning of Charleston in 1861, Rousseau, 34ff. For a summary of the theological perspective current at Maynooth (and by presumption at Carlow) see Rousseau, 38ff.

17. For an excellent summary of the theological perspectives current at Maynooth (and by presumption at Carlow) see Rousseau, 38ff.

18. Louis Delahogue, *Tractatus de Ecclesia Christi*, 5th ed. (Dublin: O'Toole, 1848), 143. "Concerning the agreement necessary among [world's] bishops, as that of the episcopal body, in order that some [papal] definition be recognized, [as] an infallible judgment."

19. Delahogue, 156.

20. Delahogue, 241. *"Christus Petro et ejus successoribus, aut ecclesiae, nullum concessit potestatem directam, aut indirectam in regum temporalia."*

21. Bailly, cited in Rousseau, 40-41.

22. Rousseau, 51-72; See also Sidney Ehler and John Morral, *Church and State Through the Centuries* (Westminster: Newman, 1954), 207-208.

23. Rousseau, 72.

24. James Brennan, "A Gallican Interlude in Ireland," *Irish Theological Quarterly*, 24(1957) 219-237 and 283-309. See also in this regard Guilday, *Life* 68-69, n.15 that gives some background on the Gallicanism of Delahogue.

25. Patrick W. Carey. *John England and Irish American Catholicism, 1815-1842: A Study in Conflict* [unpublished dissertation] (NY: Fordham University, 1975).

26. Gerald McCool. *Catholic Theology in the Nineteenth Century* (NY: Seabury, 1977), 67ff. Other insights on nineteenth century Catholic theology, especially J.S. Drey, are dependent on the work of John Thiel, *Imagination and Authority: Theological Authorship in the Modern Tradition* (Minneapolis: Fortress, 1991, esp. 72-94. John England visited Austria several times and worked with the Leopoldine Society there and through correspondence. He also made a number of trips to Europe to seek funds for his work in the United States. It is likely he was fluent in German and was familiar with the theological currents in Tubingen at the time because of the trips made to German-speaking countries. See Peter Clarke, *A Free Church in a Free Society: The Ecclesiology of John England, Bishop of Charleston, South Carolina, 1820-1842* (Greenwood, S.C.: Center for John England Studies, 1982, 520 who refers as well to the 31 reports and letters of John England to the Leopoldine Society written in German that are housed at St. Francis Seminary in Milwaukee, Wisconsin.

27. McCool, 71ff.

28. Guilday, *Life*, 71-73.

29. Cited in Carey, *England*, 31.

30. *The Cork Mercantile-Chronicle*, Sept. 5, 1819, cited in Carey, 30.

31. Guilday, *Life*, I, 95-96, n. 18.

32. Guilday, ibid., I, 123; Guilday, "Arthur O'Leary," *Catholic Historical Review*, 9 (1923-1924): 530-545.

33. LeBuffe, 48-49.

34. Guilday, "O'Leary," 540.

35. Carey, *England*, 83-96, esp. 89, n. 13. According to Locke the social compact establishing the civil order was not "between ruler and ruled, but between equally free men, Paul Edwards, "John Locke," *Encyclopedia of Philosophy* (N.Y., Macmillan, 1967): vol. 4, p. 499. Locke was also a strong advocate of religious tolerance, ibid., 501. Needless to say, Locke has been referred to as the "resident philosopher" of the American political tradition. See also Paul Sigmund, *The Selected Political Writings of John Locke* (NY: Norton, 2005) xvi ff.

36. Locke, "First Treatise of Government," in Sigmond, 42, 87.

37. Daniel F. Kearns, "Bishop John England and the Possibilities of Catholic Republicanism," *South Carolina Historical Magazine* 102 (2001): 47, 60. DeTocqueville is cited on page 60 of Kearns. See also Carey, 95-96, n.29.

38. Kearns, "Bishop John England," 48; Philip Pettit. *Republicanism: A Theory of Freedom and Governmen.* (NY: Oxford, 1997), see particularly his discussion of communitarian romanticism characteristic of the republicans, 120ff.

39. Kearns, "Bishop John England," 48.

40. Patrick W. Carey, *People, Priests, and Prelates: Ecclesial Democracy and the tensions of Trusteeism* (Notre Dame, 1987) 282 and Carey, *England.*, 79ff., esp. 113f.

41. Stanley Hauerwas and Charles Pinchas, *Christian Among the Virtues: Theological Conversations with Ancient and Modern Ethics* (Notre Dame: Univ. N.D. Press, 1997).

42. Kearns, "Bishop John England," 33, 48; Pettit, *Republicanism*, 33-41.

43. Pettit, *Republicanism*, 12. "Non-interference" / "non-coercion" appear congruent with Vatican II, *Dignitatis Humanae*, 1 of which Roger Haight observes, "no one can be forced to act contrary to his or her beliefs." *Christian Community in History: Comparative Theology*, vol. 2 (NY: Continuum) 2005, 399.

44. Cf. Carey, *England*, 4, 45-46.

45. Christopher Kauffman, *Tradition and Transformation in Catholic Culture* (NY: MacMillan, 1988), 102-103 for a concise insight in this regard.

46. A copy of the Diocesan Constitution is provided at the end of this book. Chapter three examines the document closely.

47. Thomas Corcoran, "John England, 1786-1842, *Studies*, 17 (1928): 24-25. There was a controversy over the authorship of the most nationalistic of the textbooks, *School Primer of Irish History*, which was published anonymously. Anglican Archbishop Magree in a speech in the House of Lords attributed the authorship to John England, according to Corcoran.

48. Guilday, *Life*, I, 91.

49. Finbar Kenneally, *United States Documents in the Propaganda Fide Archives: A Calendar* (Washington: Academy of Franciscan History, 1966): vol. III, no. 1143, Jan 28, 1817.

50. Kenneally, *United States*, no. 1432, March 19, 1817. See also *Works*, V, 145; III, 254 for England's own account of the request.

51. Kenneally, *United States*, no 1147.

52. Cited in Guilday, *Church in Virginia*, 117.

53. J. O' Connell. *Catholicity in the Carolinas and Georgia* (N.Y., Sadlier, 1879): 90.

54. Read in *Works*, I, 9.

55. *Works*, I, 11.

56. Kearns, 53.

57. C. S. Peirce, "What Is A Sign?" in *The Essential Peirce,* vol. 2, Peirce Edition Project (Bloomington, IN: University of Indiana, 1998), 4-10. Lou McNeil, "C.S. Peirce's Theory of Inquiry: Reading the Signs of the Times," an unpublished dissertation, Toronto: University of St. Michael's College/ University of Toronto, 1982) 168ff. Jeanne Evans, *Paul Ricoeur's Hermeneutics of the Imagination* (NY: Peter Lang, 1995), chapters 2, 3, and 4, esp. 127f. Paul Ricoeur, *The Rule of Metaphor* (Toronto: University of Toronto, 1977).

Chapter Three

Living and Leading within a Minority

> No great advance has ever been
> made in science, politics, or
> religion, without controversy.
> Lyman Beecher

The United States and Its Milieu

The War of 1812 and Its Consequences

The country to which John England sailed was itself in the midst of revolutionary times not unlike those in Ireland. Though the United States had fought and won its independence from Great Britain in 1776, it had only recently concluded what some have called its second war of independence in 1812. This war was undertaken by and large at the instigation of expansionists who burned with the ardent zeal of a proselytizing republicanism. Western frontiersmen had cast their eyes upon Canada with the hopes of annexing this large outpost of British colonialism on the North American continent.

Great Britain, however, exercised firm control over the trade routes between North America and Europe. The British attitude and domination of trade played into the hands of the American war party that strove hard and finally won the support of New England commercial interests for war with the British. The war ended a virtual stalemate. For all their shouting, the Americans found that there was little real support for the effort anywhere in the nation, even on the frontier with Canada. The frontiersmen's designs upon Canada failed miserably. The nation was humiliated with the burning of its capital, Washington. Nonetheless, the Americans did win several major battles that assured them their more modest and most valid goals: freedom of the seas and surety that American citizens would not be impressed into British naval service, which had happened frequently in the preceding years. When the war ended in 1815, an era in American history also came to an end. Great Britain was no longer a threat to American sovereignty. More importantly from a political perspective, the frontiersmen emerged as a potent new factor in the American political arena. Furthermore, among these frontiersmen was a newly discovered national hero and symbol of the frontier's more radical democratic aspirations—Andrew Jackson. Jackson, who had won the celebrated battle of New Orleans during the war, quickly secured his reputation and image as a man of the "little people," a man of the expansionist frontier following the war.

Having for the first time pushed the national Congress in the direction of their own interests (the coastal states had originally opposed the war but eventually capitulated, though they gave only minimal support to the effort), the frontier states found and solidified a new identity. The frontier, the war and Andrew Jackson by the close of the 1810s proved to be harbingers of radical institutional changes on the American scene.

Constitutionally a republic, the United States was not by any means a radical democracy. The revolution of 1776 had taken pains to insure the government from the hands of a democratic rabble. In effect a republican oligarchy was established. Only the white, male and landed person held franchise. The electoral process for choosing the president had been placed squarely in the hands of the respective states. In no instance was the popular vote alone determinative. The members of the United States Senate likewise were chosen, not by popular vote, but by respective state assemblies or legislatures that, in turn, chose the president through the mechanism of the electoral college. The plutocratic and oligarchic nature of the nineteenth century U.S. federal government is outlined well by Robert Caro in the second volume of his biography of Lyndon Johnson. Money, commercial interests and planters held firm rein through most of the century on federal authority even as Jacksonian populism and its successors waged a counter-offensive.[1]

Jacksonian Democracy

When Bishop England arrived in Charleston harbor in late December 1820, the era of the "radical democrats" was just beginning to emerge in the Jacksonian movement. In the eight years preceding the triumph of Jacksonian democracy in the election of 1828, Richard Hofstader writes, "Democracy walked hand in hand with nationalism. The new democracy esteemed individualism and enterprise; although it began by attacking economic privileges."[2] A series of political events that began when Massachusetts scrapped its constitution in 1820 in favor of a new and more liberal one ignited a full attack upon the old federalism and its eastern oligarchy. Debates over suffrage, religious tests and the role of the courts (the last bastion of the oligarchy) enflamed the national debate to a fever pitch. Following Massachusetts and the newer states of the frontier (e.g., Kentucky, Ohio and Tennessee), New York and Virginia enacted new constitutions with broader suffrage and no religious tests. The currents of popular democracy soon engulfed the entire nation. This assessment must be balanced by the growing recognition of the social or communal moorings of Jacksonianism. There is no question of the deeply populist roots for the radical Jacksonian democrats, yet as populist movements that were to follow, its breath of inclusion was not total. It was during the presidency of Andrew Jackson that the Choctaw peoples traversed the Trail of Tears on their journey from North Carolina to the Oklahoma Territory that led to near extinction.[3]

Though the Jacksonian movement included some members of the frontier evangelical movement, the clergy and the churches by and large saw the movement as godless, mob-ridden and morally corrupt liberalism. Even the symbols of the movement, Jefferson and Jackson, were themselves widely understood not to be "believing Christians." Jefferson was believed by many to be an avowed Deist. Jackson, nominally a Presbyterian, was popularly and unfairly understood to have lived with his wife for two years before she received a divorce from her first husband. She and Jackson were unaware, in fact, that the divorce had not been granted. With the attacks Jacksonianism unleashed upon the established leaders and institutions of American society, a radical and disorderly mob did seem to be emerging. As a result of the strident calls for rapid and far-reaching change, "even people with the most nominal religious interests were beginning to regard the breakdown of Christian ties as a major cause of radicalism."[4] As a result the clergy generally rallied to the side of the opponents of Jacksonianism, first the Federalists and later their successors at the polls, the Whigs.[5]

By 1832 serious discussion was given the notion that the antidote for such radicalism was to place the government on a sound religious basis. *An Inquiry into the Moral and Religious Character of the American Government* was a popular book that appeared in the 1830s promoting the prevailing Whig view that the United States had a "national religion as well as a national government."[6] Some Whigs even proposed public taxes in support of the churches. During this era the courts emerged clearly as the protectors of the Federalist/Whig tradition. Soon some courts did not permit the sworn testimony of unbelievers (and Catholics in a few cases) because such persons held themselves unaccountable to God in an afterlife. Consequently they could not be regarded as trustworthy.[7]

As often happens the rise of one movement generates quickly the development of its opposite. Jacksonian democracy had the effect of revitalizing (temporarily) Whigism and giving impetus to "revivalism" in the churches. Something approaching an accommodation of these opposites arose with transcendentalists who saw "the cause of democracy as the cause of pure religion not less than of justice."[8] For George Bancroft and Orestes Brownson popular democracy (with which John England earlier had identified himself) was the cause of practical Christianity. Thus after England's death the transcendentalists would bring a significant segment of the religious community to the side of popular democracy. But this is to get ahead of myself.

In *The Age of Jackson*, Arthur Schlesinger suggests that the major contribution in the religious sphere of Jacksonian democracy was "the growing secularization of society." Its substantial effect was to direct the church toward what many in this century believed its true function: "*to lead the individual soul to salvation,* [emphasis mine] not interfere in politics."[9] If Schlesinger's appraisal is a fair one, then John England, who was very much a popular democrat and seemingly a Jacksonian, must have his thought closely scrutinized regarding his model for church ministry. Was it a highly individualistic one, as some Church historians have recently suggested, or a more social interpretation and understanding both of the role of the church and the individual? Our answer to this question must be framed in light of England's frequent contextualization of individual liberty within the exigency of the common good and social responsibility. He wrote, for example, "The individual shall honestly prefer the public good to his private emolument... [its] neglect... offends that God who is the author of the social compact." [10]

During the same time in South Carolina, the molder of opinion in political matters was John C. Calhoun. He served as the Vice President of the United States from 1825-1832, resigning so that he could enter the United States Senate from South Carolina. He remained a member of the Senate until his death in 1850. Calhoun is best remembered for championing the cause of nullification, i.e., the political proposition that an individual state could nullify federal legislation upon the ruling of the state courts that such federal legislation was, in fact, an infringement upon the prerogatives of the state. An ardent and frequently embattled Southern patriot, Calhoun alternately aligned himself with the Whigs and the Democrats, depending on which offered the best advantage to the Southern cause at the moment. The question he grappled with was whether the conservative, aristocratic South (the South he represented) should ally itself with the Whigs against the mob of radical Jacksonian Democrats favoring universal suffrage or with the radical Jacksonian Democrats in their fight against the domination of Northeastern business interests?[11] Calhoun, after vacillating, ultimately chose the Jacksonian Democrats. The South, during the same period, generally voted with the Whigs. Later by the 1850s the Whigs were to endorse abolition nationally, while it was the Democrats that clearly appeared sympathetic to the Southern plight. In retrospect, then, Calhoun from the viewpoint of a strictly Southern anti-abolitionist, pro-slavery bias was seen as the rejected prophet of the Southern cause! During the late 1820-1830s, Bishop England, like John Calhoun, placed his sympathies with the cause of the radical democrats and against both the business interests of the North with its accompanying economic liberalism and in favor of the separation of Church and State.

One may see here England's nuanced understanding of the individual and society. The practice of religion that, for accountability and ethical reasons must be free, was valued on the same basis as Augustine would have. Moral culpability requires free will, one of Augustine's contributions to the theological tradition. But liberalism in the economic sphere and a rugged pursuit of economic self-interest were rejected by John England (as a good Jacksonian and socially aware Christian) as antithetical to a broad range of Christian virtues. The tenor of his position was summed up well in his understanding that the common good, in contradistinction to Northeastern business interests that favored an unrestricted free market exploited the small farmers of the South and West and was an affront to the commonweal of the nation. This was a principled position that some current critics fail to recognize or appreciate. In it there seems little ground to attribute an acritical accommodation to liberal, Enlightenment individualism.[12]

Immigration, Immigrants and Nativism

When the Treaty of Ghent was signed in 1815 it concluded a series of wars only one of which was the American-British conflict of 1812. In the subsequent recession that settled upon the previously warring nations in Europe, wages plummeted and welfare escalated. As a result many European nations were gladly bidding farewell to the thousands of their citizens who began journeys to the United States.[13] The immigrants to the United States were heavily Catholic, and at this period the Irish constituted a significant proportion of the total. Prior to the arrival of these immigrants, American Catholicism had been largely an Anglo-American and Franco-American community. Its membership was chiefly found around the southeastern corner of Pennsylvania, the state of Maryland, the south of Louisiana and in scattered but significant minorities of people along the Mississippi and the Gulf of Mexico. Smaller French communities were scattered through the Upper Great Lakes Region. These areas had traditionally afforded Catholicism the greatest toleration. A characteristic timidity, which had plagued the English Catholic settlers of Maryland, would also be apparent in its daughter, the English-speaking American Catholic community. The small company of priests that had constituted the leadership of the church during the colonial and early national periods had been extremely cautious regarding the establishment of a hierarchy. Their caution, it should be remembered, was not without grounds. They recognized that the Protestant-Episcopal Church (Anglican), for similar reasons, had not sought a bishop during this period. It would seem that this comparison limped somewhat. An Episcopalian bishop at this time would have been directly related by appointment and consecration to the British Crown, but not in the case of a Catholic bishop. But the point could still be made that a Catholic bishop was regarded within the tradition as a lord or prince carrying with him in his dress the insignia of the aristocracy.[14] The expectation of severe opposition, perhaps even persecution, voiced by these pioneer priests (even Charles Carroll of Carroll Town agreed) seems to have been more a symbol of an inferiority complex and timidity that Thomas McAvoy suggests was inherited from English Catholicism.[15] Nonetheless, it was engrained into the American Catholic consciousness from the moment the first Catholic settlers set out for the colony of Maryland. Lord Baltimore, the proprietor, warned the captain of the ship and its passengers to refrain from any public reference about their faith. Calvert had the Protestant passengers of the maiden trip board the ship at the stated point of departure. The Catholics, however, were picked up at an obscure port in the south of Great Britain so as to avoid any possible talk about a "Catholic" colony. Upon arrival at St. Mary, Maryland, Calvert insisted on preventing any public show of Catholicism.[16] Decades later when an increasing number of immigrants began to arrive, this reserve disappeared. The Irish, in particular, were to introduce a bolder, more public and, eventually, more aggressive tone to the American Catholic Church.

Throughout the early national period there was a progressive movement in the United States toward broader religious toleration and pluralism.[17] Original legal restrictions set by various religious tests seem to have been largely ignored if not quietly removed from the statutes during the period 1776-1827. This relatively enlightened attitude may well have been due in great measure to the paucity of Catholics in even the most Catholic areas, Maryland and Pennsylvania. Catholicism could hardly have been seen as much of a threat to anyone. The attitude may be illustrated in the fact that John England was widely accepted in the rural Protestant churches of the South during the period 1821-1823.[18] Furthermore, active church membership and interest in organized religion was quite low in the country at this time and that would account for a degree of indifference to "intra-Christian" rivalries.

By 1827, however, the number of Catholics also had increased significantly and a new awareness of an American Catholicism in its midst sharpened Protestant attitudes. According to Ray Billington, the Jubilee Year proclaimed by Leo XII in 1827 and the converts that were entering the Catholic Church were two factors that stirred up a heightened consciousness of Catholicism.[19] Another significant factor in the changing awareness and perception of American Catholicism was the First Provincial Council of Baltimore in 1829. Not only did the hierarchy, which consisted of ten bishops, become more visible, the decrees issued were ill-considered in terms of their impact upon Protestant ears. The council warned against "corrupt translations of the Bible," the "perversion" of children in schools with a strong Protestant atmosphere and it urged priests to baptize non-Catholic infants in danger of death.[20] These decrees were issued in the midst of the traditional pomp and regalia of a Council that would smack, of course, of aristocratic and courtly presumptions to American sensibilities. Finally there was the apparent victory of the "monarchial" bishops over the embattled democratic parish trustees. Each had contended for control of the church's property and the right to appoint pastors. The impression Protestant Americans received in all this, according to Billington, was that Catholicism was a "sworn enemy" of democratic and American institutions. With the concomitant rise of fundamentalism in the form of the revivalism of the period, wilder and wilder rumors developed regarding Catholicism. Horror stories from convents, tales of despotic, Catholic monarchs in Europe hatching plans to take over the United States, as well as the belief that Catholics generally were liars, criminals and a shiftless people inundated the nation from 1830-1850.[21]

Faced with increasing hostility toward Catholicism, Bishop England would be a beacon of progressive inculturation both in institutional and pastoral questions. He would succumb, however, to the temptation to prove Catholicism and himself truly American on the slavery question which is undoubtedly the tragic aspect of his career. His failing in this regard may well have been the tight focus he placed upon his service to his own community of faith and its institutional expression and a severe lapse in his attentiveness to those outside the circle of his own community. In this instance, the church's propensity to accommodate the traditional expressions of society and culture, together with his Southern context, contributed to his failure to expand his vision. In almost all the other instances of his life, England allowed himself to be stretched by one or the other of these two contexts. In ante-bellum Charleston as regards slavery, neither stretched him as he should have been.[22]

The Catholic Church and the Papacy in the Early Nineteenth Century

What was true in the rise of Jacksonianism in the United States was paralleled in the Catholic Church at large. Popular democracy and liberalism generated a conservative reaction in both. A revival of papal influence after Pius VII's release by Napoleon in 1815 can be attributed to the security ordinary people sought in light of the revolutionary and rapid changes that swirled around them. The early Lamennais and De Maistre, while accepting notions of a constitutional monarchy and representative government, were ultimately to influence the reviving forces of Catholicism in opposition to the encroachments of liberalism on the church. Both of these men condemned popular sovereignty and specifically the theory of a social compact. The theory that England had embraced regarding the social compact was grounded in God as its author.[23] It was England's use of what was most appropriate of the modern world that is notable. It reflects an astute inculturation. The dialectic of his era was the contestation between the concentration of authority and power and the emergent populist forces that promoted decentralization, accountability and the balance between powers. Unlike England, the period's dominating revisionist, ultramontane understanding of the papacy saw not only the pope as infallible, but his supreme sovereignty was regarded as a check over national abuses. Lamennais, for example, embodied both progressive and ultramontane perspectives in his promotion of popular democracy in Europe while aligning with a strong papacy to counterbalance the influence of the rising nation-states. While the first half of the nineteenth century did not always see a consistent, unbroken line of development in an enlargement of papal claims, the progress was steady.[24]

There were four pontificates during John England's adult years. Pius VII (1800-1823) was for a time the prisoner of Napoleon. A humble man, he promoted spiritual renewal in the religious orders. Cardinal Consalvi, noted for his efforts to win back the Papal States through negotiation after the removal of Napoleon, was bitterly opposed by Metternich and the conservative to reactionary monarchs who were in the ascendancy after the fall of Napoleon. Consequently with the death of Pius VII in 1823, Consalvi retired from his position at State and was sent to the Propagation Office. It was Consalvi, then, who would have read John England's Diocesan Constitution when it was sent to Rome for approval. Leo XII, Pius's successor, was more hostile to modernizing trends than his predecessor. He condemned religious toleration as a drift to indifferentism. Yet, paradoxically, it was under Leo that many of the independence-minded and "liberal" bishops in South America were appointed.[25] Consalvi was surely a major factor responsible for this.

Leo was succeeded by the more liberal, but short-lived, Pius VIII (1829-1830). Like Pius VII, the new pope had opposed the rule of Napoleon. He furthermore was much more disposed to accommodate the liberal forces of the time. Pius, however, died soon after his election and was succeeded by the much more conservative Gregory XVI (1831-1846), who had been in charge of the Propagation Office. Gregory eventually chose as his Secretary of State Cardinal Lambruschini who would be a dominant force throughout Gregory's reign. During his pontificate, Gregory rejected and virtually condemned the separation of the Church and State and certain understandings of freedom of conscience in *Mirari Vos* (1832) and *Singulari Nos* (1834). This signaled the ascendancy of the anti-liberal forces in the Catholic Church.[26] It was an indication of the beginning of the Catholic leadership's withdrawal into itself as a result of the liberal onslaughts of the nineteenth century. In spite of this, it was Gregory XVI who paradoxically appointed the notoriously "liberal" John England to negotiate a concordant with the government of Haiti. Thus the "liberal" John England, appointed to the episcopacy by the notoriously conservative Pius VII in 1822, was further affirmed when he received a diplomatic assignment from the even more anti-modern, anti-republican Gregory XVI. This should cause us to be suspicious, at the very least, that some contemporary projections onto John England and some other nineteenth century Catholic leaders seem not to fit the circumstances of the time. The subtlety of John England's thought, as we have seen, is miscast if it is simply typified as assimilationist. Such an aspersion reflects more current political and religious debates and ignores earlier understandings of individualism, accountability, decentralization, and divine right.

Catholicism in the United States: The Trustee Question

In the United States itself, Catholicism by 1820 had grown only moderately. John Carroll had been appointed bishop of Baltimore in 1789. He had realized quickly that the organization of the church through his own efforts would be severely limited in such a far-flung diocese. (It was coterminus with the new nation.) At his urging Baltimore had been created a metropolitan see in 1808 with suffragan sees located at New York, Boston, Philadelphia and Bardstown, Kentucky. None of the men appointed to these new dioceses were native to the United States. Two, however, had served for several years in the country.[27]

Discipline was the major factor the young church faced and the trustee system was the greatest irritant to its peace and harmony. This was due in part because of the notion of congregationalism that some of the Irish introduced into the United States. Another factor was the nature of American law regarding corporate ownership. There were no provisions for the "church" to own property. Rather trustees of a corporation or an individual could be the only legal possessors of title to real property. Following the example of the Protestant community prior to 1829, Catholics established parishes with trustees holding title to the property. Because of the inheritance problems resulting from the laws and the experience of the church in Europe with a bishop's heirs' possibility to claim title to church property, the bishop as sole trustee was not quickly and unhesitatingly resorted to at this time in the United States. The role of the immigrants' memories of the trustee questions (*jus patronis*) in their homelands also is well addressed by Carey. One might question, however, Carey's underestimation of the republican-democratic influences of the American experience that came to bear upon them.[28] Not being fully familiar with the legal traditions, U.S. Catholics consequently did not place in their corporation charters clear guidelines to distribute and restrict authority in the management of the property. As a result the trustees had sole and unrestricted authority, in most instances, over all parish affairs from a legal point of view. Unscrupulous or contentious trustees soon created turmoil throughout the country. During this early period, trusteeism was a phenomenon in the coastal cities and only later spread west. A major issue that also arose during the trustee controversies was the *jus patronus* (the right to appoint the pastor). Although a major issue that was controverted, the *jus patronus* was not probably the basic underlying factor of trusteeism. The difficulties had been gathering from John Carroll's time and first came to a head in the 1810s. In Philadelphia the confrontation between Bishop Conwell and Fr. William Hogan became the focal point of a series of such outbreaks. In the Philadelphia affair, the bishop and the trustees stood toe to toe conceding nothing to each other for nearly a decade. The tragic climax was reached when Rome intervened. Rome issued the document *Non Sine Magno* condemning the excessive claims of the trustees.[29] The bishop was removed from the administration of the diocese and Francis P. Kenrick was appointed coadjutor-administrator. Bishop Conwell was also deprived of voting privileges at the First Council of Baltimore in 1829.[30] This acrimonious affair unfortunately shaped many American Protestant impressions of Catholicism. It cannot be disputed that a democratic spirit was a factor in the lay trustees' desire to have a say in the management of their parish. In pleading the right to name their own pastor, they stated that those who pay the salary should also have the right to hire and fire. It would be inaccurate, however, to suggest, as earlier chroniclers of the period have, that the trustee movement reflected a type of "an emotional republicanism" and "a form of American liberalism."[31] In most instances, the agenda of the trustees seemed concentrated on ethnicity and local conditions within a parish that were coupled with holding the pastor accountable. It should be remembered that the early bishops themselves frequently complained that canonical pastors, whom they could not replace since such pastors held irremovable status, were not appointed because of the "quality" of a large share of the priests who chose to migrate to the United States from Europe. Some trustees saw a clear parallel between their cause and the European tradition of the *jus patronus*. In Europe the *jus patronus* had been granted to the patron, the financial supporter, of a given church congregation. In some instances even the government exercised this right in Europe. Since in the United States there was no government support for the church and no private benefactors (patrons), such patronage rights surely could be claimed, they reasoned, by the members of the congregation.[32] The reasoning also reflected clearly the congregational and Protestant influences of the United States as well as in some instances the independence of Irish congregationalism during the period prior to Emancipation.

There were other factors also involved in the lay-trustee controversies. Not the least of these were ethnic considerations, as we noted in passing above. Many of the parishes where trusteeism was most persistent were Irish dominated. These parishes, such as Norfolk and Charleston, strongly resented the appointment of French-born pastors. A common, if not valid, complaint of the Irish was that the Frenchmen preached so poorly in English. In the Irish's efforts to be American, these French-born pastors were seen as an embarrassment. Yet, Thomas McAvoy, I believe, correctly maintains that French clergy were more readily accepted into sophisticated American circles than were the Irish. This would, of course, belie the Irish claims against the French on the basis of their not being sufficiently American.[33] It would lead one to speculate that class may also have been a factor. In any case, Billington is likely incorrect when he asserts that the trustees "constantly" tried to appoint native rather than foreign pastors. They often were, in the early years of trusteeism, anti-French or pro-Irish, and fought for Irish pastors whether native-born or not.[34]

When John England received the news of his nomination to the see of the Carolinas and Georgia, he was also briefed concerning the trustee problems that existed in Charleston. The controversy between the trustees of St. Mary's Church and the Archbishop of Baltimore had begun in 1815. The dispute arose over a question regarding Fr. Robert Browne's claim that he had been assigned to the parish as an associate pastor by the late Archbishop Carroll. Fr. Felix Gallagher, the pastor, supported the claim. Carroll's successor, Leonard Neale, however, asserted that the diocesan records indicated that the appointment had only been a temporary assignment made in response to a request by Fr. Gallagher. The priest, the Archbishop claimed, made the request for replacement for himself while absent from St. Mary's because of personal reasons. Archbishop Neale therefore had appointed Fr. Cloriviere, a French-born priest, to replace Fr. Browne in the parish. Whatever may have been the legal right of the Archbishop, the least that can be said is that the move to appoint a French native to the parish was impolitic. With ethnic feelings as they were, such an appointment to a predominantly Irish congregation was sure to exacerbate the situation. As a result, during the next four years the two Irish-born priests, Gallagher and Browne, along with the trustees, remained intransigent to the arguments of Neale and his successor, Ambrose Marechal. During this period Browne even made an appeal to the Propagation Office that ruled against the Archbishop, although this decision was later retracted. Unable to move beyond dead center for nearly three years, the Archbishop then conceived the plan of establishing a diocesan seat at Charleston as the antidote. Indecision and ethnic feelings had prevented Marechal from dealing with the situations in Charleston and Norfolk effectively. Rome undoubtedly thought this was the case also when they decided to appoint two Irishmen to the new dioceses over the objections of Marechal. His position in the whole affair is a bit hard to fathom. In his list of suggested nominees for the new see, he did not include any native Americans, such as Fenwick, whom he sent to resolve the conflict in Charleston. He urged, however, that neither an Irishman nor a Frenchman be appointed. In other words, his communication to Rome had broad categories of people excluded from consideration (including "no American priests are qualified") leaving only a few personal friends as acceptable.[35]

It was when Marechal had finally taken some decisive action sending the Jesuit Benedict Fenwick and an Irish-born priest, Fr. Wallace, after the long period of vacillation and misjudgment, that the strength and forthrightness of these two priests contained the conflict and created a modicum of peace shortly before the arrival of the newly appointed bishop of Charleston. The matter at Norfolk was neglected entirely during this period.

England himself must have been all too aware of the inept handling of the situation in Charleston over the years. One of the alarming developments in this bungled job of administration was the existence of some letters that indicated a move had been underway to persuade Fr. Richard Hayes, an Irish Franciscan and a personal friend of John England, to proceed to Utrecht for the purpose of being consecrated a bishop for the "Independent Catholic Church of the United States."[36] So worried was Rome, though some feel that it was exaggerated, that the Diocese of Richmond was created to prevent such a Jansenist bishopric being established there or in Charleston.[37]

Much has been written regarding the Franco-Irish skirmishes in the early nineteenth century American Catholic Church. Gabriel Richard, S.S., of Detroit, asked explicitly that an Irishman not be sent anywhere in the United States. The Irish, on the other hand, were unstinting in their characterization of the French-born clergy and the bishops generally as hostile to American institutions and culture. Proponents of each camp made strong points and each, in all likelihood, was right given the objectives and strategy they deemed best for the church.[38] Bishops Marechal and England, regardless of their better intentions, were both victims to a degree of the polarities that reflected their French and Irish constituencies and backgrounds. The Franco-Irish conflict was significant in John England's activities throughout his lifetime in the United States. As has been seen, the consequence was that the relationship between England and Marechal was not calculated to produce the best of possibilities from the start. Things hardly improved with the appointment of Archbishop Whitfield, an Englishman, as Marechal's successor. When Whitfield sent out the invitations to his episcopal consecration he excluded from the list not only Bishop England, but also two of England's closest allies in the hierarchy, the two Bishops Fenwick, the one of Boston and the other of Cincinnati.

Among the Irish "dissidents" John England emerged as the champion, the Irish hero and protector. He was the man to whom the dissidents felt they could turn. And they did. He became the symbol of Irish aspirations, republicanism, individual rights, a moderated form of Irish congregationalism and assertiveness. Surely, because of the prominent role of the American Irish in the trustee questions and John England's constitution for the diocese, the Irish were indeed seen as trying to "democratize" the church. The constitution that he established for his diocese played no small role in insuring his stature among his like-minded contemporaries. To a great extent the battle between the French and the Irish was based on cultural and personal considerations. There is validity to the belief that there were some clearly divergent ideas about the church in the positions of John England and his opponents in the Franco-American bloc that may have run along the same fault line as the Whig-Jacksonian Democrats on a wide range of political and social values.[39] The priests native to Maryland and Pennsylvania also associated themselves with the positions of the French group that derived much of its influence from the presence of the French Sulpician priests who served as the faculty of the seminary in Baltimore. Bishop England constructed much of his vision of the church around his practical involvement with the hopes and struggles of the laboring immigrants arriving from Europe. The others seem to have shaped their vision of the church from the more established Anglo-American cradle of Catholicism in Maryland and later Philadelphia. These latter Catholics represented economically and culturally a far different experience in this period (1820-1832) than that of the Irish or any of the other Catholic ethnic groups which soon were to constitute the far greater part of American Catholicism. Daniel Kearns writes,

> The importance of John England's vision to the integration of immigrant Catholics into American politics cannot be overstated. . . . A Federalist culture of conservative and quiet hierarchy personified by the squire-like Charles Carroll fell to a republican vision that allowed Catholics to take part in American life. . . . . Through such figures as Martin Spaulding and John Hughes, Catholic bishops inspired by England turned the Church into a social force that could no longer be ignored.[40]

It should also be mentioned here, however, that while John England himself was theologically shaped by influences from France (as we saw above), the priests who served on the faculty at St. Mary's Seminary in Baltimore had arrived there in the years 1792 and later on the heels of the turmoil and chaos of the revolution at home and because of the chaos of the revolution represented a very different, perhaps chastened attitude toward pre-revolutionary positions.

John England's First Pastoral Letter

The efforts of Benedict Fenwick while administrator at St. Mary's Church, Charleston had done much to still the turmoil and provide some direction to the parish. England's own words some years later indicated that "peace was in some degree restored. . . . by Doctor Fenwick. . . . by removing some of the causes of previous irritation.[41] Quite obviously all the problems associated with the trustee question were not resolved. Upon his arrival, Bishop England recorded that he found "the mode in which the church property had been hitherto invested, liable to serious abuses, and having, in several instances, been the occasion of incalculable mischief." [42] In his assessment, England was clearly of the opinion that pastoral rule did not arise from the people as he might have argued would be the case for the secular realm. He writes very succinctly, "Ecclesiastical rule was not [referring to the parish at Charleston] in the pastor, but the people."[43] This, he noted, was the source of the divisions and loss of direction in the parish's life.

Whatever the circumstances were specifically in 1820, when he departed for the newly established diocese, John England was aware and concerned with the schism that had only recently been defused by dint of the personal qualities of Fathers Fenwick and Wallace as conciliators. This recent wound in the local church was obviously in the forefront of his thoughts when he wrote his first Pastoral Letter to the people of the diocese. It was the first such letter issued in the United States.[44]

Having arrived shortly after Christmas, 1820, the new bishop had begun immediately to draft the letter to his flock. It was in many respects a cautious letter, particularly in light of the later Pastoral Letters and writings and the forthright positions taken in them. A very traditional conception of episcopal authority was presented. This was certainly a prudent and understandable position for a man newly appointed to such an office in a diocese so recently marked with disorders centering on the question of episcopal authority. While the tone of the letter was quite different in some respects from his later writings, it did set the agenda, so to speak, for his new administration. It is an important document that gives us a clearer idea of how the bishop viewed ministry and church.

Faith, Authority and the Church

The Pastoral was short. It occupies only six full columns in the Reynolds edition of England's *Works*.[45] It began with an overview of salvation history as recorded in the Sacred Scriptures. This biblical approach was to be characteristic of the first four national Pastorals (of the Councils of Baltimore) that were the compositions of Bishop England. The unfolding of salvation history was to be found in the tale of creation. Adam walked in original innocence, yet by "presumptuous disobedience" he lost his innocence and happiness. Nonetheless God did not abandon Adam and his progeny. Salvation was offered, but on condition that "although his [humankind's] salvation did not originate with man. . . . without his cooperation it could not be accomplished."[46] The conditions for salvation therefore were twofold: belief and practical obedience. England saw these two conditions as an antidote to humankind's "presumptuous disobedience" because "belief humbled [humankind's] understanding; obedience checked his will."[47] In this manner God was at one and the same time punishing humankind's disobedience, healing its weakness and redeeming it from its own petty willfulness. Humankind's duty therefore was to discover God's Will and to uncover what God taught and commanded. This entailed an examination "of facts, not opinions" which, of course, meant a thorough study of the Sacred Scriptures. In the Scriptures could be found both the content of God's Will and the authoritative office through which that Will was communicated to us. "[A]nd when upon Sinai he gave the law, he thundered before the multitude, and called the teacher up to his presence: upon the authority of Moses, Aaron was consecrated. . . to the priestly office."[48] Although the authority and priesthood of the Old Testament were to expire, Jesus replaced both. He passed his own priesthood on to his disciples. He made known to them as well all the mysteries of the Kingdom "that they should teach them to the nations." But these twelve men were mortal and it was necessary that they likewise should pass their commission on to others and so "by prayer and the imposition of hands, they did qualify others." The bishop concluded: "And thus do we find in the new law the same principle which governed the old; the authority to teach and to minister in the church specially bestowed upon particular individuals. . . . and continued by regular succession to after-ages."[49] Of the apostles, one was clearly preeminent in power, Peter. With Matthew 16: 18-19 and Luke 22: 31-32 as his texts, the bishop demonstrated what he held to be the "office" bestowed that just as surely as Jesus established "a church which was to last to the end of the world, its government was to be coeval with its existence." Peter therefore was succeeded until that very day when Pius VII possessed the same "office" and "power." It was unquestionably Rome, the bishop noted, that had preserved the succession and was the "mother and mistress of all other churches."[50] John England then turned to his own appointment as their bishop. "Thus we are placed in the midst of you, unworthy as we are, yet vested with the apostolic power, having, through the Holy Spirit, received that power from Jesus Christ Himself."[51] He had been placed "over them as a father" to teach the doctrines of truth, to guide them to a very deep concern about their duty to God and the practice of their religion. In the Pastoral he also made mention of the impossibility in providing pastors to all who were desirous of one. Among the difficulties was the wherewithal necessary to support materially the pastors of the diocese: "They who preach the gospel should live by the gospel (II Cor. 9)." Few localities in the diocese had sufficient numbers of Catholics to supply an adequate income for a priest-pastor.

The pattern of the Pastoral also unfolded for the members of the new diocese the priorities the bishop wished to set. With some apparent hesitance, given not only the trustee questions that confronted him but also the "democratic spirit" that pervaded the entire country, he delineated the concept of authority in the church. The faithful were essentially called in faith to be obedient to the lawfully established teaching and ministerial authority of Christ. Given the context of the trustee problems and his unfamiliarity with the exercise of episcopal authority, the emergence of this question as central in the Pastoral was understandable. Episcopal authority, service and ministry were necessary, he continued, to teach those who "have not become acquainted with the doctrines of the Redeemer, or, knowing his doctrines, stand in need of the administration of his sacraments."[52] It was essential not only to good organization but also absolutely necessary for the provision of the ministry of Word and Sacrament. The argumentation that grounded England's ecclesiology was presented forthrightly in his first Pastoral. Humankind's salvation was dependent upon its faith and practical obedience. It was obliged to uncover what God wished it to do. It was the church that had received both the "deposit of faith" and the authority to rule the believers. Therefore the church taught the believer what to believe and what to do in regard to salvation. It was seen that the Word, Sacraments and the Church were all channels of God's grace. The presence of this grace in humankind's history as it unfolded was accomplished through the divine commission given the apostles and their successors in the episcopate. For the moment, we can observe that Bishop England's theology of Church was consistent with his times. However, we will see later the practical wisdom and the pastoral practice he brought to this theology. Both will effectively recast his ecclesiology without compromise. God is the source of revelation and salvation and, consequently, ecclesial authority, not the community.

The Christian in Civil Society

In the final part of the Pastoral, England's attention turned to the civil responsibilities of Christians. He reminded the people of their responsibility to preserve the public peace and maintain the "liberal institutions by which you are so well protected."[53] He quickly added how greatly he admired "the excellence of your Constitution." England had been apparently quite enamored of the United States for some time. Earlier he had resolved to be sent as a missionary to the country and later, in his first Pastoral, he expressed his determination to become an American citizen. In light of the fact that he later refused a bishopric in Ireland while residing as bishop in Charleston sharply highlights his commitment to his new country and the values it represented.[54] Perhaps in the flush of his recent arrival and in being so newly enamored by it all, he continued in the Pastoral that he had

> been desirous to behold your eagle grow in strength and beauty as his years increased,—whether he rested with majesty upon the bases of wisdom, the moderation and the fortitude of your government or lifting himself on the opinions of your prosperity, and surrounded with the halo of your multiplying stars, fixed his steady eye upon that sun of rational freedom, which culminates for you, as it departs from the nations of the East.[55]

Later letters and orations were to develop these themes more fully. It is clear, however, that the "liberal institutions" referred to had or would mold England's thinking on the consultative process. Consultation from parish through diocese to the national church and on to the universal church was to be a frequent cause in his writings. In writing, for example, to Rome in June 1824 about the state of the Church in the United States, England reported of the Americans

> they know that in the Catholic Church the power of legislation resides in the Pope and the Bishops; and they would be greatly impressed if they would see the Church in America regulated in accordance with laws emanating from a Council of Bishops with the approbation of the Holy Father. The conformity of this mode of procedure with their own principles and practice is so striking, that it would easily gain not only their obedience but also their attachment. But they will never be reconciled to the practice of bishops, and oftentimes of the priest alone, giving orders without assigning any reasons for the same.[56]

Constitutionalism was the ideal mode by which to define clearly and assign responsibilities. It was the effective means by which "liberal" institutions could effectively be incorporated into the Church's own decision-making processes. England embraced these twin principles enough to bring them to bear upon the organization of his own diocese. To define and assign responsibilities, within the divine commission to preach the Gospel, was in England's mind hardly an alien concept in relation to the long history of the Church having done so. He distinguished governance from revelation. The one is of human origin, the other divine. The Church is the instrument that serves the Gospel. It was not itself of the same stature as that which it serves. As Francis Sullivan and Richard Gaillardetz have clarified in the post-Vatican II era, the pope, the college of bishops and the *magisterium* have authoritative roles in the interpretation of the revelation handed on through the ages.[57] John England would appear almost prescient, even as he may not have had the resources for, as we may, as clear an articulation of the principles: The papacy, the college of bishops and the *magisterium* serve the revelation. They do not constitute it.

Organization of the Diocese: The Turmoil and Problems

As recorded in his journal, the bishop began immediately a visitation of the entire diocese. He traveled from town to town, visiting and searching out any Catholics that could be found. This was a pressing necessity for, as he wrote, "Upon . . . arrival [in the diocese], the bishop [himself] found only two churches occupied, and two priests doing duty: one at Charleston and one at Augusta."[58] He appointed Benedict Fenwick, who had agreed to remain and help in the diocese for a year, his Vicar General and then left on January 15, 1821, for Savannah, Georgia. (This was sixteen days after his arrival in Charleston harbor.) With him was Fr. Robert Browne, the same involved in the trustee conflict with Archbishop Marechal. The day after arriving in Charleston, England had granted the faculties of the diocese to both Fathers Gallagher and Browne. Archbishop Marechal had suspended both priests earlier. Their reinstatement in ministry would presage England's far less severe attitude, yet effective one, in dealing with the trustee question.[59] After they arrived at Savannah, Fr. Browne was appointed pastor, serving at the pleasure of the bishop. Browne, however, accompanied the bishop on the remainder of the trip in the state of Georgia. In the absence of their new pastor, the bishop appointed John Dillon, a local Savannah layman, to read the prayers of the Mass on Sunday. This was a pattern that was set in community after community as the new bishop appointed lay-readers to serve in place of priests who were simply not available.[60]

By the time he had been in the diocese a year, John England found the trustee problems still surfaced. On February 16, 1822, he wrote in his journal that the vestry of the Hassell Street Church, St. Mary's, Charleston, was still inflexible in its "uncanonical claims." To remedy the situation, he moved decisively, and as strongly (at this point) as any of his confreres in the American hierarchy. He recorded in his journal, "I also regulated that no clergyman should under pain of suspension *ipso facto*, to be incurred, officiate. . . . in any church, the property of which was not vested either totally, or in trust, in the bishop and his successors."[61] In September 1822 John England recorded the unhappy results of a committee of the Hassell Street Church. It was a draft of a new set of rules regarding church property. The draft was to have reflected the guidelines given the committee by the bishop. He wrote, "The rules were worse than the former. I therefore gave up all hopes of bringing the church to be useful, and determined to Interdict it as soon as my lease should expire."[62] His assessment of the trustees' position that gave them sole control over the finances and property of the congregation was that "it is folly to attempt raising the edifice of Catholicity upon Calvinistic foundations. I shall not attempt it."[63]

If the bishop's position appeared indistinguishable from the usual stance of the American hierarchy, it was because, at this point, he instinctively reacted as did they. However, only a short time later he significantly modified his position. Yet at this earlier period his openness to new possibilities was indicated by the fact that he was more moderate than most of the other bishops when he spelled out the regulations. "The money matters [are] to be managed by a committee to be chosen by the laity. . . . and to be commissioned by the bishop or his deputy, and to be accountable both to the bishop and priest as well as to the laity for their management of the funds."[64] Authoritarianism or high-handed hierarchical aloofness was not part of the man.

As indicated this position was further modified as England became more familiar with the problem. It was in serious discussion and consultation with John Gaston of North Carolina that he came to understand more clearly the complexity of the issue and the sentiments of the trustees. John Gaston was a well-known North Carolinian lawyer, politician and state supreme court justice. England reported in his journal on May 19, 1823, just a little over a year following the original policy decision, "Consulted Mr. Gaston upon the best mode of drawing title for Catholic churches and after much discussion we agreed the best mode was to vest the legal interest in the Trustees, who were to hold the property to be administered under the control of the Bishop."[65] The complexity of the varying state laws regarding ecclesiastical incorporation had become clearer to England, who had developed a sophistication in this matter unmatched by his brother bishops. It was their insufficient grasp of legal matters and consequently their inability to deal with them that led Bishop England to be so critical. Carey gives a great deal of attention to the difference between John England's handling of the trustee problems and others in the hierarchy, whom he designates the "anti-trustees." These latter he associates with the French-born and French-educated bishops in the United States, who are seen as opposed to republicanism and liberalism and who accordingly fanned the flames of nativism with their rhetoric. They rejected the notion of the separation of temporal and spiritual jurisdiction within the Church. In this last matter, England did agree with them.[66] They, however, appeared to be opposed to *all* democratic processes in the Church, such as due process, increased lay participation through advice and consultation or any mode to balance Church power along Lockean lines. They also wished to draw the Church out of the greater part of the arena of public morality.[67] It was along these very lines that John England was most sharply critical of his fellow bishops and priests when he wrote the Roman authorities at the Propagation Office in 1833: "The clergy in general was composed of foreigners who did not comprehend the nature of those laws [regarding church property] and the churches were led into servitude without their knowing how to prevent or remedy the evil."[68] The context for this accusation was his appraisal of the trustees' aspirations as legitimate outgrowths of the American experience. The bishops, to England's mind, never comprehended this legitimacy.

A Diocesan Constitution

As the inexorable task of organizing the diocese progressed, the new bishop found that he had to structure the diocese and his administration of it with a constitution. He published on September 25, 1823, therefore, a Constitution for the Diocese of Charleston with the following comments recorded in his journal for that day.

> Having paid great attention to the state of several churches in America, and studied as deeply as I could the character of the government and of the people, and the circumstances of my own flock, as well as the canons and the usages of the Holy Roman Catholic Church, and having advised with religious men and clergymen and lawyers, I this day, after consultation and prayer in the Church of St. Finbar, published the Constitution by which the Roman Catholic Church under my charge is to be regulated, and I trust with the blessing of heaven much disputation and Infidelity restrained. It was subscribed by the clergy and many well-disposed laymen.[69]

John England had been in the diocese over two and a half years before he declared his decision to establish a constitutional form of government. It was not precipitous. Nonetheless he was accused of acting precipitously and unilaterally by some. From the time he had arrived in the country, Bishop England had badgered the Archbishop to convoke a Provincial Council "for the purpose of having established some uniform system of discipline. . . . and of having common counsel and advice upon a variety of important topics regarding the causes and remedies of those disastrous contests which have torn. . . . this afflicted church." England, as we shall see several times, could be contentious. This first letter (of a business nature) to Marechal was not calculated to initiate a warm relationship. Among other things he wrote the French-born Archbishop, "If I had five or six good priests who could preach well in English. . . ." This could not have been anything but an irritant to the Archbishop, who had not yet made personal acquaintance with England. In light of the fact that the common complaint of the Irish involved with trusteeism was that the French-born priests were such notoriously poor preachers as to embarrass them, such a reference to the absence of good preachers among the Charleston Catholic clergy, even now, appears to be an unnecessary reflection on the French-American clergy.[70] He had argued continually that only through common counsel could a satisfactory remedy be found against "the evils of trusteeism." He concluded another letter in August, 1821: "I thought a Synod could make better regulations than an individual."[71] In a fourth letter on the subject, dated December 22, 1822, England said of the Provincial Council proposal, "If you refuse to call it I shall lament that we are left divided to meet our several difficulties."[72] Finally, he decided to act on his own since the Archbishop was apparently adamant in his refusal to call a council. Though England made a decision to act apart from the body of bishops, he still felt a compulsion to keep the Archbishop informed of his activities and plans. On January 15, 1823, he wrote Marechal: "I have been led fortunately to adopt all the principles of the document which you have been sent." [73]

The bishop of Charleston believed that the national Church needed a uniform code of discipline so that, as he wrote, the accusation would not be leveled at him or any of the bishops by laity—"Why do you require more than other bishops?" Though the opposition of the Archbishop prevented the convocation of a Provincial Council and Bishop England was forced to move ahead on his own, he was never comfortable without Provincial regulations reflective of the unity among the nation's bishops. In March, 1827, he wrote the Archbishop, "I feel also and acknowledge the serious inconvenience of having unlike customs and dissonant discipline within the same province. . . . I am further desirous of having the Statutes and customs of my diocess [sic] based upon the decisions and regulations of a Provincial Synod." [74]

Reactions to the Diocesan Constitution

With the publication of the constitution on September 25, 1823, much criticism was directed toward the bishop. Some of it, such as that of

Bishop Dubois of New York, was patently unfair. England referred to this particular criticism in a letter to the Archbishop on April 26, 1827.

> The Bishop of New York in a letter to me some time in the beginning of this year passed an indiscreet censure upon me, for having without the advice and concurrence of my brethren of the Province made serious and important regulations in my Diocess [sic]... although my brother of New York was correct in principle he was not so in its application.[75]

Within three years, however, Dubois would appreciate England's approach much more. Dubois was critical of the decrees of the First Provincial Council of Baltimore. He felt that they placed too much emphasis upon episcopal authority. A better solution of the Church title and administration question, as he saw it, was to invest authority in three trustees in each parish who would operate under a constitution limiting both their own and the bishop's powers.[76]

Archbishop Marechal viewed the constitution as sponsoring "democracy," which in his eyes, of course, was incompatible with Catholicism. Bishop Conwell of Philadelphia felt it gave too much freedom of action to the laity. Other bishops, Brute of Vincennes (Indiana) and Whitfield among others, were united in an assortment of reservations and criticisms. Bishop Kenrick of Philadelphia summed them up well when he wrote Paul Cullen, later the first Irish cardinal, "He (England) also eulogizes his Constitution, which no other bishop admires, for though it checks the Trustees it organizes a System which under every form is highly objectionable."[77] Kenrick believed the constitution worked only because of the personality of John England. In itself he felt the document dangerous because either it gave the laity real power in relation to the clergy or, if it did not, it would lead to dissatisfaction. Kenrick went on in this review of the *Works* to observe that "under no circumstances can they (the laity) claim rights over the temporalities of the church."[78] England's constitution, in actuality, delegated such authority to the laity but made clear that their delegation was received from the bishop. Kenrick, nonetheless, was both critical and apprehensive about this question in the constitution. Archbishop Whitfield had written Rome criticizing England's republicanism. Rome itself wrote Marechal at an earlier period asking for a copy of the constitution. The Vatican did nothing, however, after reading it. England himself wrote Rome describing the success he experienced with the constitution: "I have embraced a constitution for the church of this diocese . . . the constitution and its laws has stabilized both Carolinas."[79] Criticism of the constitution had also been carried to Rome by Fr. Anthony Kolhman, who had served in New York before beginning his work in the Roman Curia.[80]

Defense and Analysis of the Rationale for a Constitution
John England had developed a keen faculty for relating political theory and practice to the operations of the Catholic Church. He sent a letter to the Holy See in 1824, requesting approval of the Diocesan Constitution. In it he argued flawlessly the case for approval. After outlining the substance of the constitution he concluded:

> This Constitution is now in force on the diocese of Charleston and is accepted by all—hence according to State laws, it is now the standard for Catholics, and all our affairs in consequence thereof are progressing peacefully. After much and many prayers, and frequent consultation with jurists and trustees, and after many changes, I finally sanctioned it. The clergy and nearly all of the laity affixed their signatures to it. Only one condition was appended, *reserving to the Holy See the faculty of summarily abrogating it in case anything were found there contrary to Morals or to ecclesiastical discipline.* [Emphasis mine.] All its provisions are before us, and no prescription unfavorable to the Holy See appears in the sanction.
>
> But the people desire to have the constitution printed, so that they may have a standard by which they may be guided. I have learned by experience that the genius of this nation is to have written laws, to have these laws at hand, and to direct all their affairs according to them. If this is done, they are easily governed. If it be refused, a long and irremediable contention will ensue. By fixed laws and by reason much can be obtained from them; but they cannot be compelled to submit to authority which is not made in manifest by LAW.[81]

Actually there was a very long delay in the *printing* of the constitution for distribution that England refers to at the second South Carolina convention. Guilday can easily be misunderstood in this regard.[82] There was no delay in *implementation* of the document, since the earlier legal incorporation of the diocese in the State of South Carolina had effected the instrument upon which the bishop operated. The last parish, incidentally, to approve the constitution was St. Mary's Church in Hassell Street in 1830, a testament to the bishop's ability to genuinely allow the parishes to make their own decisions in these matters.[83]

John England enunciated well what has become seemingly a principle in the American Catholic experience: written law defining clearly stated rights and duties in terms, as well, of checks and balances. The bishop's point was not and did not abet the specter of private rights over against the community's claims upon the individual as it developed later in the American tradition as a result of current rulings in the U.S. courts regarding the Bill of Rights.[84]

The idea of a constitution for the diocese was the result of a number of factors. One certainly was England's earlier involvement in the fight for Irish emancipation. This developed a strong predisposition in his spirit to written law/legislation to assure freedom and order. Another factor was the state legislation (South Carolina) that imposed a new set of circumstances upon the Catholic Church in the matter of the incorporation of Church property. A third factor surely must have been the sheer joy that the republican constitutional form of the diocese brought to Bishop England as an apologist. He was able to point to it in argumentation with American Protestants of a "No Popery" bent who believed Catholicism and republicanism were incompatible.[85] Bishop England's use of the constitution in his apologetics is illustrated in the following:

> But where the society makes no constitution. . . . but has merely persons chosen as trustees. . . . These trustees have the power to make all regulations and to change them as they may think proper. . . Hence I was convinced at an early stage that the remedy that was most natural, most safe . . . was to designate, in such an instrument as the law would recognize and sanction, the line that separated the rights of the clergy from those of the laity.[86]

The constitution *vis-à-vis* the trustee question was a finely tuned instrument. It represented a successful effort to bring the laity into the decisionary process of the diocesan and local church. It strove at the same time to assure the freedom of the ministerial office from excessive dependence on or restriction by the temporal competency of the laity. In this latter case, England saw an affinity between the Veto question in Ireland and the trustee question in the United States. In either case, be it lay domination (government) of the Church in the Irish question seen in the influence the British Crown sought or lay members of the congregation in the American case, both were considered hindrances to spiritual and prophetic missions of the church.[87] The role of the church was to comfort its flock, but it was equally charged to challenge the flock to follow the values of the Kingdom of God and not those of human culture alone. Conversion was never lost sight of by the bishop.

The implementation of the constitution of the diocese was effected with the state of South Carolina's issuance of the papers of incorporation. The constitution was far more than a mere charter, however, in the life of the diocese. The constitution called for annual district conventions at which accountability for the administration of the diocese, spiritual and temporal, was rendered. Between 1823 and 1838, these conventions were held on a district basis: two in North Carolina (1829 and 1831); nine in Georgia (1826-1832, 1835); and fifteen in South Carolina (1823-1838, excepting 1832 and 1836; however, two conventions were held in 1837); in 1838, the constitution was amended and one annual convention replaced the district meetings.[88] For the next two years, 1839 and 1840, the diocese met as a unit in Charleston. In 1841, Bishop England returned late in the fall from Europe, tired and sickly. He died April 11, 1842. The diocese remained vacant for over two years before his successor, Ignatius Reynolds, was appointed. During the interim the constitution fell into disuse. His successor never revived it.

The success of the constitutional government of the diocese brought peace and harmony to a strife-torn church. It brought the scattered Catholics of the diocese together in an annual convention that gave them a sense of purpose and identity as Catholics. More recently another bishop, Joseph Brunini, of the missionary diocese of Jackson, Mississippi (1967-1984) mirrored John England. He shared a somewhat similar personal background. He was raised at the margins of the larger community society of Vicksburg, Mississippi. His father was Catholic-Italian and his mother Jewish. The family was of considerable standing in the community since Brunini's father was a lawyer and somewhat prominent in the state social and political circles. Bishop Brunini understood the values we recognize in John England. He too initiated an annual, and later triennial, gathering of diocesan Catholics along with annual district meetings for these very same purposes: 1) consultation with and affirmation of the lay Catholics living in an alien religious culture as well as 2) to foster their social cohesion as a community. In both cases it was the vibrancy of Catholic life at the margins of both the church and the larger community that could introduce new experiences to the Church. What is also notable is Rome's response or lack of it. Much as with the case of John England, Rome did not exhibit any hesitancies nor prohibit nor censure this model of consulting the faithful. If one were to argue that in both cases the diocesan see or local bishop was just not significant enough to warrant a Roman response, we should recall that Rome not long after the constitution's implementation assigned Bishop England as a legate to Santo Domingo to resolve difficulties that had arisen there. (Bishop England, of course, remained the bishop of Charleston.) In the more recent instance, a young priest served Bishop Brunini as his closest advisor and protégé who was none other than Fr. Bernard Law, later the luckless Archbishop of Boston, but notable at the Vatican.

Guilday offers a balanced assessment of Bishop England's noble experiment. If it has not reshaped the Catholic Church it was through no fault of either the people of the diocese, the bishop or practical and theological insight. It was its failure to inspire more generous financial support.[89] Had that happened, or alternately had the innovation been at the center rather the margins of the life of the Church's structure, the story may have ended quite differently. Yet, we surely have seen in the developments of John England's life that creative bursts and visions seldom occur at either the center of the culture's elite or in stable and prosperous times.

Notes

1. Robert A. Caro. *The Years of Lyndon Johnson: Master of the Senate II* (NY: Vintage, 2002), 1-49.

2. Richard Hofstader, et. al, *The American Republic* (Englewood Cliffs, Prentice-Hall, 1959) 390. The individualism of which Hofstader writes need not be understood to be libertarian. Hofstader's writing did not require an awareness to nuance questions that have arisen in more recent years and that are better phrased in the work of Sean Wilentz, *The Rise of American Democracy* (NY: Norton, 2005), who is sensitive to the distinction between individual rights and any overtone of libertarian or Enlightenment privatism that could be too broadstrokedly attributed to republican impulses. He emphasizes this time and again the Jeffersonians opposed dominance based on class as the source for the loss of liberty, 57. John Adams is understood, as the other founders of the republic, to

emphasize "selfless virtue," 76. The Jacksonian Democrats are clearly portrayed as opposed to "Whig humanitarianism. . . with [its] abstract political theories of inequality and [its] Enlightenment rationalist affinities." 491. Wilentz also makes the important distinction between urban and rural republicans that appeared to underscore the conflict between the Jeffersonian and Hamiltonian parties. The rural "lacked the elaborate Enlightenment defenses. . . that were common in the city groups' addresses," 61. The value of Hofstader is, indeed, that the era represented the emergence of the individual from a strong social and conservative matrix. But that individual, to the republicans of the period, largely was a citizen first who had responsibilities for the commonweal.

3. For an excellent treatment of this thirty-year period, 1820-1850, see Arthur Schlesinger, Jr., *The Age of Jackson* (London: Eyre & Spottswoode, 1946), esp., the chapter, "Jacksonian Democracy and Religion," 350-360. Sean Wilentz, *American Democracy,* 182-518. Also Daniel Rogers, "Republicanism: the Career of a Concept," *Journal of the Early Republic,* 12 (June, 1982)) 11-38.

4. Schlesinger, 351.

5. Schlesinger, 3, 17.

6. Schlesinger, 352-353.

7. *Works,* V, 263.

8. Schlesinger, 360.

9. Schlesinger, 360.

10. *Works,* VI, 358 cf. also VII, 73.

11. See Schlesinger, 209ff. esp., 244.

12. Contrary to Harvey Hill, "American Catholicism: John England and 'The Republic in Danger,'" *Catholic Historical* Review, 89 (2003) 240-257. Wilentz is much more perceptive in this regard. He recalls that the rural Jacksonians frequently betrayed a religious foundation in their outlook and rhetoric, 61. He also notes that J.C. Calhoun, who alternately supports but eventually separates himself from the Jacksonians, stood for a very different vision of republicanism, 178, 533ff. Wilentz deals far more effectively with the significant differences within the Democratic Party during John England's lifetime.

13. By 1837, there were 105,000 paupers in the United States of whom 50% were foreign-born, Ray Allen Billington, *The Protestant Crusade* (N.Y., Rhinehart, 1952) p. 34.

14. In this matter see Thomas McAvoy, "The Catholic Minority in the United States, 1789-1821," *Historical Records and Studies,* 39-40 (1952) 37. As regards the influence of the English upon the shaping of the American Catholic Church see Mary Peter McCarthy, *English Influence on Early American Catholicism* (Wash., C.U.A., 1959). Another valuable background study for this concern is Elwyn Smith, "The Fundamental Church-State Tradition of the Catholic Church in the United States, "*Church History,* 38(1969): 486.

15. McAvoy, "Minority, 1789-1821," 37.

16. Thomas O'Brien Hanley, *Their Rights and Liberties: the Beginnings of Religious and Political Freedom in Maryland,* (Westminster, Newman, 1959): esp., 77ff.

17. In regard to this see above page 24 and note 50. An excellent presentation of the anti-Catholicism of this era can be found in R.A. Billington, *The Protestant Crusade.* This is in striking contrast, for example, to an earlier period in North Carolina (as well as other states, with the exception of New Jersey) as shown in Stephen Weeks, *Church and State in North Carolina,* (Baltimore, Johns Hopkins, 1893). Although John T. McGreevy addresses the period immediately following upon Bishop England's death, he helps us to understand Bishop England's position. It was an era that struggled with the dichotomy of oligarchical authoritarianism and the republican principle of government as rooted in the people. McGreevy, chapter one.

18. *Records* 6 (1895): 29-55, 184-224.

19. Billington, 37.

20. Thomas F. Casey, The Sacred Congregation, *De Propaganda Fide and the Revision of the First Council of Baltimore* (Rome, Gregorianum, 1957): 116, 138 and 94.

21. Hill, "American Catholicism."

22. John Quinn, "Three Cheers for the Abolitionist Pope," *Catholic Historical Review,* 90 (2004) 67-93. John T. Noonan, *A Church That Can and Cannot Change* (South Bend: Notre Dame, 2005) 17ff.

23. *Works,* VI, 358.

24. Thomas Bokenkotter, *A Concise History of the Catholic Church,* Rev. ed. (NY: Image, 1999) 261-275 and 284-288.

25. Kenneth Scott Latourette, *The Nineteenth Century in Europe: Background and the Roman Catholic Phase* (NY: MacMillan, 1976). This Protestant scholar gives an excellent summary of Catholic developments at Rome, esp., 238-260. See also for background on this period of Catholicism, "Gregory XVI," *The New Catholic Encyclopedia* (NY: McGraw-Hill, 1967), vol. 6, 784 (hereafter, NCE), which gives the context of *Mirari Vos* in the political upheavals of the Papal States as well as generally in Catholic Europe under the influence of Lamennais; see also the Catholic Church *vis-à-vis* liberalism in the early 19th century.

26. Thomas Bokenkotter, chs. 25-26 for an excellent summary of the issues during these pontificates. Ann Freemantle, ed., *The Papal Encyclicals in Their Historical Context* (N.Y.: Putnam, 1956). She gives an excellent summary of the pressures exerted upon Gregory XVI by the conservatives *Zelanti* and Metternich, 126-128.

27. Much has been made of episcopal appointments in the early years up to 1840, yet seldom were American citizens appointed any time during this period. Marechal and England both made a great point about appointing native-born, yet both more frequently recommended English, Irish or French clerics in their

communications to Rome, Guilday, *Life,* II, 317; I, 441. During this period twenty-nine bishops (Carroll to Loras) were appointed, of whom five were born in the United States, twelve were French-speaking natives, nine were Irish, and one each came from Italy, Austria and England. Also see Guilday, *Life,* I, 439-441; Marechal's "Letter to Cardinal Fesch," cited in Thomas Hughes, *The History of the Society of Jesus in North America: Colonial and Federal–Documents,* vol.1, pt. 1 (London: Longmans-Green, 1905), 526.

    28. Carey, *People,* esp., 17.

    29. Rome issued the document *Non Sine Magno* condemning the excessive claims of the trustees, e.g., the *jus patronus* as cited by Guilday, *Life,* I 356-358. Robert F. McNamara. "Trusteeism in the Atlantic States: 1785-1863," *Catholic Historical Review,* 30(1944) typifies the trustee movement rather casually as "an emotional republicanism" and "a form of American liberalism."

    30. Guilday, *The History of the First Council of Baltimore,* (N.Y., Macmillan, 1932): 86. For an understanding of trusteeism during this period see *Works,* V, 109-213; John Tracey Ellis, *Documents of American Church History,* (Chicago, Regnery, 1967) esp., Marechal's "Pastoral of 1819, "223-227; P.K. Guilday, "Trusteeism," *Historical Records and Studies,* U.S.C.H.S., XVIII (1928) 7-73.

    31. McNamara, 135-154.

    32. "The Old Catholic," (*Norfolk Herald,* Aug. 7, 1822), cited by Guilday, *Church in Virginia,* 155. Carey, *People,* 26f.

    33. Thomas McAvoy, "The Formation of the Catholic Minority, 1821-1860," *The Review of Politics,* 10(1948): 13-34, and Sr. Mary Carthy, *English Influence on Early American Catholicism* (Washington: Catholic University, 1959), 83.

    34. Billington, 40. Carey, *People,* 135ff. who notes that class and politics often played a significant role in the trustee controversies.

    35. Guilday, *Life,* I, 251-252.

    36. On the entire question of the Charleston schism and the Jansenist scheme see Guilday, *Life,* I, chapters 6-9.

    37. Guilday, *Life,* I, 285.

    38. Sr. Dolorita Mast, *Always the Priest: Gabriel Richard, S.S.,* (Baltimore, Helicon, 1965) 292, 319. See also Guilday, *Life,* II, 371, I, 31. A strong proponent of the Irish position is Andrew Greeley, *The Catholic Experience,* (Garden City, Doubleday, 1967): 63-100. Sympathy for the French-American position is found in any of Thomas McAvoy's works as in the bibliography. John England's own scathing criticism of some of his fellow bishops was detailed in his "Report to Rome," (1824), *Records,* 8(1898): 460, esp., nos. 7 and 10. Gabriel Richard represented another distinct group of French priests not associated with the post-revolutionary migration of 1791. He reflected and led the older settlers of French-Canadian origin.

39. Kauffman, 104-106. England appeared to understand the French Sulpician leadership of the Franco-American bloc as unrepublican and wedded to the *Ancient Regieme*. Peter Clarke, *A Free Church in a Free Society* (Hartsville, SC: Attic, 1983) helps us to understand this particularly in the cases of consultation, subsidiarity and cooperation as found in England's episcopal leadership, esp., 467-469.

40. Kearns, 66.
41. *Works*, III, 253.
42. *Works*, 254-255.
43. Guilday, *Life*, I, 317, quotes England, "*regimen ecclesiaticum non in pastoribus, sed in populo fuit.*"("Ecclesiastical rule was not in the pastors, but in the people.")
44. Guilday, *Life*, I, 301.
45. *Works*, IV, 232-235.
46. *Works*, IV, 232.
47. *Works*, IV, 233.
48. *Works*, IV, 233.
49. *Works*, IV, 233.
50. *Works*, IV, 233.
51. *Works*, IV, 233., 234.
52. *Works*, IV, 234.
53. *Works*, IV, 235.
54. *Works*, III, 254: V, 145.
55. *Works,* IV, 235.
56. "Journal," *Records*, 8(1898): 462.
57. Francis Sullivan, *Magisterium* (Mahwah, NJ: Paulist, 1983), 24-34. Richard R.Gaillardetz, *Teaching with Authority: A Theology of the Magisterium in the Church,* (Collegeville: Michael Glazier, 1997) and *By What Authority,* (Collegeville, MN: Liturgical Press, 1996), 57ff.
58. *Works*, III, 254.
59. "Journal," *Records*, 6(1895): 33-35.
60. For example see the "Journal," *Records*, 36, 53, 55, 187, 201, and 218. In each instance as the bishop left the flock he had gathered, he appointed lay-readers to lead them in the absence of a resident priest-pastor.
61. "Journal," *Records*, 202.
62. "Journal," *Records*, 206-207.
63. "Letter to John Gaston," January 9, 1823, *Records*, 18(1907): 385.
64. *Records,* 385.
65. "Journal," *Records* 222.
66. The Preface to the Diocesan Constitution, *Works,* I, 92.
67. Carey, *England,* 221-267.
68. *Records*, 8(1897) 317.
69. "Journal," 223.

70. Letter to Archbishop Marechal, March 1, 1821, cited by Guilday, *Life,* II, 77-78.

71. Letter to Marechal, August 8, 1821, cited by Guilday, *Life,* II, 86.

72. Guilday, *Life,* II , 90.

73. Guilday, *Life,* I, 409. It should be noted that the date of this letter, January 15, 1823, and its contents indicate that the process of consultation was well known and underway, at least, nine months before the publication of the constitution.

74. I Guilday, *Life,* II, 98, March 29, 1827.

75. Guilday, *Life,* II , 105, April 26, 1827.

76. Thomas Casey, *The Sacred Congregation de Propaganda Fide and the Revision of the First Provincial Council of Baltimore, in the United States* (New York: Kenedy, 1879), 73.

77. *Records,* 7(1896): 293, for other criticisms see Guilday, *Life,* I 360, 362; II, 257, etc.

78. Kenrick, *Brownson's Quarterly Review,* 7(1850): 156-157.

79. Kenneally, I, 1467, 1909 and "*obtinui amplexam constitutionem pro ecclesia huiusce dioceseos...constitutio legibus utriusque Carolinae stabilita est....*" 874.

80. Guilday, *Life,* II, 131.

81. *Records,* 8(1897): 458-459. Actually there was a very long delay in the printing of the constitution for distribution that England refers to at the second South Carolina convention.

82. *Works,* IV, 318. Guilday, Life, I, 349-350. Implementation was effected by the diocese's legal incorporation in the State of South Carolina. See below.

83. *Works,* V, 425-426.

84. John Witte, Jr. *God's Joust, God's Justice: Law and Religion in the Western Tradition.* (Grand Rapids: Eerdmans, 2006), 243-262.

85. Carey, *England,* 269-275; *Records,* 8(1897): 318.

86. See *Works,* III, 224-243.

87 *Works,* III, 511-512; II, 461; Carey, 273.

88 See the "Constitution," V, 93.

89 See Guilday, *Life,* II, 496f. who gives a fair appraisal of the constitutional system of John England.

Chapter Four

A Vision from the Margins

> In questions of power let no more be heard of confidence in man, but bind him down from mischief by the chains of the Constitution.
> Thomas Jefferson

Introduction

This chapter will be an outline and commentary on the text of the Diocesan Constitution of 1839. The observations offered here do not pretend to be exhaustive. The commentary will turn mainly, but not exclusively on those aspects of the constitution that reflect John England's creative adaptations of Catholic ecclesiology rather than an exploration of the details in diocesan administration. In doing so we will understand better not only the possibilities of shared governance within the Catholic tradition, but also we will more adequately understand that these possibilities exist *within* the tradition and are not simply reflective of an "Americanist" or Enlightenment accommodation.

In most cases the commentary is made by invocation of other statements of John England that elucidate his vision in the constitution as a reflection of Catholicism's effective implantation in the United States. The key issue with which I wish to deal is whether John England's embrace of republican constitutionalism constituted too great an accommodation to modern notions of individualism. The issue turns on whether the "freedoms" spoken of in the constitution reflect a valid understanding that the democratic person must be guaranteed "freedom from" coercion or whether such freedom fails to support the more religious perspective that humans are created with the "freedom for" something larger—the transcendent Creator God and that God's purpose in the creation of humans. The critique raised against the efforts at inculturation by men such as Bishop England remain whether such efforts have, in effect, abandoned the Catholic and Christian tradition that freedom is not merely a negative "freedom from" but more precisely a freedom to pursue the end (teleological) for which humankind exists and finds its realization. The vision of the Christian faith community as it has developed through the centuries, is that its faithfulness and, therefore, its fullness must be virtue driven. The Christian's goal is to live virtuously and not simply to fulfill the minimal obligations of law. Whether it was the theology enunciated by Paul, Augustine, Aquinas, Luther or, most recently Hauerwas and the "virtue ethics" ethicians, lawful obedience falls short of the value acknowledged in a virtuously lived life. The Catholic and Christian ethical tradition generally has clarified this well. Law establishes only the minimum expectations of the citizen or the believer. Law, however, cannot establish virtue as the standard of public behavior short of becoming a theocracy.

John England believed, as the eighteenth and nineteenth century constitutionalists did, that the delicate balance of power needed to assure the citizenry their bedrock religious and moral freedom required a statement of minimum standards that would assure both social and personal authenticity. Such a minimum was "freedom from" coercion or force since citizens, as children of God, cannot embark on the pursuit of their ultimate human destiny or final end (theological teleology) unless they are *free* to do so. To do otherwise would be to deny the centrality of free will, as Augustine would remind us. Pressure, duress or force flies in the face of the Christian tradition as it has grown and developed in its self-understanding through the centuries. As we will see, a freedom to pursue their God-given purpose is accomplished by the assurance that they will not be hindered. However, if to pursue their God-given goal is not facilitated by law to that degree law fails its citizens and consequently, constricts the "freedom from" required by moral imputablity. Critics, who espouse the separation of Church and State and suggest that a "freedom from" fails to address adequately the religious, social and public need for shared values and moral standards, fail to understand the very nature of the Gospel message as "good news" to those who recognize that a life in common is a life that calls for constant attendance to the other's experience and point of view. Such attention, by necessity, means the civil community must acknowledge the teleological purpose of each individual and, as in the case of theoretical judgment and practical judgment, cannot universalize people's experiences in propositions or statements adequate to individual experiences of life.

In this chapter we will closely assess John England's instincts that a republican constitutionalism was the finest instrument to insure the laity's rights and obligations.

The Charleston Constitution and Roman Reactions

The constitution that John England used in the administration of the Charleston diocese (1822-1842) was unique in the Catholic tradition. Constitutionalism, the distribution of authority or the concern with "balance of powers," was the energy in the political thinking of the period. It supposed the leveraging of rights, duties and the authority to rule. Yet, it was also a movement against which much of the energy of Catholic Europe was expended. Such a paradox typified the struggles of the "liberalizing" forces within the Catholic Church during this period. England pointed out, however, that the Catholic Church itself had a long tradition of constitutionalism in its religious orders.[1] He saw the Dominicans as the best and clearest example of republicanism in the religious life. His position was not idiosyncratic. John T. McNeill has pointed out that the Catholic Church manifested a propensity toward representative government even before it became apparent in secular institutions when it relied upon conciliar structures and sanctioned the constitutions of the Benedictines in the fifth century.[2]

Another example of what may appear to a later generation as paradoxical, if not contradictory, yet indicative that Bishop England was not seen in Rome as either idiosyncratic or a maverick, was his appointment by Gregory XVI in 1832 to be Apostolic Delegate in Haiti. Rome had not only been aware of England's republican sympathies and constitution, but also earlier that same year Gregory's encyclical, *Mirari Vos,* had *seemingly* condemned the concepts of the Church and State separation, freedom of conscience and religious liberty (that England held) on both religious and moral grounds. The bases of the condemnations were that pluralism rejected the objectivity and certainty of truth and that the ground for public or secular authority was based in the people rather than delegation from God. Yet, the effect *Mirari Vos*, which was promulgated while John England was in Rome on a visit, had upon the bishop's position *vis-à-vis* Rome was apparently negligible. His newspaper, *The United States Catholic Miscellany,* did not publish the encyclical, nor make reference to it for over two years. When it did, there was no defense of the document offered beyond saying that it was being printed because so many anti-Catholic newspapers had commented upon it inaccurately. The *Miscellany* and John England both remained undeterred in their support of republican constitutionalism, the separation of Church and State and freedom of conscience.[3] England's position rested on what he believed was the proper interpretation and intention of *Mirari Vos* and both circumstances and canonical tradition seem to support the belief that Rome may very well have appreciated his interpretation.

While Rome's condemnation of individual freedom of conscience was clear and emphatic, it was what Rome believed to be the consequence of such freedom of conscience (freedom from coercion), namely *indifference to divinely revealed truth* that was the object of its condemnation. Bishop England did not conceive the condemnation to be directed at individuals' freedom of conscience, insofar as such freedom is the theological basis for personal moral culpability and the substratum upon which we may reach judgments regarding social justice. Rather the consequence of the separation of church and state as well as freedom of conscience, *as the encyclical described them*, led to indifferentism. Such indifferentism was manifest in much of the anti-religious rhetoric of the Continental proponents of republicanism and the separation of Church and State. It is this alone that Bishop England and others believed Gregory XVI intended to censure.

The separation of Church and State and religious liberty are, Gregory wrote in his encyclical *Mirari Vos*, "evil deceits increasing in every quarter that require, if you please, that everyone be ready with the profession of the [true] faith [Catholicism] that [is needed] for eternal salvation." The pope continued, "[A]nd from this rotted indifferentism has flowed such erroneous and absurd thoughts, that deleteriously claim to vindicate this as freedom of conscience."[4] Gregory XVI was concerned that the true purpose of human freedom, moral culpability and the pursuit of our supernatural end, was in question among the continental proponents of republicanism.

From Gregory's vantage point such continental supporters of these radical new ideas failed to understand the obligation to form properly one's consciences. To his mind, they were partisans and aimed to destroy established order that was necessary to and concomitant with free will and social justice. The possibility that Catholic tradition could be reconciled with their "non-coercion" position, for that reason alone, was deemed impossible because it would have meant to embrace relativism and indifference. Quite obviously England as well as many others, including Lamennais against whom the encyclical was directed, concluded that they were not, indeed, promoters of religious indifference or epistemological relativism—indeed, just the opposite to their mind. Their position did not uphold the limitless or absolute personal liberty (*imprudentissima libertas, immoderata libertas opinionem*) that *Mirari Vos* condemned. And they certainly did not deny the supernatural end of humankind to which God directed humankind. For them, quite clearly, the shared *telos* of the human family as God the Creator had constituted it was the bond that united the human family as a social unit with a shared understanding and experience of what their life fundamentally meant. We need to recall that the Vatican often condemned ideas because of the *manner* in which they were presented inasmuch as they were seen to be destructive attacks upon the community's (the community of faith's) well-being.[5] Such condemnations, therefore, were not necessarily doctrinal condemnations. Rather the manner in which such "radical" ideas were proposed and propagated constituted "sheer madness" and the destructive impact they had upon civil society. This is illustrated well by the wording in *Singulari Nos*. Gregory XVI wrote,

> We have studied the book entitled *Paroles d'un croyant*. By Our apostolic power, We [sic] condemn the book: furthermore, We decree that it be perpetually condemned. It corrupts the people by a wicked abuse of the word of God, to dissolve the bonds of all public order and to weaken all authority. It arouses, fosters, and strengthens seditions, riots, and rebellions in the empires.[6]

As we will see in all of England's work, but especially the Diocesan Constitution, this common, ultimate goal of the human family permeates the whole of his thinking. Barring an explicitly libertarian position, the very notion that rights and obligations ought to be delineated presupposes the centrality of society around which individuals must discover and shape their identity, safety and freedom. The condemnation by Rome of those who promoted republicanism, the separation of Church and State, and religious liberty was clearly directed at the unsettling political and social consequences Rome believed was the consequence of their rhetoric and tone. The use of an instrument such as a constitution could hardly, of itself, warrant condemnation since such instruments of governance were common to the Church itself. The actual reference to the separation of Church and State in *Mirari Vos*, for example, appeared more exhortative than definitive: "We cannot anticipate either a desired nor a religious outcome from these proposals to separate the church from rule [the state] . . . they seek only to disrupt [good order].[7]

John England and the early republicans could not and would not have perceived republicanism to be based in individualism. For most of them the grounding of republicanism was in a fundamentally religious principle that justice, accountability and a virtuous life presupposed a higher Being. Therefore, together all citizens are held accountable and can make no final claim to legitimacy in opposition to this higher realm. The absolute monarchies of Europe at the time taught the founders of the American Republic, and the early generations well appreciated, that absolutism constituted a system of non-accountability and that no portion of the populace was above the law. Thus on the score of individualism, the founders can hardly be guilty of naiveté. On the score of freedom from force, coercion or intimidation, they allowed that the citizen and the believer must be free to pursue (negatively or in the absence of any extrinsic pressures) the loftier purposes of the well-lived life, but not required or obligated to pursue (positive freedom directed by an extrinsic influence upon individuals) it as the leadership might desire. It was a careful and considered distinction. The absolute monarchs and the religious intolerance and wars in Europe following the Reformation were clear reminders that a positive implementation of laws or rules about humankind's final end by any one group was as likely to lead to subjective and arbitrary impositions as the relativism with which we wrestle today.

This larger context must be remembered in order to understand why Bishop England saw the fulminations of *Mirari Vos* (and *Singulari Nos*) directed toward attitudes and ideas certainly not found in constitutions of either his diocese or the United States. Both simply enshrine the rights and duties that eighteenth and nineteenth century republicans believed were bestowed by God or a higher Being so as to assure that those subject to the constitutions were morally accountable to that God or higher Being. John Courtney Murray, the American Jesuit, a century later illustrated clearly the misunderstanding and misapplication that accompanied many papal statements such as *Mirari Vos* and *Singulari Nos*. In a somewhat similar instance that indicates that a proper understanding is found in the recognition of the gap between North American and Continental Catholic theological thought, Murray made this observation,

> In his social theory Leo XIII did indeed urge Christian democracy in the sense of beneficent action on behalf of the people; but in his political theory he never really answered the great question, raised for the first time in the nineteenth century, "Who are the people?" Actually, the first great historic answer to the question was given in the United States; but the din raised by the conflict with the Continental Liberals was too great to permit the voice of America [ironically, a deist and Protestant voice giving a Catholic answer] to be heard in European canon law classrooms. In fact, to this day European authors of textbooks *de jure publico* seem unaware that there is any difference between Jacobin democracy and Anglo-Saxon democracy or between "the sovereignty of the people" in the sense of [17] '89 and "government of the people, for the people and by the people" in the sense of Lincoln. *Hinc illae lacrimae*, [Hence the many tears] spilled by an American on reading books *de jure publico*.[8]

In the following section we will assess the critique now being leveled by a few American Catholics of this continuous and two-century-old American Catholic tradition of inculturation that traces itself from Archbishop John Carroll through Bishop John England, Cardinal Gibbons, Archbishop McNichols (Cincinnati), Cardinals Mooney and Dearden (Detroit), and John Courtney Murray to name a few.

Contemporary Assessments

The virulently anti-religious rhetoric frequently used by republicans on the European continent was not that of the North American republicans, as we earlier noted. Both, however, shared the belief that authority arose from the people and was not vested as in the manner of "divine right" of kings. Many of the former held the source of authority to be fully secular—that is, vested solely in and received from the people. The latter, among whom were both Locke and Montesquieu, believed it was rooted in the natural naw tradition of a people unabashedly religious and that law, as in Aquinas, was grounded in the Divinity or higher Being. David Schindler, Michael Baxter, and other revisionist critics insist that an intractable problem exists because the public language that flows from a republic steeled in a principle of the separation of Church and State cannot and does not have the ability to support a value system amenable to religious believers.[9] It does not, they warn, because such individualism is the hallmark of a secularism in which the rational individual and social authority derived, not from God, but from the citizens leaves no room in the public debate for God-talk or religious ethics. Religion is divorced from philosophy and can be afforded validity only in its private expression. Clearly there is something to be said for this position. What place, indeed, does religious ethics have in political discussion if it cannot demand the concurrence of the interlocutors and on what score could a religious ethics lay claim to a role in a pluralist context? The most pressing challenge, of course, is how can such a society provide a coherent ethics at all for so autonomous a citizenry? The conundrum also, however, is to what degree can such language and practice be enshrined in either law or civic ritual without at the same time reducing religious faith to a generic, homogenous commonality acceptable to all. On the opposite score, would we expect it to bring to bear some degree of coercion, if not physical, social or psychological, in its pursuit to build a coalition of agreement approaching (surpassing) a consensus? The approach John England takes is driven far less by academic rationality than by pastoral, pragmatic and non-dogmatic practice. In other words, he was motivated by the Gospel. The pursuit of virtue, while logically resting upon principle, was always applied and esthetically implemented according to the practical virtue that assures the most beautiful and good for the canvas that is the society. Bernard Lonergan made the point well: "moving the issue forward" is the criterion of Christian success in many instances. Issues move forward incrementally and in the effort that avoids breakage in the bonds of community relationships. "Incremental," of course, does not confute the possibilities of significant paradigm changes.

In John England's time issues surrounding religious language and ritual in the public arena were situated in a social context quite unlike today. Religious language was somewhat large in the *lingua franca* of the American Republic and religious ritual, one under which Catholics at the time often chafed, was reflective of the Protestant spirit and virtually omnipresent. The Protestant Christian nature of religiosity conformed well enough to Protestant ecumenical sensitivities of the time so as to accommodate a broad swath as well of those who may no longer held to specific Protestant or traditional Christian practices but who recognized and were comfortable with the cultural residue of their past Protestant heritage. This was possible to a great extent because the republic was relatively still quite homogenous. The fact that Native American and African-American religious cultures were largely excluded or forcibly absorbed illustrates the point well. Yet, as the years were to pass, numerous groups came to recognize that their own language and rituals were either excluded or driven "underground," such as the Catholics, Jews and Mormons. The accommodations made necessary in the public language to accommodate these latter groups into the mainstream of the nineteenth century would come to model the inclusiveness time would bring to bear on the republican principle that neither individuals nor communities of belief should be coerced or badgered, physically or psychologically, into a homogenous religious outlook. In the eyes of the American republicans the reasoning was not argued on the basis of individual rights as community peace and well being. Such peace was purchased, not in the silencing of any position, but in protecting each position. Thus did the nineteenth century republicans see themselves assuring the freedom of religion. The position certainly did not make appeal to reason or logic alone, but to an esthetical appreciation for social tranquility. A free conscience could not be regulated by civil law without infringement upon religious principles themselves. Love itself cannot be mandated; it is freely given or it is not love.

Laissez faire capitalism in a latter era, likewise, represents an individualism not characteristic of this period when the balance of power between not only the executive and the legislature, but also citizens and communities, was recognized as necessary to a society heterogeneous in its interests. Aside from Ayn Rand's objectivism, it is hard to imagine anywhere in the American tradition a failure to place emphasis on the community or social interests. Certainly this was not the vision that the early republicans held. Baxter and others may be correct that the challenge has become exponential in the sense that accommodation to ever greater heterogeneity baffles the Christian's belief in the certainty of

Divine Revelation, but to abandon the challenge of heterogeneity would appear to be a far greater threat to social well-being and some core Christian beliefs. A proper response to such a challenge must, however, secure two things that were true for the early American republicans and remain true for our situation: 1) To maintain and strengthen a people's identity *does* require common symbols, rituals and experiences. These are the very things that are central to social stability, identity and purpose and usually reside in a socially shared religious faith. Yet, few would argue today that any kind of pressure, force, or coercion to dislodge identities based on symbol-systems, rituals and socially shared experiences would be effective, let alone a likely recipe for successful community building reflective of the teaching of Jesus. 2) "Rights language" is not a modern or contemporary invention. Developed societies have always enshrined rights and duties in law, whether primitive taboos, Roman law, canon law or English common law.

If "free market capitalism" and Ayn Rand "objectivism" have combined to create a root metaphor of solipsistic individualism in our society, such cannot be projected back onto John England whose insights about religious orders and monastic republicanism argued strongly for the origin of "individual rights" within a community. Such religious communities respected the rights of its members but also served as mediating communities providing several layers of identity to its members. Monks held authority to elect their ruler, the abbot, who then exercised a social role holding rights of its own. Monks also exercised their rights as Benedictines and as Franciscans. The abbot's authority *came* from the monks just as in the modern republic authority rises from the people and presupposes their possession of rights. On the other hand, the dress, ritual celebrations and shared life experiences as either Franciscans or Benedictines created identities that were, indeed, distinct and so plural within the larger Church. They were men (or women), Frankish or Germanic, they were Benedictines or Franciscans but they were all Catholic. Overlapping identities necessitate overlapping rituals, even as both the rituals and identities are not identical. So while abbatial authority was received by virtue of the election (but not episcopacy or apostolic succession)—that is appointment—this did not negate patriarchal authority nor contravene balance from other centers of authority. In the end, even the religious language varied community to community without, at the same time, preventing the development of a religious language that transcended the differences, while being distinct.

Such transcending religious language today is too often the result of mere homogenization (some type of force) of values, but it not need be. The transcendence of value language that becomes inclusive may be realized through rational strategies or in the relationships. The former will bring some pressure for conformity to bear. The latter are much more sensitive to affect and esthetics and rest on a pragmatic and concrete coalescence. John England sought such unity through consultation, dialog and relationships. In other words he sought and believed unity was accomplished in the art of ministry well done. This is a central to Pedro Arupe's notion of inculturation.

Critics such as Baxter and Schindler paradoxically appear to abandon the balance found in the relationship of reason and esthetics and appear to land on a propositional and logical strategy they believe will assure the social unity, perhaps, all of us desire for the public arena's moral system and ethics. Yet, their call for religious language or discourse that is specific to a particular belief system rests largely on the very principles they explicitly reject, the logic of Enlightenment rationalism that emerges from individual thinkers and not social exchange reflective of a community of diverse experiences and discourses—for example, the diversity found in the Eastern and Western Churches or Gospels of Matthew and John. Can we actually presume that the discourse (on unquestioned values) about "thou shalt not kill" ranges any more broadly between Islam and Christianity than within Christianity itself?

Republican discernment or polity is not in any way a contradiction to the manner by which religious authority itself may also be exercised. Historically the church has not always rejected popular acclamation, for instance, in the selection of bishops. Such acclamation may have well been, in fact, somewhat similar to opinion polls today. Grace (the non-historical) and nature (the historical) are not as estranged as we may have once believed. God in God's dealings with humans, as has always been acknowledged, must resort to human tools or instrumentalities. The human, as Rahner and Lonergan have so aptly taught us, cannot receive any revelation from God save through the devices of human experience. C.S. Peirce would more specifically note that all knowledge is through signs. Theological justification of this basic unity between the two orders (the natural and the supernatural) has found articulation in the recent emergent synthesis first advanced by Henri DeLubac and later by Karl Rahner.

Religious and secular experiences, the natural and supernatural orders, cannot be hermetically sealed off from one another. Humankind has a single purpose according to the created nature (the natural law of being) given it by its Creator. In differing ways both these theologians argued that "pure nature" is only an abstraction for a believer. Rahner's description is that we live in a *supernatural existential*. As a consequence it is only a question that we come to thematize what already (transcendentally) exists or has reality. Newman called it the illative sense. DeLubac's position has been characterized as "already always" as regards the presence of the supernatural in humankind's very existence. In each case the world of grace and the world of history, the sacred and the secular, for the believer are not totally or even separable realms. The difficulty presented by Schindler's and Baxter's understanding of secular (perhaps more appropriately, pluralist) social context and religious language is the degree to which they believe the two are incommensurable. Given their position, they are impatient, even fearful for the health of the religious communities.

Yet, Murray's point about the rights inherent in the religious liberty of every individual is as applicable to the early nineteenth century as it is to our own times. A republican democracy needs to reflect its pluralistic composition. Murray wrote, "The spiritual issues were always clear to Gregory XVI . . . but the former Camaldulese monk had no grasp of political issues. . . . The inherent rationality of democratic development was obscured to the churchmen in a fog of false ideology that pretended to justify it."[10] England's own response, if his actions are any indication, was much the same as Murray's. The papal condemnations not only were not targeted at his position, they reflected a romantic spirituality that paid no heed to political realities. To put it bluntly, John England had lived at the margins of an English Protestant-dominated society in eighteenth century Ireland. He understood the reality that a minority or oppressed group cherished a basic "freedom from" as the prerequisite to positive decisions that could follow upon such political and personal freedom. He knew well how Catholics felt "unfree" because they could not participate in the Protestant ethic of the public society in which they lived. Minorities needed protection from the tyranny of even well intentioned majorities. Baxter seems to recognize this. He asserts, "How can differences over the nature of community be adjudicated when those differences stem directly from theological convictions about God, creation, redemption, and so on?" Because Schindler does not satisfactorily address these questions, Baxter concludes, "Schindler can give us only a thin account of what his followers are to do now. . . . These are crucial questions precisely because [the effects] of liberalism *are* [emphasis his] as corrosive as Schindler says they are, so much so that now we find the liberal state effecting, so to speak, the withering away of the Church."[11]

Baxter's extensive critique of Murray, in concert with David Schindler, fails on its face. As noted in the foregoing citation, Baxter is a bit apocalyptic as regards the withering away of the Church in the liberal (read, autonomous, individualist and rationalistic) state in the face of the evidence. The degree of adherence to religious bodies in the United States belies such an assertion, particularly when set in comparison with those societies in which the separation of Church and State has not been as widely or long practiced. Whether on the grounds of practice or adherence to a tradition, American society remains in the Western world, perhaps, the most publicly religious society. If the trajectory is supposed to be one of ever mounting secularization in all the Western democracies, the period of comparison would be difficult to delimit. On what basis can one assume the broad practice of genuine Christianity, as opposed to superstition, prevailed to a greater, or lesser, degree during earlier periods in Europe? The evidence is hardly compelling that established religion did exceedingly well prior, during or following the Reformation. Most disconcerting, however, in the critique is the ideology that is present. Earlier it was noted that Cardinal Dulles observed that a systematician's logic, if too consistent would guarantee a less successful theology. This was the fate of the schoolman and scholastics, Catholic and Protestant. It appears to be the fate to which some theologians have returned. These are scholastic debates with scant relevance to the actual experience of individuals or communities. Indeed it may be a spectacular example that human reason and logic alone are not the final word in knowing. Murray's critics themselves appear trapped in a modernist conundrum of rationalism of a type.[12]

A solution to the critique offered by Schindler, Baxter and others may well be in an esthetics as Baxter himself notes. He uses Hans Urs von Balthasar's theology to make a very good point. The example he provides of Archbishop Oscar Romero and his successor Archbishop Saenz is quite suggestive, but I am not convinced he applies it to its best advantage. Von Balthasar's theological esthetics may, indeed, be an important discovery of the way to build the "good community." The community, however, that has a clear self-understanding of its supernatural/natural goal is one that knows clearly and passionately because it treasures and loves its individual and communal life. C.S. Peirce frequently made this point as well. Baxter suggests Von Balthasar's theological dramatics lead one to discover in Oscar Romero's life and death the cause and meaning of justice. This precisely is a major route of epistemological discovery. Yet, Baxter does see or apply the same theological dramatics to the "Americanists" (and for us, John England), which is surprising, even though the intensity in the drama of the lives of the men are not the same, the revelations that are their lives are epistemologically parallel. The same is true of the American Catholic experience and it surprises me that Baxter cannot see this. The oversight may be due to too tightly held an ideology. The values of the American Republic John England valued and celebrated as part and parcel of his Catholicism reflect a "civilization of love" (Schindler's term) whose purpose is that given it by God. That purpose specifically has been the call to be patient and tolerant in our life together, cognizant that God's ways are not those of human clarity or logic alone. In both English and American polity, the theological esthetics embedded in their Christian heritage seem to mandate an ever broader community of respectful care among people of different faiths or no faith and different classes on the basis of "fellow-feeling" and, sometimes, simply practicality. The theological dramatics are seen in the young bishop from Ireland, who had fought the Crown's claims in the Anti-Vetoist controversy on the basis of what was right, not on the basis of law or precedent, and on the basis of what would work to create a content Ireland. Truth was in the unanimity of the community.

Philip Pettit's argument that political and social freedom is grounded on a "freedom from coercion" is not adequately addressed by the critics. The critics prefer to believe that genuine human freedom can only be narrowly teleological—that is the "freedom for" what God set as an almost pre-determined purpose to human life. Unfortunately, one may come to believe that such an end is based upon a deductively rationalist theology as opposed to either an inductive or abductive (hypothesizing) theology that submits its understanding of divine revelation to plausibility structures found in inductive evidence or Peirce's abductive esthetics. The abductive esthetics of Peirce or the theological dramatics of Von Balthasar better serve the practical theologian than scholastic systematics and rationality. Theological dramatics also points to persons of faith who appreciate most the protection people on the margins require and which the privileged, perhaps academic, cannot fully appreciate. John England's background afforded him the opportunity to appreciate the value of such protection from coercion. Such appreciation is the knowledge that love imparts.

John England's theology was not academically prescient of the theology of DeLubac, Von Balthasar or Rahner nor the philosophy of Peirce. However, he and Murray fully grasped the substance and effectively wed faith, reason and esthetics to discover in their circumstances the presence of God's activity. For the Christian God is never absent and so we live a "graced" or supernaturally natural experience of the ever-present God. Every human being, therefore, draws upon the same longings and sense of purpose. It is this shared experience and the language we so haltingly give to it that sanctions the dialogue communities enter upon in their diversity. The experience gives rise to language (symbol), as Ricoeur noted, but that language need not be and should not be solely that of the church. It must, indeed, be public and communicative across plural thematizations of shared or analogous human experiences; otherwise our cultural and rational presuppositions place limits upon the activity of God.

An issue about which Baxter is legitimately concerned is the privatization of the religious experience. Is it effectively banned from public discourse? Quite possibly it is in many quarters. To suggest, however, that Murray and the many "Americanist Catholics" who preceded him privatized religion and consigned it to the periphery is a stretch and too facile an understanding of these great leaders. Why? Because Baxter does not deal concretely with the issues, but proposes that the role of the Church is to be a "contrast society."[13] In what manner can dialogue proceed, if it rests upon a language that is not shared or that is imposed? In the end, such a stance appears to retreat into another era when theology made claim to being the "Queen of the sciences" and could draw all from its own bosom. The "contrast society," as in Matthew 5:4, the "city on the hilltop" that is unambiguous in its witness, without the balance given in the contrasting analogy in Matthew 13:47-50, the parable of the good and bad fish caught in the net cast, devolves into sectarian exclusivity and obfuscates the very clarity the Gospel intends to offer.

Bryan Stone, who writes from a Reformation tradition, also relies largely on Alasdair MacIntyre, John Howard Yoder and Stanley

Hauerwas, as does Baxter. Both insist upon Christian faith language in dialogue with other religious believers (Islam, Hindu, Buddhist, etc.) and non-believers. To their credit each also insists that the dialogue must be Christ-like—that is, it must not force or attempt to coerce others, but neither author wrestles honestly with the communicative issues involved in a dialogue in which one partner is wedded to his own faith language that cannot be altered without substantive loss to accommodate the dialogue partner. To do so, at least Stone explicitly states, would cede the field to one's dialogue partner.[14] Each fails to deal adequately with the pragmatic or practical dimensions we have seen John England, Murray and others address so well. The critics who turn to MacIntyre fail to grasp the importance of his reminder that Aristotle and the Thomistc traditions hold to the distinction between theoretical reasoning and practical reasoning.[15] Theoretical reasoning easily leads us to affirm that the human family stands united as regards the virtue of love, perhaps even "we must love our neighbor as ourselves." The challenge is what is love? Practical reasoning is the application of the theoretical. What is "to love" in this particular situation? Is the loving thing a hug? Is the loving thing the discipline given a youngster who has slapped a sibling? In the latter instance, a hug is lovingly inappropriate. It is so only because of particularity. Love cannot be lived theoretically, but practically. On the other hand, because practical reasoning cannot give us universal truth, MacIntyre and the tradition seem to pose a serious question for the critics. It cannot be all that difficult to recognize that the notion of "freedom for" (i.e., to pursue our supernatural end) established by civil polity in its law and/or rhetoric would be a specious freedom because of its very theological problematic. It would smother the practical with the theoretical. On the other hand, we have already seen that John England, and earlier and later American Catholic progressives, never assert that the civic polity establishes an "absolute freedom from," a notion, of course, that would itself undermine the constitutional principle of duties and obligations to the common good.

Murray, as a public theologian, did not use explicit *teleological language*, and quite happily so, but rather sought to clarify the shared experiences that might later arrive at shared language. John England, however, used such teleological language in its proper place, a diocesan constitution or Church document. The *public* language both used was larger and more inclusive and, yet, reconcilably Christian and Catholic. It points us to realize that our freedom as persons is to fulfill our nature.

This was fully in accord with the natural law tradition to which both adhered. It was a language that called their interlocutors to reflect on their shared experiences and to clarify the expression given them. This is in full accord with Aquinas's insight that "grace builds upon nature." All humans find their true freedom in being truly and *authentically* human and that graced experienced, for the believer, is one that is shared even with the non-believer. The manner in which we articulate or identify what constitutes *authentic* humanity divides, perhaps, secular and religious understanding, but it is also what will, if anything, be central to our mutual understanding. The dialogue is not beyond reason if, as we noted above, it is also submitted to a theological dramatics or esthetics. Yet, to plumb the depths of our human longing is the *shared (transcendental) experience* of all the human family and the ground upon which all can meet. Time and again the early republicans, as well as John England himself, asserted the role of *personal virtue* to assure the well-being of the democratic *community*. They all assumed the priority of the common good over individual good and, even given the relative pluralism of their era, they understood the shared experiences that made all of us human and intelligible to one another. Whose expression sets the language in the public arena? Only particular circumstances can determine that, but from the standpoint of a theological esthetics, Christian language must be patient and careful if it is to be the language of virtue. It must go the extra mile since it is likely that religious language finds itself enriched if it does so.

John England's Retrieval of Catholic Republicanism

A major factor in Calvinism or Reformed theology, and it was Reformed theology that set in place much of the religious outlook in the early republic, stressed the humanity's sinfulness in such a way that virtue in society could flourish in an environment that needed to stabilize a delicate balance between the exercise of authority, leadership and the will to power. Law, somewhat paradoxically for a Calvinist tradition that also stressed the primacy of faith over law, came to supplant virtue in American republicanism, a factor that can be traced, no doubt, to the English common law tradition. Virtue seemed to have little room to flourish in the public arena and its agenda.[16] In this respect, the American tradition came to associate closely the observance of law with virtue itself. The consequence was that religious ethics became increasingly marginal to public life. The tension that existed, however, was that the classically trained person of the late eighteenth and nineteenth centuries was very aware of the Aristotelian, even its Christian Thomistic expression as regards theoretical and practical reasoning and the practice of virtue. A natural law ethic existed alongside the tradition that observance of the law was primary. Practical adherence to natural law theory floundered on the fact that generally so many disagreed about what was or was not expected or virtuous in any given situation. A genuine understanding of the principles of the natural law theory was reduced to a popular series of affirmations that isolated natural law thinking to the arena of religion and situated the legal system as the public arbiter of behavior. The understanding that the natural law was law only in an analogical sense escaped most people's purview. As with the virtues, the principles of natural law served as the horizon or yardstick by which humans were to adjudicate behavior through appropriate application to particular circumstances. The Aristotelian tradition had assisted generations of thinkers as well as John England to appreciate that if there was a lack of clarity or universal agreement about what exactly was the natural law, the disagreement was in practical application, not theoretical judgment. The republican tradition both dissented and agreed with the Greek and medieval view of virtue, law and ethics. However, in each case, "rugged individualism" was not the option chosen. It was, instead, a dialogical turn to a community of practical reasoning premised on the priority of the common good. Kearns offers a practical insight central to understanding John England's appreciation of the manner by which Christian virtues were to be lived in a society of law. Without religious liberty and the distribution and balance between authorities in society, the concrete situations of religious pluralism would be lost and with it the depth and profundity of the plentitude of humanity's religious encounter with God. The question for England and his generation was largely not a question of individual rights in contestation with those of the community, so much as of the balance between conflicting interests. According to Kearns, John England came to his position because of his experience as a member of the Catholic minority amidst Protestant evangelicalism in South Carolina. Indeed, a degree of wariness as regards evangelicalism can also be found in his response to his Carolinian milieu. As wonderful as he frequently described it, he also noted its imperfections. Kearns writes,

[T]he bishop never bent from an absolute belief in the separation of church and state. The rise of evangelicals in search of a nation under *their* [emphasis mine] God caused [John] England to spew forth torrents of invective:

'Good God! Then is America fallen so low? Is her intellect so debased? Are these states become such a link of ignorance, as that all rejected falsehoods of Europe are to find this as their asylum? Are we, who have led the way in the career of rational, well-regulated society, to crave after the bigots of Europe.'[17]

John England's appeal to rationality was not naïve. He dealt with a quite different agenda than the majority Protestant population, namely the limits that needed to be placed upon the right of believers to impose their sincerely held faith upon the minority. Reason for John England (as in the Catholic theological tradition) was required as an integral part of the social discourse. Faith without plausible explanation is mere assertion as I Peter 3:11 suggests. Furthermore, the thought of a Catholic bishop was at a distance from the popular Protestant belief and principle: *faith alone, bible alone and grace alone.* It may well be more upon this latter "popularized" (vulgarized we may say since Martin Luther was quite sophisticated and nuanced in his application of the principle) catch phrase that, along with the English common law tradition, contributed to an American sense of the privatization of religion. Quite clearly, the Baptist tradition, along with other dissenters in the British tradition, came to emphasize the individual relationship with Jesus as Savior as well as private interpretation of Scripture over which no external body should exercise control. Certainly on a popular level, the consequence was also that the Scriptures were not to be sullied by the philosophies or reasonings of humankind. If this is correct, we can little doubt the public dialogue would come to exclude religious language as such popular perceptions developed. It is to these factors that religious privatization and fideism may be traced more than to subsequent interpretations of early American republicanism. For John England, as we will see, Catholic substance took exception to such reductionisms to which both Luther and Calvin were subjected.

Constitutionalism, on the other hand, was to John England an eminently Catholic tradition. In its Catholic expression it was found in religious life—such as religious orders, from as early as the sixth century. It was neither intrinsically privatist nor rationalistic. This is the core of Bishop England's gift at inculturation to a hierarchical church in the midst of a republican constitutional society: the retrieval of the Catholic tradition of republican polity in the religious life and synodal or conciliar gatherings of bishops and theologians. The dialectic, of course, was that this tradition ran parallel to a monarchical episcopacy that John England trusted could be reconciled.

Yet clearly the issues of democracy and religious liberty were troubling, even disturbing, as we have seen, for Rome in the first half of the nineteenth century. How else does one explain *Mirari Vos* and *Singulari Nos?* While John England would appear to espouse the American political and constitutional milieu with the fervor of a recent convert, he actually had been a proponent of these positions when he was still in Ireland. So it was that we noted the surprise that first met his earlier appointment to the episcopacy and consequently, after serving in Charleston, when he received an additional appointment as a papal nuncio to negotiate a concordat between the Vatican and the Haitian government. While he obviously espoused the very republican and democratic principles that Gregory had expressed both grave concern and condemnation, they also were the very principles that were central to a successful negotiation of a new concordat between the Vatican and Haiti.[18] If this unexpected action on the part of the Vatican is to be understood (like so many paradoxes during this period), it must be seen in the overall context of the Vatican's interests. As would be the case in its relationship with the American Republic, the Vatican, for political reasons, consistently proved itself practical rather than ideological. It tolerated political and social conditions of which it disapproved for the sake of its membership's survival and healthy growth. Catholics, for example, in the United States were never pressed on the issues of religious liberty and the separation of Church and State. On the other hand, it cannot be supposed that the Vatican's political wiliness was amoral. Indeed, political and pastoral accommodation were and are justified only in the case that the issue involved was not one that is intrinsically evil. Whatever else we may say of such condemnations as those in *Mirari Vos a*nd *Singulari Vos,* they quite clearly should be understood in a much more qualified sense than often is the case. The Vatican clearly understood its own "condemnations" in a twofold manner. Firstly, they were directed at persons perceived as "radical" and destructive of good order and social tranquility, as we saw earlier. But secondly, the Vatican would have understood diplomatic actions in the face of values understood as dangerous, not as compromises of theoretical reasoning or principles, but the virtuous application of those principles to assure the well-being of *all concerned.* It is the *pastoral* sense, the ability to recognize the wise implementation of principle and the avoidance of destructive ideology. Such an approach was viewed as consistent in Rome and, consequently, John England was not viewed by the "anti-republican" Gregory XVI as anything less than orthodox.

This is particularly pertinent when we recall that the categorization of "liberalism" is too sweeping and misleading particularly when coupled with the concepts of individual rights, republicanism, separation of Church and State, and individualism. From another perspective, the best of the American pragmatic tradition may help us understand a dynamic that has always existed in the human family. In a broad stroke, since we cannot spend time exploring the details here, it found its best articulation by Charles Sanders Peirce later in the century. The pragmatism that Peirce held was not mere functionalism such as we might associate with contemporary popular forms or a sheer expediency that suggests "being pragmatic is to do what is necessary to get something done *without* consideration of *long-term impact.*" For Peirce, pragmatism was a method to ascertain meaning, but most importantly such meaning was not identical with final truth. His was a non-foundational approach. Meaning was yielded by the logic used to determine what "something" was and what was or would be its consequence, if it were. It was not a consideration whether that "something" was good or true, but that it had consequences and, on that score, was "real." Such logic, however, was not the totality of our "knowing." Inquiry, instead, was also like the hypothesis or the esthetics that allows or drives the scientist and researcher to "see the lines that connect the dots." This is the method that opened the inquirer to the good and the beautiful, the truthful. Ethics is needed to assess or appraise whether the lines are correctly drawn, named or stated. If they are, then, logic calls us to draw conclusions that move beyond specific or particular instances to general principle or formulae. This is the dialectic of the American (human) experience, the interplay of the individual and a community of inquiry or discovery. The particular leads inevitably to the recognition of the general or universal and the truth that underscores both. Hypothesis (esthetics) is the contribution characteristically of individuals; the ethical and logical contributions, respectively deduction and induction, are the contributions of a community. This interplay between esthetics, logic and ethics (Peirce's firstness, secondness, and thirdness) is also central not only to the way in which we come to know, but also to the way we can grasp the role of leadership within a community and the interplay of the particular and the general. It was a philosophical insight particularly American and republican. Peirce gave it articulation, John England was one of many who had practiced the pattern long before its articulation. Peirce drew the lines between the dots.

The Roman reaction to the Diocesan Constitution is unsurprising, particularly if we recall that England's argument for it ran along the lines of those offered for Roman approval of a constitution by religious congregations of men or women. Leaders, the esthetes, emerge from communities validly insofar as they validate the communities' unarticulated experience. Such experience comes to articulation in the community's resonance and validation. In 1824 Bishop England had sent a draft copy of the constitution and an explanatory cover letter to Rome. The Vatican dutifully made investigations of complaints that had been forwarded to Rome in its regard.[19] In the end, Rome made no effort whatsoever to abrogate, censure or modify the Diocesan Constitution. Republicanism was, in some senses, an "old friend" under a new name, but certainly also with a new dynamism.

Rome could not have thought its response, therefore, in the least bit unusual and Bishop England too showed no great surprise at the response. Reporting to the convention of South Carolina Catholics in 1833, he said, "I have also had it (the Constitution) *reexamined* [emphasis mine] at the Holy See, where it was found not to contain anything objectionable. I could not look for its approbation because the power of making the regulations which it enacts, resides within each diocese for itself, subject only to the Apostolic See, to prevent their containing anything incompatible."[20] We should notice here, as well, a pre–Vatican I presumption in favor of decision making at the diocesan level. Thus, this tacit approval by the Vatican was given in spite of the chorus of objections raised by a number of members of the U.S. hierarchy.[21] We should note also that the prefect of the Propagation Office at this time was Cardinal Consalvi, who had been Pius VII's moderately liberal secretary of state. (In the last several references we use the term "liberal" in its more popular meaning, as in generous and open to innovation, not in its more academic social-scientific sense as the autonomous individual.

The Constitution of the Diocese of Charleston

The Process of Development and Approval

The edition of the constitution examined here is the one of 1839, the second and final one.[22] The Italian copy of the original 1823 edition in the archives of the Propagation Office, Guilday assures us, "shows but few amendments" in the edition of 1839. The proceedings of the second South Carolina convention gave examples of two minor amendments made to the constitution: simplification of the membership requirements and of the warden's responsibilities.[23] Surely the most significant amendment was in 1838 when the district meetings gave way to an annual diocesan-wide gathering. In the advertisement that accompanied the constitution in the Reynolds edition of England's *Works* (and following the preface) we were told that the principal changes were "one annual convention . . . and also . . . one board of General Trustees . . . One or two [others] of trivial moment," such as the definition of faith, were also substituted/added. In any case, the advertisement further stated, "The amendments had been submitted to the bishop, to the conventions of South Carolina and Georgia, in 1838; subsequently to the vestries; then to the conventions of the same states in 1839; to the several congregations of North Carolina in that year, and having received, in every instance, their unanimous approbation, were confirmed by the bishop." Another change was in response to Bishop David of Bardstown. David objected to the definition of faith found in the original edition of the constitution. England had written originally, "Faith is the sincere disposition to believe all that God has taught." This, David objected to as inadequate. England agreed and stressed that faith was certain. He wrote, "Faith is the belief . . . [of those things] which He hath revealed to us, even though they . . . [be] beyond the comprehension of our reason." [24]

The first district to vote approval for the constitution was South Carolina on November 25, 1823, in convention at Charleston. No record of this convention, which might have given us an idea how many people gathered to approve the document, is available. We have already noted England's personal testimony to the process of approval as found in his journal, the preface to the constitution and his letter to Rome explaining it to the authorities there. One of his observations is, "The clergymen and laymen who attended the several meetings [re: the first South Carolina convention] upon this subject were unanimous in their approval of the Constitution."[25] Yet, just how broad a consensus was given in the voice of that first convention is unanswerable, since the other two districts, the states of Georgia and North Carolina, came under the constitution with their respective conventions later in 1826 and 1829. It is beyond question however that the bishop allowed the districts and the congregations to enter freely into union under it. This was witnessed, for example, by the delay of the Church of St. Mary at Charleston in accepting it until sometime in 1830. When England addressed the seventh convention of South Carolina, he made reference to the congregation/s that had not yet approved the constitution. The bishop's deep and genuine republicanism is seen here. "It is true some of our brethren who formed very strange notions not only of the Constitution we have adopted, but took equally erroneous views of my mode of administration, have kept aloof for a time. They have been permitted to follow their own plans without interruption; they adhere to our faith, they observe our ecclesiastical discipline. It is not my intention to interfere with their peculiarities."[26] It would appear from his journal that England wrote the constitution himself and submitted it (after a great deal of consultation) to the conventions for approval. Likewise, it seems there never was a widely printed and distributed edition of the constitution available until 1839.[27]

We should exercise some caution in an assessment of John England. "Napoleon wished to give the Spaniards, for example, a constitution *a priori*," Hegel wrote, "but the attempt fared badly enough. For a constitution is no mere artificial product; it is the work of centuries, the idea and the consciousness of the rational in so far it has been developed in a people." Hegel then continued, "What Napoleon gave the Spaniards was more rational than what they had before, and yet they rejected it as something alien to them."[28] Many have suggested, not without reason, as much of John England's "top-down" approach as well. What appears as a serious shortcoming, however, in the process of development of the Diocesan Constitution, can be judged less harshly because of the Diocesan Constitution's success. As we shall see, it seems to have responded to the conscious rationality and political context of an American Catholic people and their republic proclivities. They, as immigrants not formally educated, belonged also to a tradition to a great extent estranged from its own republican dimensions in earlier history. Yet, they accepted and appreciated leadership that offered cohesiveness to their Catholic and newly found American heritages. England exercised, certainly, something akin to a "top-down" approach since he wrote the constitution himself and gave it to the people of the diocese. Such can easily be associated with a type of paternalism certainly. But some caution is warranted lest we simplify and dichotomize. It is a shibboleth that clearly finds validation, for example, in the misguided vision of the British and other European colonial powers in the nineteenth century that believed that they bore the "white man's burden" to civilize the world. In the case of John England, however, another model seems more appropriate. It was more something of the nature that Gramsci underscores with his "organic intellectual." John England's constitution is a perfect example of a teacher leading and preparing his people from within their aspirations. He allowed, for example, the Cathedral parish freely to opt not to operate under the Diocesan Constitution until the Cathedral parish freely joined shortly before Bishop England's death. While Bishop England operated decisively, it was not imperiously.[29] It reminds one of Winston Churchill's supposed comment to Franklin D. Roosevelt as World War II was coming to an end. Roosevelt asked why Churchill was looking backward so often over his shoulder. "Mr. President," Churchill replied, "a leader must be sure he is not too far in front of the people."

The Preface of the Constitution

Government of the Church
The preface to the constitution introduced the reader to the concept of authority in the Catholic tradition. The church was divided into two parts: one of divine institution, the other "of human regulations." The part that was of divine institution came under no one's authority. On the contrary, it was what humankind was obligated to submit to without fail or question. The second part, namely that "of human institution" was dependent however upon the first, since the two parts could not stand in contradiction to one another. The adage, "We must distinguish, but cannot separate" seems a fitting description of the bishop's position. Therefore it was the "invariable and essential" rule of the Catholic tradition that the authority to exercise this "human regulation" was given only to those who were appointed by the Lord Jesus as "the judges and witnesses and preservers of his institutions."[30] The preface made a further distinction regarding the authority of "human regulation" within the

church. This was further broken down into 1) ecclesiastical discipline and 2) temporalities or property. Both were properly within the authority of the hierarchy—and therefore "spiritual" authority in the sense that they regulate the intangible dimensions of community life. The economic or financial independence of the Church was a long-standing concern dating, at least, to the question of Lay Investiture in the eleventh century. Such authority was distinct from political or civil authority that regulates the external and visible aspects of the community's life. While the church's temporalities were tangible and external, they, in the life of a spiritual community, exist only in service of that spiritual role. If such service provided by the Church's tangible assets contradicts solid reason, faith becomes implausible and spiritual authority non-binding. Faith may precede reason, but cannot contradict it. In his apologetics England operated within this mind-set, a very Catholic one. Elwyn Smith pointed out,

> In comment on England's thought, we would note only that there is a sharp contrast between his concept of the "spiritual," which retained the concreteness of its meaning in the medieval tradition, and that of some Protestants to whom the spiritual meant primarily the subjective and invisible. . . . The persistent misunderstanding between Catholics and Protestants in America on the meaning of these terms has exacerbated friction.[31]

The Catholic sacramental tradition absorbed profoundly the belief, based upon the experience of the ages, that what is *of God* (*de jure divino*) and what is *of history* (*de jure humano*) must be held in permanent tension. It is also a reminder that John England clearly offered (I use the term anachronistically, of course) an inculturated vision of Catholicism in America. Bishop England's notion of the "spiritual" would possibly be expressed by us today more adequately as "religious" authority. This religious authority pertains to those who hold religious offices (institutions) or derive such authority from religious belief/action (discipline). The authenticity of their office elicits from the believer obedience whereby the good of the community precedes consideration of private, rational good. It is not blind obedience, but the recognition that virtue (the good and the beautiful) is not founded solely upon reason alone. The "invisible" affects that hold the community or family together, insofar as these are not irrationally pursued, take precedence over individual or private good.[32] As the founders of the nation balanced power in the visible realm, John England strove to balance faith and reason, logic and affect in those arenas more "spiritual" and less tangible. The locus of authority in ecclesiastical discipline was made abundantly clear. It "was necessarily. . . under the exclusive regulation" of the bishop. The search to define leadership roles for the laity, therefore, was in the only remaining area of church authority: the regulation of temporalities or property. But given what we have just reviewed, how could this be done?

Significant leverage may be found, nonetheless, in the hierarchal tradition. Christian religion rests on divine revelation and consequently the interpretative norm. While ordinarily and properly placed in an appointed or anointed office, the reality is that such religious authority interprets authentically and governs well within the context of a discernment process that is consultative. From the beginning, when differences arose among the first Christians, we find the New Testament witnesses to meetings and consultations among the leadership (Acts 15). It is a pattern that had always been presumed (if not necessarily always followed). Whether it was the first council at Jerusalem or the numerous regional and universal councils that followed in the first centuries, the tradition has always recognized this. It is attested to in the consecrated religious life and in the interplay between the *magisterium* and the theologians throughout history as well. The discernment process centers the exercise of ecclesial authority. John England's constitution gives great play to this. The cross-over effect that the assignment of consultation regarding temporalities as the area of lay competence (and therefore consultative or passive voice) rests in the fact that, assuming goodwill, financial and other material considerations will in the end affect the entire range of ministerial efforts undertaken. A moral relationship is established whereby the partners exert influence and authority over each other and the action/reaction that reverberated within Christianity for centuries as a result of the Lay Investiture question can be obviated. Bishop England's movement of the issue parallels the 1983 *Code of Canon Law* which mandates a consultative voice to laity in parish finance councils, even as the moral interplay of parish councils as advisors to pastors on a much broader scale develops a momentum not officially or juridically defined. In the *Code of 1983* Bishop England's vision, however, is still not found on the diocesan level. The *Code* does not obligate the bishop to operate under the same consultative mandates as those assigned to the local pastor. Clearly the theological issue for the Vatican has been another principle of hierarchy that has become more difficult to explain in the developed world—that is, those appointed and anointed by divine right or commission (priests and bishops) cannot be under the supervision of those not so appointed or anointed (the laity). Yet, consultative processes quite wisely, while not supervisory, are urged, even mandated for priest-pastors who themselves share in the same sacrament of appointment (Holy Orders) as the bishops themselves. If the distinction between the ordained priesthood and the priesthood of the laity is to be that of "kind" and not simply of degree, the same is not officially said to be true of the distinctions between bishop, priest and deacon. Yet, we discover the *Code* urges accountability and consultation upon the priest and deacon in their relationships with the laity, but refrains from making the same suggestion to the espiscopacy. John England was surely ahead of his times in this matter.

Since the Church in the United States did not receive funds from the government, but was rather founded upon the voluntary system, several problems presented themselves. John England was particularly interested in the problems he saw arise from the fact that "the church had no divine power of taxation" and so must struggle to support herself through a fully voluntary approach. The constitution's preface addressed three questions, 1) How was money to be raised and property to be obtained? 2) Who would hold title to such assets of the church? 3) And finally, how were the assets to be expended? Since the Church—that is—the hierarchy could not tax on the basis of any command left by Jesus to do so, the obvious answer presented itself: the laypersons, as the beneficiary of the ministry of the Church, should pay for it. Certainly the early Church made just such an argument itself on numerous occasions. Therefore the laypersons must likewise be allowed in some manner to determine the uses of the money that they gave to the Church. It was observed that all through the centuries the management style of the Church's temporalities could and did change. Initially "all this power rested in the apostles and they distributed portions of it amongst others," namely the deacons according to England. Later in some places this authority to regulate temporalities was placed in the hands of the laity "by the bishop to aid the priests and deacons." One great and abiding principle, however, remained throughout the ages: the bishop "had at least a *negative* upon the management of Church property"—that is, he had a veto that, of course, could neither be easily over-ridden nor appealed. If one wished to pursue either course it required submission of the question to Rome.

The Purpose of the Constitution

Lay trustees had asked for some say in the management of Church temporalities. The preface noted that such claims were not based upon the principles of the Catholic Church. The trustees followed rather "the example of churches which protested" against Catholic Church doctrine and discipline. "The Constitution of this diocese was formed, for the purpose of preventing in [the] future the recurrence of evils of this description within its limits." The purpose of the constitution, however, was more positively stated later as

> to lay down those general principles of law, and to show their special bearing in the most usual cases; and then upon the mode of raising, vesting, and managing church property, to fix the special manner on which the great principles that are recognized by the Church should be carried into practice.[33]

Thus while assailing the trustees, the constitution was to remedy the problems along several lines in the trustees' position. As was seen earlier, the substantive basis of the trustees' argument was generally the concern that the layperson be allocated significant authority and responsibility in the management of Church affairs and further that some system of "law" be instituted to assure this. This does not contradict the fact that the issue surrounding *jus patronus* and ethnicity were also clearly emotional and not simply a matter of lay-clerical prerogatives. As the issue of trusteeism, however, matured in an individual's mind the question of accountability of Church authority clarified itself as the principle of the trustee movement.[34]

There were at least three factors operative in England's mind as he framed the constitution for his diocese. The first of these was the Irish milieu out of which he had come. Diocesan and national organizations of the Church had been widely recognized as a need in Ireland both by its leadership and its people. When he arrived in the United States, this was the context out of which he operated as he visited throughout his diocese. It was also evident in his incessant pleas with Archbishop Marechal, that began within months of his arrival, that a provincial council be called.[35]

The second, and obviously most pressing and explicit motive, was stated in the preface: to counteract the abuses of trusteeism, a basic concern with a modern form of lay investiture. A third factor was his creative contribution. This was underscored at length near the end of the preface. There he demonstrated not only the compatibility but also the notable parallels between Catholicism and republicanism. "The portions of our church government are very like those of the government of this Union." There followed a list of the parallels between the two. The bishop and state government held authority not as deputies of the pope or the president, but with the same authority by which the latter held authority. As the states were bound into a federation, so were the parishes bound into a single diocese, and the diocese bound into a single [world] Church. Both the state and the diocese had the power of legislation so long as they did not contravene the general law. As the majority in Congress bound its members and their districts, so the General Council bound its bishop members and their diocese. The executive, whether pope/church or president/state, was subdivided. The same applied as well to diocesan administration. All the subdivisions had legislative authority appropriate to themselves. Left unsaid by Bishop England was the power of the veto without legislative possibility to override. Yet, his mind would be clear. As in the Anti-Vetoist controversy, no social institution could gainsay the Church in its task, when faithful, to divine revelation. The notion of republicanism endows the faithful with the cohesive identity associated with the citizenry. That ecclesial citizenry, endowed also with God's charisms, plays its role to assure the Spirit's effective presence in the ecclesial body. Lacking that mutual (and Spirit assured) faith and cooperation, Church and State fail as institutions. Indefectibility is an ecclesial gift—that is a communal one.

The Principles of Constitutionalism in John England's Other Works

Though it had never been stated in the preface, John England's principal apologetic concern was evident. In Ireland he had frequently heard the charge of the "No Popery" crowd. They generally held that Catholicism was not compatible with any government that was not itself Catholic. In the United States the same theme was voiced regularly. John England, now in a position to do something to prove the charge false, did so. Having established his diocese on a constitutional basis, he could concretely argue that a republican governmental style was compatible with Catholicism and was, in fact, lived out in his diocese.

In his address, "On Charity," delivered at the Boston Catholic Cathedral, May 14, 1841, this theme of Catholic republicanism was hammered home in the unmistakable style of the apologist. The occasion was a day of a general fast in memory of President William H. Harrison, who had died little more than a month after taking office.

> Look through the records of the world, and see where the principles of true republicanism are first to be found. They had their origin in Christianity, and their earliest instance is in the Church of which we are members. Her institutions are eminently republican.[36]

Surely Bishop England's claim is a bit exaggerated. Philosophically, Plato, Aristotle and Cicero could have made as great a claim, if not greater. The struggles of republicanism in ancient Greece and Rome made their marks as well. However, the remark is not without its merit. England in this address reminded his listeners that on the field at Runnymede had been the Archbishop of Canterbury and with him the Catholic bishops of England. Indeed in pre-Norman times when one of the English kings wrote the pope asking for a code of laws for his realm, the pope responded, "I can give you principles, not laws. Your duty as monarch is to consult your men of wisdom, acquainted with the wishes and necessities of your people."[37] Republicanism, he maintained, was found throughout the ages in the Catholic tradition. This theme of the reconcilability of Catholicism and republicanism had been pursued earlier in his "Address to Congress" in 1826. There he also made frequent reference to history. William Tell, some of the Swiss republics, the Republic of San Marino and the wars of independence then being waged under Simon Bolivar in South America were all illustrations of the compatibility. In this same address Bishop England interestingly even makes reference to "St. Peter, the president of the apostolic body." [38]

The bishop's claim on the compatibility issue was modestly but compellingly noted in "On the Catholic Doctrine of Transubstantiation," a letter to a Protestant clergyman, the Rev. Dr. Bachman. "Now, Sir, if your (Protestant) republicanism and ours be estimated by the numbers of reigning sovereigns in our several communions, we shall pretty nearly be on a par."[39] Whether we take seriously England's inflated claims for his

Church's development of republican principles is not as important as the recognition of his effort to establish clearly their compatibility.

The tradition of constitutionalism within the Catholic Church—in the religious orders of men and women—was a strong argument for such compatibility, even if it was not universally accepted during *that* period by his Church's leadership. It was this tact that the bishop followed in his sermon, "At the Habiting of an Ursuline Nun." In it he commented upon the antiquity of the Ursuline constitutions and of the principles of republicanism found in them. Among the facts he noted were that the superiors were elected at the suffrage of the membership, the terms of office were limited and there was accountability for the conduct of each office.[40]

England's zeal for republican values was nearly consuming. It was a central force in much of his writings. It was also a major factor in his strained relations with the French-born clerics in the United States. This subject was referred to earlier. An example was the stinging rebuke England laid at the door of the French-born clerics as being un-American and anti-republican.[41] The context of the republicanism of the French revolution was recognized by England as a factor for the understandably negative attitudes ("not precisely of the description that was required in the new republics") taken by many of the French-born clerics who migrated to the United States after the French revolution.[42] It should come as no surprise, therefore, that republicanism framed his model for the government of his diocese or that its theoretical underpinnings were such a major focus in the preface to the constitution.

Title One: Doctrine

Any citations not followed by a reference in the remainder of this chapter are simply *verbata* from the title and section of the constitution under discussion.

Faith, Revelation and Infallibility
The first title of the constitution dealt with the doctrine of the Catholic Church. The stated principle was simple. People were bound to believe what God revealed and only what God revealed. The corollary was evident. There could be no picking or choosing among the *revealed* doctrines. All were truth; all were to be believed. However, people could not expect that their reason could comprehend all that was to be believed.

Thus the definition of faith: "Faith is the belief, upon the authority of God, of all those matters which He hath revealed to us, even though they should be above or beyond the comprehension of our reason." These truths are "above or beyond" reason, but not contrary to it. In the Gospel of love, one comprehends that reason can divide; on the other hand, it is love and care alone that transcend and unite. Reason is not the final arbiter, but neither is assertion of faith free from all restraint.

The strength of the bishop's Catholic tradition quickly showed itself in the paragraph following this definition. He noted, "How do we know what God has revealed?" The answer, he said, was "from an infallible witness." And who or what was the infallible witness? "God hath spoken . . . by His beloved Son, who hath on earth established his church . . . and . . . commanded all persons to hear and to obey that Church as the infallible witness of his doctrine and precepts." England then described "that Church." It was a "visible body" with "one visible head" professing the "same faith," using the "same sacraments," teaching the same "holy" doctrines within the "unbroken succession" of pastors back to the apostles. The "church" therefore was the judge of the "true sense and interpretation of the Scriptures." The Church, for England, the Catholic Church, was the *infallible witness* of God's revelation.[43] England's language here may be nuanced differently today, but his intentions seem clear. England did not believe the Scriptures were simply subject to the whim of the Church. "No one would presume to say that it is from the judiciary [that] the legislature derives its authority because the explanation of its authoritative acts is given to the judiciary. [In a like manner] the church is not the mistress of the Word of God."[44] John England's notion of the Church was quite institutional, reflecting largely the outlook of Catholicism in his time. Yet, even as we speak of his institutional bias in his understanding of the Church, we must recall that in the period prior to Vatican I ecclesial institutionalism had somewhat of a different overtone. England was far from alone in the belief that "the infallible witness of God's revelation" rested in the infallibility [indefectibility] of the Church, not the infallibility of the pope. While we cannot project post–Vatican II ecclesiology onto John England, his larger point, contextualized properly, stands. The *church* [the faith community], not the papacy as such, is the receptor of the revelation and its steward. We do not find in Bishop England any indication that the institutional Church was the proprietor of revelation. Thus while the bishop may not have fully recognized the complexity of historical conditioning, he trusted deeply in the ability to discover the fact and reliability of divine revelation within history.[45] As other Catholics of his time, he trusted deeply in the *certainty* of the divine revelation as "received," (taught or explicated) oftentimes in contradistinction to the medieval theologians, who were, in fact, more cautious about *certainty,* not because of his adherence to Enlightenment values, but in opposition to them. If popular science during his era proposed certainty in its discoveries because of its ability to demonstrate, a large portion of the religious community countered with a defensive argument for the equal certainty of its revelation from God. We need not be terribly troubled by this, since we have come to recognize, whether in the case of reason or faith, all of us must act on the "truth" we have at the time. As C.S. Peirce so amply illustrated in "The Fixation of Belief," we act not on doubt, but belief. The issue revolves, for both Peirce and John England, around plausibility and the responsibility persons, appreciating their historical condition, have to decide and to act. As Peirce also wrote, "It is absurd to say that religion is a mere belief. . . . Religion is a life, and can be identified with a belief only provided that belief be a living belief—a thing to be lived rather than said or thought.[46] To demand demonstration or absolute certainty would raise serious questions about one's inability ever to act when situations demanded action. The alternative would have been to believe that the failure to act when not absolutely certain was virtuous rather than a possible occasion of evil through omission. John England's attempt to reconcile "the old and the new" remains as relevant today as it was then. The plausibility he associated with Christian revelation provided sufficient certainty that he could intelligently act on it. The vagaries of science or faith left him powerless or incapacitated to act.

The Church and Salvation

In the closing paragraphs of title one, there was included a profession of faith in the declarations of the Council of Trent and in the Roman bishop as the Vicar of Christ. The title's final paragraph summed up the denominational stance of the document. "This true Catholic faith, without which none can be saved, we do at this present, freely profess and sincerely hold." A note was appended to this formulation of *nullus salus extra ecclesiam.* Quoting a declaration of the bishops of the Irish Catholic Church, John England made it clear that one could be in good faith and still not believe as Catholics did. In such cases, the person was left to the merciful judgment of God. Our responsibilities to such a person, Bishop England advised, were the duties of charity and social life. Francis Sullivan's work, *Salvation Outside the Church*, helps us to understand England's theological locus in the works of Bellarmine (1542-1621, Suarez (1548-1619) and DeLugo (1583-1660). According to each, the obligation to be a member of the Catholic Church rested in the recognition and "sufficient knowledge" of such a Gospel obligation. Those who did not have such knowledge were not bound, provided they possessed some measure of religious faith.[47] Suarez, for example, refers to "implicit faith in Christ" that arises from belief in God. He wrote, "God does not usually, even in a case of necessity [baptism in Christ], exercise extraordinary providence so that such means [baptism] can actually be had and applied. Rather, it is normal for the desire or wish to use such means to suffice, as is clearly the case with regard to baptism and confession."[48] DeLugo was even more explicit. "The possibility of salvation for such a person is not be ruled out by the nature of the case; moreover, such a person should not be called a non-Christian, because even though he has not been visibly joined to the church, still, interiorly he has the virtue of habitual and actual faith in common with the church, and in the sight of God he will be reckoned with the Christians."[49] We refer to these theological sources to remind ourselves that John England was not only a committed missioner in a marginal community in the American South, he was also theologically conscious and subtle in his application of the tradition to such circumstances. Finally, the bishop's personal, face-to-face relationships also fed his knowledge. Another person might believe differently than the bishop (or the Catholic Church) and still be recognized as of "good faith" and subject to God's judgment alone. How could one not believe this in friendships and work relationships and be a follower of Christ? Only isolation feeds an opposing ideology.

Analysis

An Overview

There has to be a touch of irony in reading this part of the constitution. In it we discover an essentially juridical orientation to the concepts of revelation and doctrine. There was no mystical flair, no spiritual sentiments expressed. Indeed, a cold, rational, theological jargon quite typical of nineteenth century Catholicism characterized the treatment. This last aspect is a bit surprising in the light of the style England exhibited in his first Pastoral and, even more so, in the four national Pastorals attributed to him. These Pastorals, the latter ones in particular, were highly salted with citations and allusions to the Scriptures. In the first title of the constitution, admittedly a legal-style document, this was not the case, in spite of the fact that the subject matter was much the same as that of the first pastoral. We may easily conclude that he was quite conscious of the genrė as distinct from that of the preacher or teacher.

Notions of Truth and Certainty

The construction of his theology of revelation should be understood within the context of his era. The theological and epistemological framework of Catholicism in the first part of the nineteenth century differed greatly from our own time. "We come now to the matter of fact and *deduction* [emphasis mine]," he wrote, "God did reveal His knowledge . . . what He once asserts as the truth, will be truth forever."[50] Elsewhere he wrote that "we assert that it is possible to know with certainty what our Saviour has taught. . . . Faith is built upon certain knowledge."[51] For England there was "an indissoluble connection between faith and infallibility."[52] It was this link between revelation and infallibility of the Church's witness that appears to the contemporary reader to cast a pall of rigid institutionalized authority over England's conception of God's revealing Word. Contemporary notions of revelation and faith stress the community of faith's struggle to penetrate the meaning and truthfulness in what is revealed. Such a stress was alien to the bishop's Catholic mind and times. His concept of faith, on the contrary, stressed the value that "faith is lost at the very moment that any deliberate doubt is willfully entertained in the soul."[53] The sense and spirit of this thought would appear to prevent the Christian from framing a truly searching question of faith. But the intention was quite otherwise. His intention clearly was that God had revealed truth to us and this truth could be grasped and understood. Ultimate truths, because of the testimony of the Church, could be found and known with certainty. In this regard, then, faith could and was certain.[54] *We* might best understand his emphasis to be that knowledge gained through faith was certainly as definite as any other knowledge, given the limitations of the time and history. It was a period when both people of science and people of faith believed in final truth in a manner quite different than we may today. If the constitution's view of infallibility in the witness of the Catholic

Church appeared somewhat triumphalist, England's position was more modestly phrased in a later diocesan Pastoral letter. "We do not deny that abuses and superstitions have existed in the Church and may yet occasionally and even extensively exist, but we deny that the doctrine which the Church has always held and does now hold is favorable to abuse or founded upon superstition."[55]

The crux of the distinction for us is between the Church's infallible witness to revelation and its authority in the arena of "human regulation." In this latter category the Church could, and often did err. Nonetheless, the impact of the commission given the apostolic college to "go forth and teach" remained stupendous. The Church's doctrinal teaching was an infallible witness to absolute truth. "When the great majority of the bishops united with their head, the bishop of Rome . . . thus concur in their testimony, it is evidence of truth: we will infallibly come to a certain knowledge of what God has revealed."[56] England held the infallibility of the Church in the sense already referred to—that is, indefectibility—and not in the sense that we have more recently come to associate infallibility as an aspect of the papal *magisterium*. For John England's era the struggle with truth and interpretation was the struggle of the tradition and its community to come to grips with the reality of their religious experience of revelation. The challenge John England wrestled with has come to fuller articulation in recent theology as the struggle to understand that the community of faith is guided by the Spirit and cannot be abandoned by the spirit of truth in that struggle. Contemporary jargon alludes to such knowledge, meaning and ethics as culturally or socially established. It offers a ready foundation for the culture's relevance to people's certainty in beliefs. On the other hand, there is a bit of defensiveness found in England's stress upon "certain knowledge." As Gerald McCool has observed in *Catholic Theology in the Nineteenth Century*, the Church's reaction to the Enlightenment and rationalism devolved by the time of the nineteenth century into the Church's own assertion of a deductive and rational certainty itself based upon revealed first principles. DeLugo was also a proponent of such a deductive theology and was a major figure who directed post-Tridentine theological thinking decisively to a deductive logic. The neo-Thomists asserted the importance of natural reason over against the Romantics and displayed a high degree of defensiveness *vis-a-vis* both the advance at the time of the physical sciences and the Age of Reason. This led the church and, most likely, John England as well, to stress the certainty of their own knowledge. In particular, the influence upon John England may rest in work done in the earlier part of the century by Hermes and Drey, each in their quite different ways, who attempted to give a compelling and satisfactory explanation to theology in the face of modern science. Hermes appealed to revelation's certainty not in its theoretical dimension, but in its practical one. In the practical order moral mandates often are found to demand action of us and we must and do readily dispense with any theoretical doubt we may have. Drey simply relied upon the traditional arguments that held that divine revelation's moral imperatives, as a romantic articulation of meaning had held, were culturally received *and* verified. Both these ideas find currency in Bishop England's presuppositions and thought. Both were contemporaries of John England and were widely noted.[57]

Parallel Texts on Teaching Authority

While England's position on the authority of the teaching Church was not extraordinary or innovative, neither was it simplistic.[58] Using an analogy from the political order, he wrote in his first "Letter of Reply to 'Truth'" that as the Supreme Court of the United States did not rule Congress because it possessed the authority to interpret the laws of Congress, neither did the Church, the interpreter of the Scriptures, become, in virtue of that office, the mistress of the Word of God.[59] This is consistent with Vatican II's declaration *Dei Verbum* (*On Divine Revelation* 10). "This *magisterium* is not superior to the Word of God, but its servant." England quotes Augustine, "I would not believe the Gospel were I not induced thereto by the authority of the Church."[60] As England would elaborate it, "Thus before the Scriptures were known to the Christians, they knew the Church; and they recognized its infallible authority in teaching the doctrine which had been revealed, and of which it was made the witness and depository."[61] Reformers, such as Calvin, with his dialect of Word and Spirit, rejected precisely this type of high ecclesiology. But for the bishop, following the romantic understanding of culture found in Drey, the issue was, "What witness exists to testify for the validity of the Bible's claim of authority?" The obvious answer was the Church, understood as the community of faith (or culture) whose practically reasoned life in the Gospel over the centuries assured us of its meaningfulness and truth. Calvin's heirs in the American South would have a difficult time comprehending this line of argumentation.

The greater fear of "individual infallibility" is what he believed he saw in the Protestant principle of private interpretation.[62] He was clearly not an Enlightenment thinker and rationalist since epistemological certainty resided in the witness and life of the community through the ages in a classic romanticist sense. It is true, however, that the bishop failed to appreciate the ecclesiologies of Calvin or Luther and the importance each placed upon the visible Church.[63] The (visible) Church, in his mind, was duty-bound and indefectibly driven to testify to what she had received. This was seen in the preface when absolute precedence was given to that which was of "divine institution" and, of course, that romantic reality was the faith community.[64] In the court of public opinion the trusted witness of such communities of faith through the centuries in a variety of cultures constituted a compelling argument and foundation for the trustworthiness and certainty of the Church's witness.

The infallible witness of the Church, however, was not merely a romantic assertion that was to be accepted a-rationally. Jesus's miracles attested to his preaching, England writes, so miracles continued to attest to the witness of the Church.[65] The argument and evidence for the plausibility of faith and the practical certainty with which we take it today may evoke and may differ greatly from England's perception, but we continue to turn to evidence as a basis for the *plausibility of our faith* without as great a reliance upon a naïve type of romanticism. But the evidential nature of England's apologetics certainly does not reside in a position such as proposed by Plantinga and Wolterstorff in what I may suggest is a return for theological first principles that constituted little more than assertion. If such principles are plausible they do reside in the culture and communities that carry them over the generations, but more as they reflect *effective communication across epistemological communities.* The communicative process, as Habermas teaches us, is sensitive to the "signing" and the cultural grid through which both experience and knowledge are filtered. People must have a sufficient motive for faith, otherwise it becomes solipsistic and/or socially incommunicable beyond the confined circles of one's world. The motives for an effectively communicated message or experience combine both plausibility structures and affectivity that offer the hope that the human family might not break down into warring, incommensurable epistemological isolates. Peirce writes, "The *raison d'etre* for a church is to confer upon men a life broader than their narrow personalities, a life rooted in the very truth of being. To do that it must be based upon and refer to a definite and public experience."[66] This did not mean for John England that reasonably placed faith meant "*our reason* could discover the truth of the doctrine submitted to our minds."[67] We might have supposed, then, that John England too would have had some reservation about rationality, as George Lindbeck does with a cultural-linguistic model of theological communication. We cannot investigate the issue in any depth here, but the nature of the Incarnation raises certain challenges for the Christian who wishes to see how s/he can be both theo-centric and christo-centric. If the experience of God's revelation in Jesus is expressed solely in the cultural-linguistic model, then, in some manner it is culturally confined and its communication as a consequence hindered. Thus, while anthropology speaks meaningfully of cultural relativism, this does not address in any satisfying way the theological and communicative relativization (or historicizing) of the meaning of Jesus's revelation, because the expression given to Jesus's revelation in history may well be historically relative, but what "core human" (and self-transcending) content it possesses and in what way can we come to understand it remains central. Reason remains the fulcrum for Christian faith-tradition and its communication. If "faith seeking understanding" means anything beyond revelation's encoded cultural-linguistic delimitations, it requires the individual not be sublated into the group. The individual must have an instrumental potentiality (*obedientalis potentia*) to understand, comprehend, and appropriate.[68] This last is rooted more in the romantic thinker's understanding that God created graced individuals than in rationalist autonomy. The perspective on practical reasoning (esthetic wisdom) given to this pragmatic, pastoral interpretation of England and his ministry requires us to conclude he did not simply assimilate Enlightenment thought.

Within these restricted bounds, the Church's infallible witness as regards the reasonableness of Divine Revelation would have been comprehensible to some of England's Protestant contemporaries. But the confusion continued to exist between most Protestants and Catholics when the relation of Church infallibility was directed not only to indefectibility regarding revelation, but also extended to the area of ecclesiastical discipline and moral teaching. England himself had a difficult time to provide a clear explanation because of the stress placed upon the "practical obedience" owed the Church authorities. "We are bound by faith to believe that God gave Peter and his successors, the full power of feeding with doctrine and sacraments, and regulation and governing by ecclesiastical discipline the universal church."[69] Here, Lindbeck would prevail. John England's language and culture did not have the tools at hand to offer a clear explanation of the Church's claim to practical obedience in regulation and discipline. It still may not, but faith *knows* more than or in addition to reason alone.

In an attempt to make this intelligible to his Protestant friends, England resorted to political analogies. The United States president has full authority to govern according to the United States Constitution. Would anyone be so naive as to suggest this delegation of "full authority" to govern negated the limitations of the constitution and the law? So it was with the pope and the Church. They govern within the constitutional limits of the Word of God. When therefore the exercise of ecclesiastical discipline moved beyond or outside the limits of revelation, our "certain knowledge" of its correctness was not guaranteed. Yet, herein lies the difficulty. Filial or practical obedience was due the Church in the areas of discipline. The question of Catholic loyalty therefore remained problematic to many Protestant readers. This tension would become the Gordian Knot. The anti-papalist attacks upon Catholic citizenship in a Protestant or pluralist society were not adequately defused by England's distinctions. The visible Church loomed too large in the plan of salvation, much larger than with what Southern Protestantism could feel comfortable. Had John England the resources of contemporary biblical scholarship he may have turned to the Scriptures as his warrant for practical obedience to Church authority and cited Mt. 16:19 on the rabbinic notion of "binding and loosing" as the mandate for practical obedience. We recall, as well, the remarks made earlier regarding Peirce's insight about doubt and action. Certainty gives rise to action whether that certainty be well founded and plausible or not.

Parallel Texts on the Sources of Revelation

The bishop's notions of Scripture and tradition were laid out in broadstroke. The Scriptures were revealed doctrines given to humankind. In his second letter to Dr. Bowen, he wrote, "Its meaning . . . is not varying from age to age, but is now the same that it always has been, it was as well known in the days of the apostles as it could be and the perfection of interpretation was to preserve that meaning unchanged."[70] Though the Scriptures held a very crucial and central place therefore in England's scheme, tradition was seen as another fount of doctrine. In writing in opposition to Blanco White, he noted that there were a number of doctrines which the Catholic Church held that were not found in Scripture. Infant baptism, perpetual virginity of Mary, baptism conferred by laypersons, validity of heretical ordination "and a vast number of others" were referred to. They were all justified simply because of their antiquity in the tradition without any reference to revelation or Scripture. It appeared that tradition therefore was an independent source of doctrine and revelation. In this regard, John England did not envision revelation as it has been articulated in subsequent decades, namely as Jesus as the single source and Scripture and tradition as dual witnesses.[71] Elsewhere, as we will see, he was more creative in his use of the concept of change and continuity within the tradition, culture and life itself.

Parallel Texts on the Commission to Ministry

The bishop, to a very great extent, reflected the popular sacramental theology of his day. He drew therefore a very sharp distinction between the lay and clerical states. The sharpness of the distinction was highlighted in his denial of the priesthood of the faithful. In his second letter to Dr. Bowen we find, "But Christ commanded both kinds [bread and wine] to be consecrated and consumed at the sacrifice, which is offered by the priest and not by the people."[72] If in structure we saw a highly clericalized theory of Church authority, so too in the sacramental ministry of the church, the hierarchical dimension clearly predominated.

This theological orientation was very much the standard of Catholicism at the time, John England's *pastoral practice*, however, did not always observe it as one might have anticipated. The very existence of the constitution itself was in tension with the "clerical-laden" theology of Church authority. Another modification in this clericalization was seen in the appointment of lay readers in congregations without a resident priest, or in the absence of the priest-pastor. It might even be suggested that flexibility in his highly clerical vision of ministry is seen in his effort to develop orders of *teaching* (this was the ordinary mission of women religious in Europe) and *nursing* women. Since teaching and healing occupied such central roles in the theology of the period, it would be myopic not to credit here a degree of openness to share central aspects of ecclesial ministry beyond the circles of the ordained.[73]

Parallel Texts on the Church, Salvation and Pluralism

Final note should be made of the pervasiveness of the authority held by the visible Church. Because of their apologetical nature, John England's works not infrequently dealt with the question of indulgences. When he defined an indulgence, the Church was ascribed the delegated power to make application, to worthy members, of the partial remittance of temporal punishment due to sin. This power was received through the superabundant satisfaction of Jesus.[74] The "high ecclesiology" found in the constitution was underscored well by these ideas regarding indulgences. If it appeared he was less than orthodox on some questions in the eyes of his confreres in the episcopate, he surely was not suspect in others. Since the visible Church was so vital to England's faith, the notion *extra ecclesiam nulla salus* had to be dealt with. Obviously England was a bit uncomfortable with this ramification of a "high ecclesiology." He places therefore a clarifying footnote in the constitution as we have seen earlier. In other texts, as well, he made it clear that toleration of varying religious beliefs was at the heart of his thought.[75]

It was necessary for him therefore to thread cautiously the line that lay between this principle and that which stressed the certainty of faith and revelation found in and through the testimony of the visible Church. He was aware that for salvation the truly important thing was that each person be a member of the intangible church of all believers—and this was a universal possibility. He wrote, "Thus all they who profess their belief in what God had taught by the testimony of the church are in its visible society . . . and probably several who do not now appear in that society, may be brought by the extraordinary grace and favor of our merciful God within its bosom."[76]

The impulse of England's nature was evidenced in the original definition he gave to "faith" as the disposition to believe all that God revealed. Using this same definition in a letter to Daniel O'Connell in October 1823 he indicated the breadth of his notion about those who sought to be saved as well as a broad view of the Church. "Therefore the Roman Catholic Church extends the capacity for salvation to all who are sincerely disposed to believe all that God has taught."[77] While he later allowed for a different definition of faith, his commitment to and understanding of pluralism remained intact. In either case it was the sincere disposition, not actual propositional assent, which was most important. This was also seen in the positive value he placed upon the separation of Church and State. Such separation was necessary not because of simple expediency, but because it was an imperative of religious sentiment. Religious liberty and separation of the two spheres of authority went hand in hand. Faith needed to be freely attested or given—the result of a personal commitment. This being the case, pluralism in the experience and expression of belief was a human reality.[78] This too would implicitly suggest that God's prerogatives and Divine Revelation are reducible neither to propositions or historical conditioning. England believed the Church was necessary, but that God was not bound to work solely in and through its historical agency. The bishop's position does not hinge on the separate powers theory as much as it does upon the republican and pluralist appreciation of diversity of human experience and interpretation. It is an expression of historical consciousness.

Rome and Universal Jurisdiction

There was no question that England was thoroughly Catholic. He recognized the bishop of Rome to possess universal jurisdiction. So wedded were his instincts to this that an apparent contradiction appeared in his writings. He had written in 1815, while editor of the Cork *Mercantile Chronicle*, "Any interference of His Holiness in the local discipline, against the will of the bishop, is an unjust aggression . . . . I am led to think it beyond his competency."[79] In the preface to the constitution, he had underlined the point that the bishops were not just the deputies of the pope. In his controversial exchange with the *Mt. Zion Missionary*, he apparently espoused a position that could give the impression he saw universal jurisdiction in such a way that the bishops were, indeed, hardly more than deputies.

> We allow that if St. Peter were alive and came to Georgia, and examined into the state of the church there, he would, by virtue of his commission from our blessed Savior, have more extensive power than any other person in the church of Georgia, to make the necessary regulations; and we believe his successors enjoy, by virtue of the same commission, similar power derived from the same source, so we believe he could act in a like way.[80]

The impression one easily had from this explanation would be that the local bishop in some way may lack some ordinary power of jurisdiction in his own diocese that Peter and his successors could lay claim to. Since Bishop England was not a systematic theologian, it remains unclear how he reconciled in his thought universal jurisdiction and local autonomy. When Archbishop Kenrick attacked England's thought on the papacy in his review of the *Works* (posthumously published), Archbishop Purcell of Cincinnati came to England's defense. Purcell wrote, "Bishop England is harshly and wrongfully dealt with in his (Brownson's) last number, though not by him. The noble champion of Catholicity never meant to say that the pope was not infallible when teaching *ex cathedra*—he never did say it."[81] The specific issue in this instance was not universal papal jurisdiction, but the ambiguity of England's thought on the papacy is illustrated amply in the observations of these two friends and frequent supporters.

John England felt no need to reconcile two divergent thrusts in his apologetics found in his presentations of the local church and the papacy. In the first instance he was concerned to present the compatibility of Catholicism with republican and American institutions by underscoring the parallels. The president of the United States, for example, exercised "more extensive power" in a state than does the governor, as such. His second concern was just as vital to him: to defend the history, the tradition and the teaching of the Catholic Church. The local bishop, nonetheless, as a governor, is not simply the deputy of the pope, anymore than the governor is the deputy of the president. His loyalties led him to different emphases on different occasions. The nature of the difficulty centers in England's attempts, since he was not an academic, to reconcile the primacy of Rome (Denzinger, 466) and the conciliar propensities of the Council of Florence for which he might appear to have had some sympathy. (Denzinger, 694)[82] The same tension was and is illustrated in the very example England cited: federal and state authority in the United States. In the preface to the Diocesan Constitution the language used is federalist. The papacy and the bishops hold authority with an appearance of a certain majoritarian sense attached. It is better argued, however, that pragmatic concerns and practice hold together the relationship, not a theoretical superstructure. This is true also in the case of the American political tradition and the structure of federalism, and it is true for John England as regards the universal jurisdiction of Rome *vis-a-vis* local bishops. The pragmatics rest in the application of the principle of subsidiarity, but there are no firm and clear lines that can be established regarding what is best solved or resolved at the local level and what is best done or better referred to as an upper level of authority. At best, this dialectic between the local and the center remains as much a horizon and a goal today as it did then. To this point clear and definitive markers in such matters appear to fail. Pragmatic application, following theoretical pointers, appears to be the happy solution. This England did and this he upheld for both his diocese and the Church at large.

Title Two: Government

Title two of the constitution concerned the government of the Church. In this title there are three sections. The first treated of Church government in general, the second, the district and lay officers and the third, jurisdiction. We will look at each of the three sections in turn. By and large this title does not lead to any major controversies or insights. It offers, instead, confirmation of the bishop's basic values.

Section One: Church Government in General

Section one made it emphatic that it was the visible, earthly Church of Jesus Christ that was being discussed. The government of this Church was of divine, not human institution.[83] Its administration therefore was in the hands only of those who were commissioned. This divine commission however covered only spiritual or ecclesiastical concerns and did not include a civil or temporal competency, as we saw at the beginning of this discussion.[84] The church received its governmental shape from Jesus, but Jesus did not appoint "any special or particular mode of civil or temporal government for mankind." Nations were free in this respect to establish any form of government they wished. The Church too could and did exist under all forms of temporal rule. In a pointed response to the trustees, however, who had insisted that Church government in the United States needed to be changed, the constitution added, "Nor does therefore the difference of temporal government in their several nations require or make lawful any change in church government, so as to assimilate the same to the temporal government of the nations." The response is a classic one for Catholic hierarchy. Churlish dissent disrupts the community and the evangelical impulse of the faith community is to ask for and expect pastoral peace through obedience. Such obedience, as we have already seen, is conceived as a virtue and is recognized in its exercise, rather than in an abstract definition.[85] Virtue surpasses mere rational analysis and advances to a stage of response that is both reasonable and affectively attuned to communal needs.

The faithful at large, as John England understood it, were not the governors of the Church. A chief ruler, Peter, and his successors were appointed to *maintain unity* within the body of bishops. The office of the chief ruler Peter, was also to confirm and feed the whole flock. It possessed both a primacy of honor and universal jurisdiction. This did not mean, however, that "we are required. . .by faith to believe that the pope is infallible." The constitution underlined the fact that although the pope had universal jurisdiction he, nonetheless, had no authority whatsoever "to interfere with the allegiance that we owe to our state; nor . . . . in the concerns of civil policy."

As regards the question of infallibility, the majority of bishops, together with their head, formed an infallible ecclesiastical tribunal in questions of doctrine. In addition, the General Council had the authority "to regulate and to ordain" the general discipline of the church. Bishops individually, on the other hand, were the ordinary governors and legislators of the diocese. In the absence of the bishop, a vicar could be appointed by the bishop to stand in his stead. Upon the vacancy of the see, the vicar, properly appointed, filled the role of governor. The conciliar or synodal thrust in England's thinking, evident in this section of the constitution, was a frequent theme in his writing.[86] We adverted to the tension in England's thought about the universal jurisdiction of Rome and the local autonomy of the diocesan bishop. Clearly the difficulty is resolved in principle, if not pragmatically, in the notion of the collegiality of the episcopacy in communion with their primate, the bishop of Rome. Neither head nor body can act alone, even as *ex sese non-refomanda* indicates that the head's (pope's) infallible decisions are not subject to the review of any other—that is, appeal to another body. Such theological efforts at clarification have emerged, obviously, since Vatican I and must always be properly located in the context of the decree *Pastor Aeternus*.[87] Yet, many have continued to point out the pragmatic and concrete difficulties in the application of this principle. John England's pragmatic position is premised upon the theoretical principle as its measure and norm, but constructed on contextual realities.

Priests were in "subordination" to the bishop. This made them, in effect, deputies of the bishop. The other orders, deacon, subdeacon and minor clerks were likewise called to share, by delegation, in the ministry of the bishop. The first section closed with the reiteration of the cautious principle seen elsewhere in the constitution: "We, therefore, disclaim any right or power, under any pretext, in the laity to subject the ministry of the church to their control." The memory of the Church is long and the vestiges of Lay Investiture's lessons were not to be forgotten. Bishop England wrote elsewhere, "The altar is for sacrifice, the priest is to offer it; the pulpit is for instruction, the priest is to occupy it; the sacraments are, by divine commission, the means of grace, the priest is to administer them."[88] To protect the mission from the specter of Lay Investiture, the control of the laity over the gospel was to be avoided at all costs. To any critic of John England's inculturation of republican values or "Americanist" propensity, this must give some pause. It is difficult to see here anything that approaches an uncritical accommodation to "Americanism," if one associates with such an idea any adherence to either autonomous individualism or rationalism. England, I suggest, reflects quite appropriately the type of leadership that was later tainted with exactly such appropriation.

Section Two: Districts and Lay Officers
Section two dealt with the districts and lay officers. Districts themselves, whether parochial or supra-parochial, were formed, established or disestablished at the initiative of the bishop. Each district was to have a governing vestry. This vestry was to consist of the clergyman or clergymen as well as lay members elected by the membership. This was a notable feature given the controversy surrounding trusteeism.

Section Three: Jurisdiction
The jurisdiction of the vestry was developed in the third section. As a first principle, it was stated that the bishop, and only the bishop, had the authority to appoint clergymen to ecclesiastical offices. The same held true for the right of examining, judging or dismissing a clergyman in the performance of his office. Nevertheless the lay members of the district had a right to appeal to the bishop as regards their clergy; however, the clergyman remained in office pending the decision. Such a clergyman, were he suspended by the bishop, remained suspended pending any appeal of the bishop's decision. Other matters of jurisdiction as regards the vestry were treated in the following section.

Title Three: Property

Title three handled the major area of the vestry's authority, property. The subject was treated in four sections: i) church funds and the duty to contribute to the church, 2) to raise and manage funds, 3) funds for the support of the clergy and 4) obtaining and managing property. An introductory paragraph discussed the temporalities that were a dimension of ecclesiastical jurisdiction, the rationale for the church having funds in the first place and the necessity of owning property.

An insight into England's conception of ordained ministry is found in this section. The clergyman because of his sacred office was "precluded from following after the pursuit of worldly gain." His time was to be spent in prayer, reflection, reading and "mental anxiety" arising from opposition of weak brethren. Therefore he was worthy of respectable support. But it did not end there. "Eighteen centuries experience" of the clergy not having families of their own, the constitution stated, had taught the church that much of the clergy's financial resources were converted to the well being of the members and of the institution.

Section One: Church Funds and Contributions
Section one then briefly underscored the obligation that existed to support the church. Additionally, it was observed that a single fund, from which all church expenses were met, was confusing and inadequate. Henceforth, separate funds for each district, and others for specified purposes were to be established. A clear sense of accountability to the lay members finds testimony here.

Section Two: Raising and Managing Funds
Section two assigned to the vestry the right to determine the mode of raising funds, subject to episcopal approval. They were not, however, empowered to levy a tax upon those attending church services. This was aimed particularly at the pew system that Bishop England saw as elitist and discriminatory to both the poor and visitors. His opposition to the pew system was adamant and bitter. In his journal for March 24, 1822, he gave ten reasons for his regulation forbidding the use of the system, excepting St. Mary's Church, Charleston, and in the Augusta parish where the system was already in use. "[A]nd I have determined to bring those churches as soon as possible to conform [also] to my plan."[89] He also believed the system gave an excuse to people not to attend church, led to the exclusion of children, was not equitable in the financial burden that it imposed on members and led to trustee abuses. The constitution also forbade the vestry to fix a price for internment in a Catholic

cemetery. In the matter of legal incorporation of Church property, the allocation of funds would be for the purpose and in the proportions specified in the articles of incorporation of Church property. The holder of title was the vestry. The title would be held in trust for the incorporated district, whether parochial or supra-parochial, i.e., a district or region such as in the instance of the three districts or states that comprised the diocese. The alienation of property was subject to the approval of the bishop, as was the building of new structures. The vestry, finally, was given budgetary discretion over liquid funds in their respective districts. Its authority was explicitly restricted, however, in the areas of taxation, alienation of property or the alteration of its integrity.

Section Three: Support of the Clergy

The financial support of the clergy was treated again in section three. Because of the Church's history of lay trustees' attempts to use the salaries of the clergy as leverage to pressure them to do as they wished, this section specifically prohibited the right of trustees to withhold a clergyman's salary. Furthermore, such clerical salaries in the district budgets could be expended only upon a clergyman appointed by the bishop. This was included in the constitution as a remedy for trusteeism, no doubt, and was intended to prevent trustees of a parish hiring a priest of their own choosing quite aside from episcopal appointment. Obviously this and the pressure that might accompany payment of salaries could both be great. The constitution removed both possibilities. The pastor's freedom to challenge the congregation with the Gospel was, above all else, to be protected. We will see in what follows the counter-balance the constitution offered the laity to hold the clergy accountable. The plan was not perfect, but it is worth noting here that this complex issue, accountability and the clergy, has been addressed often through the centuries. The community of faith has relied traditionally and theologically on the Pauline stricture that the fellowship ought not seek redress in the civil courts but from within the faith community (I Cor. 6:1). The Church's history is quite consistent in demonstration of its effort to be self-regulatory, not for craven reasons, for sure. The Church's fear of secular interests' domination of its mission is well attested in history. Narrative or story ethics in the school of virtue ethics may provide fruitful insight to resolve this pragmatic dilemma. Bishop England's solution, while not perfect, attempted to place authority in tension with the distribution of oversight as we will see in the next section. The effort focused on problem solving of concrete applications rather than theoretical reasoning.

Section Four: Regulation of Church Property

The regulation of church property was the subject of the final section of the third title. In this section, the general fund of the diocese was established. Its nine purposes were also enumerated. These included the building and maintaining of a Cathedral Church, the education of the clergy and provision made for the missioners in the diocese. Only after these had been attended to were a number of other needs to be addressed by the fund: aid to poor congregations, religious orders of women, Catholic schools, widows, orphans and others which the principles of charity would dictate. This fund was to be maintained by a quarterly tax of fifty cents, an interesting departure from canonical tradition that the Church did not have the power of taxation.

The board of general trustees, charged with the administration of this fund, was to consist of the bishop (president, *ex officio*), the vicar general (vice-president, *ex officio*), five clergymen elected annually by their peers and twelve lay persons also chosen annually by the convention's house of delegates. A quorum consisted of two clergymen and three laypersons. Note should be taken of the lay majority both on the board and of the quorum required. The treasurer of the general fund was elected by vote of the annual convention. The trustees were appointed local collectors of the diocesan tax on which this fund depended. An elaborate system of accountability for these funds was developed. The trustees could expend money only in conformity with the instructions of the convention. Small, unforeseen expenditures could be approved by the board of trustees with the concurrence of the bishop, the vicar general, two clergymen and four lay members of the board. Clearly clerical and episcopal authority was not without financial accountability.

Title Four: Membership

Membership in the church corporation (established by the constitution) was the topic of the fourth title. It was dealt with in two sections: 1) qualifications and 2) lost and regained membership. Peculiarities of the secular law at the time necessitated the introductory paragraph that stated membership in the incorporated, legal association *excluded* women and children, although this certainly was not true of membership in the

Church. Bishop England was explicit and noted, of course, the tension between the legal and theological understanding of Church membership. It is best to quote from this section of the constitution, "The Church, as a *spiritual* body, [England surely means here the Church other than it is required by the laws of the State of South Carolina] consists of men, women and children: the two latter portions of which, though in full spiritual communion, are incapable of being united in this association." The theological point is as old as the Matthean Gospel where we can observe that the Gospel refers to the faith community as *qahal* or in Greek, *ecclesia*. In Hebrew, *qahal*, designated the gathering of Yahweh's covenanted, including women and children. The *synagogue*, and secular law even until recently, followed a different cultural tradition that excluded and restricted "membership" by gender and age.

Section One: Qualifications

Qualifications for membership were outlined in the first section. One had to be a resident male at least twenty-one years of age, baptized and free of ecclesiastical censures, and ascribed to the constitution of the diocese. Only members could vote for and hold offices.

Section Two: Lost and Regained Membership

The second consideration was the loss and regaining of membership. Aside from voluntary resignation, membership was lost only for these reasons: 1) defection from Catholic doctrine; 2) encouraging unauthorized clergymen; 3) obstructing a clergyman in the performance of his duty; 4) incurring church censure; or 5) non-payment of contributions in a twelve-month period. Loss of membership was premised on the "notorious and proved" facts of a situation and demanded a ruling by the bishop. Membership was regained also by the action of the bishop. Appeal to the vestry was open to a person deprived of membership.

Title Five: District Churches

The caption placed upon the fifth title was district churches and it consisted of three sections: 1) their regulation and creation; 2) their authority, obligations and procedures; and 3) the duties and powers of their officers. The district church, of course, referenced the local parishes established in the diocese. What must be noted here was the eagerness of the bishop to establish parishes at some distance from the see city, unlike his episcopal peers. He, of course, had little choice in some ways because of the vast territory of the diocese. He did not, however, cluster the parishes in and around Savannah, Charleston and Wilmington but spread them in a genuine effort to reach the people who were scattered across three states.

Section One: Regulation and Creation

The introduction to this section included the method to establish and organize a new parish or other district. The initiative in this matter was entirely in the hands of the bishop. Upon his decision to establish a district, however, he was to call a public meeting at which the prospective members would determine the local organization, the election of members to a vestry and determine by majority vote other matters delegated to them. The vestry, once elected, had the authority to determine local by-laws subject to the approval of the local membership and the bishop or his vicar.

Section Two: Authority, Obligations and Procedures

Section two designated the principal clergyman as president of the vestry, whether local or supra-parochial. A quorum was constituted by the presence of one clergyman and three laypersons, unless there was no resident clergyman, in which case subsequent approval of the vestry's actions by the responsible clergyman sufficed. The clergyman's decision could be appealed to the bishop by the vestry. The clergyman, furthermore, did not have full veto power over the actions of a vestry. He did not have, for example, a "negative power" over the vestry's decisions regarding work contracts or agreements nor over elections and appointments. These could be affected independently of him.

In a word of advice to the vestries, postponement of delicate and divisive issues was pointedly recommended: "It would be better that an adjournment should take place, to afford time for calmness and reflection, than that a hasty decision should be made and jealousy and ill-will be excited." This section also handled the procedures for presiding over the meeting of a vestry. The responsibilities in such a meeting included 1) a provision for the support of the assigned clergy; 2) maintenance of the physical property of the church; 3) maintenance of a cemetery; 4) administration of the local church corporation; 5) election of the organist, the clerk, the sexton and other officers or servants of the church, as well as the local collector for the general fund. While the bishop or clergyman could suspend the organist, the clerk or the sexton, only the vestry could remove a church warden, the treasurer, the secretary and the collector for the general fund.[90]

The vestry was to be accountable also. Therefore it had to report at the beginning of each year, both to the congregation and the bishop. Either the bishop or the congregation could demand an accounting at other times as well. Should the vestry be unhappy with the clergyman, they too had the right, upon the request of two members and notification by the secretary, to assemble, without the clergyman's presence, and discuss the nature of their dissatisfaction. An appeal in writing could then be made to the bishop. Should the bishop's decision not meet their expectations, further appeal could be made to higher ecclesiastical authorities.

Section Three: Duties and Powers of the Officers
The title concluded with an enumeration of the responsibilities of the treasurer, secretary and warden.

Title Six: The Convention

The sixth title concerned the annual convention that was as creative as any aspect of England's method to govern his diocese. There were four sections: 1) membership and assembling; 2) procedure; 3) powers; and 4) recess. This fourth and last section will not be handled elsewhere in this treatment of the constitution since it is self-explanatory and not necessary to our purpose here.

Section One: Membership and Assembling
The convention consisted of three parts: 1) the bishop; 2) the clergy and 3) the lay delegates. The bishop or his vicar convened the meeting by public advertisement, at least two months prior to the assembly. Lay delegates were to come as representatives of the districts. The term "district" here, in fact, refers to parishes. (The term was used in the constitution equivocally in reference both to parishes and the larger state districts into which the diocese was originally divided. The diocese of Charleston during Bishop England's tenure included, in their entirety, the States of North and South Carolina and the State of Georgia.) The districts (parishes) in accordance with their numerical size, received a

designated number of delegates. The determination of the number of delegates allocated each district was the responsibility of the house of lay delegates. It was also charged with the right to judge the qualifications of its own members.

Section Two: Procedure
Section two established the two houses of the convention: the house of lay delegates and the house of clergy. The norms for the presiding officer of each were also determined. The two houses were to meet separately, coming together only after their separate deliberations. In joint session they offered final approval to any resolutions requiring such.

Section Three: Powers
Certain powers or authority were explicitly denied the two houses. The powers or competency were denied in 1) doctrine; 2) discipline; 3) sacraments; 4) ceremonies of the church; 5) spiritual jurisdiction; 6) ecclesiastical appointments; 7) ordinations; and 8) the superintendence of the clergy. Each of these had been among the abuses John England associated with the trustee question. Each of these areas, of course, were regulated by the larger Catholic tradition and serve to demonstrate precisely the manner in which Bishop England sought to establish some degree of coherence between hierarchical and democratic traditions.

In the framework of Church structure, the convention was "a body of sage, prudent, religious counselors to aid the proper ecclesiastical governor." Yet, it also had the following authority: 1) to dispose of the general fund's resources, 2) to receive an accounting from those charged with the responsibilities of the previous convention and 3) to appoint certain lay officers. Quite obviously this was a mixed type of competency. The reception of an accounting and the oversight of lay appointments, however, did not greatly expand the laity's voice in the affairs of the diocese. Access to certain information and housekeeping chores were delegated to the convention, but real discretionary authority existed only in the case of the general fund. Yet, as will be seen, if any part of the constitution failed to develop, it was the general fund. Nonetheless, an important open-endedness existed to the advisory nature of the convention. The constitution read "In those cases where the convention has no authority to act, should either house feel itself called upon by any peculiar circumstances to submit advice, or present a request to the bishop . . ." he would receive it. In any case, all actions of the convention were effective only upon the approval of the bishop. The final section delegated to the general trustees in the interim between conventions, the power to dismiss and replace any officer whom the convention was capable of appointing. The bishop used this article on the power of the general trustees to change the constitution without resorting to any formal process. The specific instance was England's redefinition of "faith" in response to Bishop David's criticism.[91]

Title Seven: Amendment of the Constitution

Sections One and Two: Parts That May Not Be Altered and the Bishop's Prerogatives

The seventh and final title of the constitution dealt with the amendment process. Here the theological foundations of the bishop's thought emerge again. Those parts of the constitution that deal with matters of doctrine, divine institution or the general discipline of the Church could not be altered. The bishop alone was responsible for the matters that pertained to local ecclesiastical discipline.

Section Three: Amendment by the Convention

What remained therefore for the convention was the authority to amend those matters which concerned finances, property, appointment of lay trustees and lay officers and all matters not of divine institution, doctrine, general or local ecclesiastical discipline.

The process of amendment was thus: 1) A copy of the amendment was given the bishop who was to determine whether it lay in the convention's competency. 2) It was then submitted to both houses where majority approval was required in each. 3) It was on their approval then sent to the bishop for his approval. 4) Finally, it was sent to the several vestries of the diocese (the other district conventions, parishes etc.) for their approval. 5) Upon approval of two thirds (2/3) of the diocesan vestries, the bishop would present it to the convention, which upon approval of both houses for a second time, it became effective. Should the bishop deny the competency of the convention regarding a particular amendment proposed, appeal could be made to Rome. Interestingly, if Rome should overturn a decision of the bishop, the bishop, as the third part of the convention, still maintained the power to assent or dissent within the amendment process. This maintained, in effect, the veto right of the bishop over all actions of the convention.

An Evaluation

Wedding of Theological and Political Perspectives

In the retrospect of well over a century and a half, the constitution appears to be theologically quite in tune with its times. The notions of membership of the Church, ministry, office, authority, sacraments and mediation in the constitution were well in line with what is found in the theological manuals of the era. In this sense a close theological examination yields far less from John England's store of creativity than does the overview. More than its specific content or parts, however, it was the idea of a constitution and what is so often implicit and evocative in it, and his leadership style that are the key contributions. The impact of Bishop England's administration as a bishop does not rest solely in the individual theological and political insights he brought to the government of the diocese, but in his practical syntheses in the development of programs for action. While the theology that he learned in the seminary, no doubt, provided the ground into which he planted additional ideas, it was his constant activity in the public arena, whether as an apologist for Catholicism or as a political activist that spurred his creativity. It was in such arenas that the issues arose that set or helped set his ecclesiological priorities. His leadership called forth new possibilities that were exemplified in his fusion of political and theological perspectives. The question posed has often been whether the bishop's practical theology accommodated too greatly the agenda of a liberal, rational individualism. I believe what we have observed in the bishop's writings and the constitution itself speaks loudly that he was far from an uncritical accomodationist.

The battle for Irish emancipation clearly made, in England's mind, the separation of powers an urgent and practical matter. The mix of ecclesiastical and civil authority never appealed to him because of his experience in Ireland, and the socio-politico ferment of the Jacksonian era in the United States confirmed it. This latter movement, as did the Lockean philosophy of the social compact, made republicanism a significant, practical influence that shaped his apologetics, his determination that public policy not be based on faith alone and, therefore, his governance as a bishop. His Irish background grounded him in a communal perspective on the nature of Church and life that stood in contrast to the emergent (Enlightenment, liberal) individualism of the American Republic reflected in the Hamiltonian tradition. He also carried with him an experience of a state (the United Kingdom) that marginalized and suppressed Catholicism in such a way that he could never espouse the unity or uniformity he associated with it. He understood the pragmatic requirements of the separation of Church-State authority since ultimately the temptation would be the certainty of religious claims on the part of partisans to possibly and fatally trump minority views. For John England minority rights reflected the age-old Catholic concern for the preservation of the concepts of human free will and conscience. While his theology rested firmly upon a standard articulation of revelation, at the time, as propositional, he never wavered in his understanding that its certainty rested in faith, not reason alone. His notion of revelation evokes an affective personalist and relational tone quite consistent with much later theological developments. He was an Irish populist who, indeed, saw the ground of authority to rest in the people and *their* social contract and the civic obligations (to one another) from which government arose. But he articulated that social contract as received from God as a consequence of the social nature endowed upon them by the Creator. It was not the result of reasoned bargaining among them. At the same time, he articulated his experiences and those of the Catholic tradition in such a creative manner that they could easily be recognized as compatible with the best of the American spirit. He moved issues forward as he traveled the Eastern Seaboard lecturing audiences as varied as Catholic congregations and governmental bodies. If he did not speak to some inherent tensions in the doctrine of the separation of Church and State, it was because those were not pressing concerns at the time.

Some, on the other hand, might prefer to stress his creativity in the context of missiological terms—that is, the adaptation of ecclesial leadership and polity to the socio-political values of the people among whom one works. DeTocqueville, for example, felt that "America is the most democratic country in the world, and it is at the same time the country in which the Roman Catholic Church makes the most progress. . . . Does it follow that Catholicism leads to the democratic spirit? No. But the Catholics there are poor and almost all come from a country where the aristocracy is Protestant."[92] England's talent was his missiological vision. He addressed real people in their circumstances to his advantage. He did so especially in his effective tapping into their vision and hopes. Radical critics may pessimistically decry the efforts of those who actually made a difference in the effort to create a better world and characterize them as no more than "liberals" who accommodated a secular agenda and vacated the religious one, but such criticisms have been accompanied too often by ecclesial approaches that parallel sectarian threads of thought found in Puritanism, Jansenism and Catharism. Sectarian rivalry ensues and the theological tension inherent in the *parousia's* "already, not yet" character is abandoned to sureties properly claimed by God alone. The indefectible faith community is situated in history and incarnate in humanity. To revert to sectarian visions (not necessarily romantic) is a refusal to live *in the world*. John England avoided such a pitfall. The efforts he undertook, in the end, afford an extraordinary insight into a pattern for the inculturation of Catholicism into the democratic-republican tradition of the contemporary world. He did so, as DeTocqueville generally noted of American Christianity, by a shrewd insertion of his message into the world of the hearers. [93]

The Success of the Constitution

If tensions existed as a result of the constitutional structure, or in spite of it, in the diocese, no references were made to them as practical problems by the bishop himself. We have already seen his own appraisal that peace and harmony were the fruits of the constitution. Even his brother bishops did not criticize it on the grounds that it had failed to alleviate, let alone exacerbate, tensions within the diocese. Yet, they were very critical that it had given too much authority to the laity. This criticism, on reading the constitution itself, seems harsh, or perhaps better, incorrect. However, if it is permissible to read between the lines of hierarchical antagonism, an insight presents itself. It was also mentioned in this letter from Kenrick to Paul Cullen that John England would be appointed to New York or Philadelphia, if he left behind the constitution, which Kenrick noted England apparently would not do—"but now that hope vanishes." Kenrick's words regarding the constitution in the *Quarterly Review* were significant. "But we hold it a dangerous experiment to engraft popular institutions on those of the Church, and place the laity in relation to the clergy, which, if it gave them no real power, must prove dissatisfactory."[94] The constitution clearly defined the role, for example, of the convention in the most acceptable terms possible. "The Convention is not to be considered as a portion of the ecclesiastical government of the Church; but the two houses are to be considered rather as a body of sage, prudent, and religious counselors to aid the proper ecclesiastical governor." The phrasing was careful and quite orthodox. It was certainly calculated not to erode legitimate episcopal power or its prerogatives in any way. Nonetheless, in the very same title there was an enumeration of powers both delegated and withheld from the convention. In light of the bitter criticisms leveled at the constitution, it seems quite proper to conclude that the conventions must have successfully exercised the authority delegated to them in such a way that it was apparent they were a vital factor in the *de facto* (if not *de jure*) government of the diocese.

The question about the convention and the degree to which it was consultative or determinative can be clarified only in the practice. The bishops' criticisms therefore seem to be one argument in favor of the view that real leverage was experienced and wielded by the convention. Otherwise England could have easily explained himself to the hierarchy by simply referring to the text of the constitution. This was never his approach, however. He understood a "moral" bond had developed with the people of the diocese that some of his episcopal colleagues found unsettling. The peace and harmony that Bishop England and his critics saw as the fruit of the constitution *vis-a-vis* the trustee question can argue also that the trustees may have felt they had been granted some measure of voice and discretion. A share in the leadership of their church (churches) had been one of their principal aims, and nowhere did England appear to deny access to them on this score. His predisposition to republicanism, in fact, encouraged distinctions in roles and responsibilities and so a consequent widening in the distribution of authority, both real and moral. Yet, in the republican spirit that arose particularly from Montesquieu's framing of the idea, civic virtue and responsibility were the handmaids to authority and personal rights.

The theological tradition of Catholicism that England shared focused all Church authority in the divine commission given the apostles and apostolic succession. The socio-political influences that bore upon the bishop of Charleston from his ordination in 1808 onward were thrust in a quite different direction. Locke and more surely Montesquieu were strong influences upon the politico-philosophical scene during England's lifetime. Notions of freedom, toleration, moderation, constitutional government with checks and balances were formative in the bishop's practical activity as they were in the political societies in which he found himself in both Ireland and the United States. On the question of the separation of Church and State, Locke and Montesquieu took quite different stands however. Locke favored a stricter separation, whereas Montesquieu's notions were more conservative and leaned more strongly toward authority and aristocracy embracing the notion that Christian values and virtue must underscore republican values if good political order was to be maintained. Bishop England could have enthusiastically supported, as a Jacksonian Democrat, such civic republicanism as opposed to more individualist views associated with John Locke, at least on a popular and broader level.[95] The constitution reflected a practical and pastoral, not an academic, theology. The tensions inherent in the principles behind hierarchal and republican organizational structures and their conflictual histories and interests remained theoretically unexplored. If ever a claim may be made for a Gramscian organic leader, it may be John England. His creative pastoral and practical theology testifies to the aphorism that *theology follows practice*. This was a point that would not have been without support in Rome.[96] It must be suspected, this was the very dynamic nature in the relationship between Bishop England and the lay boards he established for the diocese in its constitution. His colleagues in the hierarchy likewise observed this fact quite nervously. Practice and experience shed new and disquieting light on received wisdom.

Notes

1. *Works*, IV, 191-226, esp. 223, see also *Works*, I, 423.

2. John T. McNeill, "The Relevance of Conciliarism," *Who Decides for the Church?*, James Coriden, ed. (Hartford, Cannon Law Society of America, 1971) 83.

3. *Works*, III, 241. Much of the information I used was found in Carey, *England*, 314, n. 103.

4. *Mirari Vos*, Gregory XVI, 1832, *Acta Sanctae Sedis*, 4(1875): Romae, S.C. *De Propaganda Fide,* 341ff. The encyclical essentially condemns "modernism" and was directed against Lamennais and a consequent letter to him from the dean of the College of Cardinals attempted to soften the blow caused by the language of the encyclical that had been written in reaction to events following the restoration of the Bourbon kings in France. The principle

objections were to the religious indifferentism and the perceived rejection of divine revelation, but both of these were viewed in the context of Lamennais's confrontation with the French bishops. Bokenkotter, 267-70. *Singulari Nos* was published in 1834 and offers a final condemnation of Lamennais.

5. *Mirari Vos*, 344. *"Praeclara haec immobilis subjectionis in Principes exempla....condemnant, qui projecta effrenataque procacis libertatis cupididate aestuantes, toti in eo sunt, ut jura quaeque principatuum labefactent atque convellant, servitutem sub libertatis specie populis illaturi."*

6. *Singulari Nos*, 6. See Bokenkotter, 267 for further comment on this.

7. *Mirari Vos, "Neque laetiora et religioni et Principatui ominari possemus ex eorum votis, qui ecclesiam a regno separari...abrumpi discupiunt."* See also commentators on principles of interpretation in the Church's Canon Law, Kenan Osborne, *Sacraments in the Post Modern World* (Mahwah: Paulist Press, 1999).

8. J.C. Murray "The Problem of State Religion," *Theological Studies*, 12(1951): 163-164, n. 10.

9. Much of this extended section addresses the issues as found in the following: Henri DeLubac. *The Mystery of the Supernatural*, "Introduction" by David Schindler (NY: Crossroad, 1998) and Karl Rahner, *Foundation of Christian Faith* (NY: Seabury, 1978) 126ff. See in particular Schindler's introduction to DeLubac, pp. xxii ff. DeLubac and Rahner remind us that grace exists in the world and the world never exists apart from grace. David Schindler, *Heart of the World, Center of the Church: Communio Ecclesiology* (Grand Rapids: Eerdmans, 1996) and Michael Baxter, "Catholicism and Liberalism: Kudos and Questions for *Communio Ecclesiology,*" *Review of Politics*, 60 (1998) 4, 743-764, take a rather different view regarding the implications. Each insists that because the human being's end or purpose is ultimately supernatural public language must speak to humankind's supernatural goal, i.e., a graced life that by definition secularism and pluralist assumptions preclude.

10. "Contemporary Orientations of Catholic Thought on Church and State in the Light of History," *Theological Studies,* 10(1949): 186.

11 Baxter, "Catholicism," 763.

12. Baxter, "Catholicism," 743-764.

13. Baxter, "Catholicism," 764.

14. Bryan Stone, *Evangelism after Christendom* (Grand Rapids, MI: Brazos, 2007) 111ff. and 180ff. Stone seems to believe the Christian narrative is compromised in every way if it is accommodated to the narrative of the other.

15. Alasdair MacIntyre. *Whose Justice? Whose Rationality?* (Notre Dame, University of Notre Dame,1988).

16. Kearns, 55 and John Witte, Jr. *God's Joust, God's Justice* (Grand Rapids: Eerdmans, 2006), 150-168 on law and covenants to provide checks and balances and 263-294 on the three uses of law.

17. Kearns, 55-56; Eugene Willging and Herta Hatzfield. *Catholic Serials of the Nineteenth Century in the United States of America,* part II. (Wash., DC: CUA Press, 1968), 220; *Works* III, 109.

18. Kenneth Scott Latourette, *The Nineteenth Century in Europe: Background and the Roman Catholic Phase* (San Francisco: HarperCollins, 1975). This Protestant scholar gives an excellent summary of Catholic developments at Rome, esp., 238-260.

19. C. S. Peirce, "The Categories Defended." in *The Essential Peirce,* vol. 2 (Indianapolis: University of Indiana, 1998) 160-178. Peirce's pragmaticism is far more developed than expressed in his famous Pragmatic Principle made popular by William James; Kenneally, III, no. 1909.

20. *Works,* IV, 341.

21. Archbishop Marechal, for example, wrote to Rome in December, 1824:*"Rumor vagatur Ill(um) D.D England Episcopum Caro(lo) poleos condidisse constitutionem democraticam, juxta quam intendit ecclesias suae dioceseos regere; atque eam misisse ac mitantut, nescio. Atamen non possum satis orare sanctissimos et eminentissimos patres ut hanc constitutionem democraticam (non) approbent, nisi lenti admodum et post valde maturum examen. Exhibitur namque quasi multum opposita bono et prosperitati ecclesiae."* Thomas Hughes, I, I, *Documents,* 525.

22. *Works,* V, 91ff. This is the 1839 edition of the constitution. References throughout are to this edition and collection.

23. Guilday, Life, I, 360, note 5., *Works,* IV, 321.

24. *Works,* II, 358; V, 93.

25. "Journal," *Records,* 6(1895): 223; *Works,* V, 93: *Records,* 8 (1897): 58-459. *Records,* 6(1895): 223-224.

26. *Works,* V, 421, *Records,* 8(1897); 458-459, and *Works,* V (1895) 425-426, also Carey, *England,* 333f.

27. See Guilday, *Life,* I, 361.

28. Cited by Frederick Copleston, *A History of Philosophy,* vol. 7, part 1 (N.Y., Image, 1965), 257.

29. See within this chapter, "The Success of the Constitution."

30. This citation as well as all further citations from the constitution refer to texts within the noted title, sections and articles of the constitution, so page citations will not therefore be used. A digested appendix is included for easy reference to the full text of each title, section and article.

31. Elwyn Smith, "The Fundamental Church-State Tradition of the Catholic Church in the United States," *Church History,* 38(1969): 491.

32. Stanley Hauerwas and Charles Pinches, "Is Obedience a Virtue?" in *Christian Among the Virtues* (Notre Dame: 1997), 129-148.

33. A condensed preface to the constitution is in the appendix to this book.

34. See above our discussion of the trustee problem and also Carey, *People, passim.* We will return to this again at the beginning of chapter 5.

35. Guilday, *Life*, II, "Antecedents to the Council."
36. *Works*, IV, 230.
37. *Works*, IV, 231.
38. *Works*, IV, 185 and IV, 181.
39. *Works*, I, 432.
40. *Works*, IV, 206.
41. *Works*, III, 240-241.
42. Cf. Kauffman, Christopher. *Tradition and Transformation in Catholic Culture: The History of the Priests of St. Sulpice, 1791 to the Present* (NY: MacMillan, 1988).
43. Works, I, 74; II, 31.
44. *Works*, II, 432; IV, 183
45. *Works*, I, 74; II, 31. The revelation in Scripture is infallible as is the witness to that revelation by the Church, ibid., 78; I, 94, 134. T.M. Schoof, *A Survey of Catholic Theology: 1800-1970.* (Paramus: Paulist-Newman, 1970), esp., 160ff. is especially helpful in understanding the "certainty" of revelation and its transmission in church teaching in the context of the nineteenth century. Contemporary hermeneutical theory would suggest very different language in the expression of these ideas.
46. C.S. Peirce. *Collected Papers*, Charles Hartshorne and Paul Weiss, eds. (Cambridge: Belnap, Harvard University Press, 1960) 6 vols. 6.439.
47. Francis Sullivan, *Salvation Outside the Church: Tracing the History of the Catholic Response* (Mahwah, NJ: Paulist, 1992), 88-99.
48. *De fide theologica,* Disp. 12, sect.4, n. 11; ed. Vives, Paris, 1858, vol. 12, 353-354 as cited in Francis Sullivan, *Salvation Outside the Church,* (Mahwah, NJ: Paulist, 1992), 92.
49. Juan DeLugo. *De virtute fidei divinae*, disp. 12, n. 104, and 300; as cited in Sullivan, *Salvation*, 96. Robert Bellarmine had articulated a similar position, cf. Sullivan, 88-89.
50. *Works*, I, 58.
51. *Works*, 66; see also 84.
52. *Works*, 58.
53. *Works*, I, 242. As regards this Catholic theological certainty see McCool, ch. 3 and Schoof, 160-165.
54. *Works*, I, 84.
55. *Works*, IV, 290.
56. *Works*, IV, 183. There is in this address a fuller development of England's teaching, see also *Works*, I, 58, 70. The citation in the text is directly from the constitution. Also interesting in this regard are *Works*, II, 291 and II, 239.
57. McCool, esp., 62-63, 138ff. and 179-180 and ch. 3.
58. England used the usual texts in support of his position: Mt. 16:13-18; 28:18-20; Jn. 14:26; 15: 26-27; 16:13; 17:17-19; and Acts 1: 16-22.

59. *Works*, I, 74. Cf. also Gaillardetz, *Teaching*, 83ff.
60. Cited in *Works*, I, 134.
61. *Works*, I, 135.
62. *Works*, I, 249.
63. John Calvin, *Institutes*, IV, 1, 3-7.
64. Harry J. McSorley has put this question well: "[What one] needs to remember is that papal absolutism and papal infallibility are not the same." *The Infallibility Debate*, John J. Kirvan, ed., (N.Y. Paulist Press, 1971), 93.
65. *Works*, I, 147. The point is not so much miracles, if one means a change in the law of nature, as much as the evidential basis for the *communication* of the plausibility for our faith.
66. See for example, "Reason and Belief in God," in Alvin Plantinga and Nicholas Wolterstorff, eds. *Faith and Rationality* (Notre Dame: University of Notre Dame, 1983) on the one hand and Jurgen Habermas and C.S. Peirce, 6.451 and 6.452-485 on the other. Extensive bibliographic material is available for both. Cf. also Thomas McCarthy, *The Critical Theory of Jurgen Habermas* (Cambridge: MIT Press, 1982), esp., chapter 4.
67. *Works*, I, 58.
68. George Lindbeck, *The Nature of Doctrine*, Minneapolis: Fortress, 1984 but esp., Ray L. Hart, *Unfinished Man and the Imagination*, (Louisville; Westminster John Knox, 1968), 171-172 and Karl Rahner, *Theological Investigations* v. 1 (Baltimore: Helicon, 1961) 171, 184, 313 etc., and Thomas Aquinas, *ST,II, II 2,3; Ia,115,2*.
69. *Works*, I, 169.
70. *Works*, II, 31.
71. *Works*, I, 161. The two-source theory of revelation would be abandoned at Vatican II in the Constitution *Dei Verbum*.
72. *Works*, II, 34.
73. See Guilday, *Life,* II, 117-118 and Guilday, *History*, 85. Need we mention the anticipation here of lay ecclesial ministries that have been promoted in recent years as consistent with the vision of the bishop who sought to involve more and more people in the public ministry of the church?
74. *Works,* IV, 295.
75. *Works*, II, 353.
76. *Works*, I, 210.
77. *Works*, II, 355. See above notes 51 and 71.
78. This is the thesis, I believe correct, of Rousseau's *John England: Church and State.*
79. Cited by Patrick Carey, *Immigrant,* 70, who reflects a more recent critical interpretation of England's position. It exhibits less appreciation for the pragmatic nature of the position the bishop took, 93-97, locating the question in a more theological and historical understanding relative to the Lay Investiture

crisis in the eleventh century. It also offers a more theoretical articulation of the two powers, State and Church, position as a basis for their separation.

80. *Works*, II, 286.

81. Cited by O'Brien, *John England: Bishop of Charleston* (N.Y., O'Toole, 1934) 68.

82. *Works*, II, 291. In this paragraph parenthetical references are made to Heinrich Denzinger and Adolf Schonmetzer, *Enchiridion Symbolorum* (NY: Herder, 1967). The references are standard and refer to paragraph numbers.

83. *Records,* 8(1897): 455.

84. See note 27 above.

85. Consult the bibliography for a sample of writing recently on Virtue Ethics: Alasdair MacIntyre, *After Virtue* and *Whose Justice? Whose Rationality?* and "The Nature of the Virtues" in Crisp and Slote, Martha Nussbaum, *Poetic Justice* and *The Fragility of Goodness* and Stanley Hauerwas, *Community of Character* and *Christians Among the Virtues*, among so many others.

86. See England on Councils, *Works*, II, 73, 179 and 219.

87. See John T. Ford, "Infallibility," in Mary Collins, Joseph Komoncheck and Dermot Lane, eds. *The New Dictionary of Theology.* (Lanham, MD: Michael Glazier, 1988).

88. See also *The United States Catholic Miscellany* cited by O'Brien, *John England,* 68.

89. *Records*, (1895): 202-204.

90. A church warden was defined at the conclusion of the title (V). He was to implement the orders of the vestry.

91. See note 24 above.

92. *Democracy in America*, (N.Y., Mentor, 1956): 155, cited in Dan Herr, *Through Other Eyes: 1777-1965,* (Westminster, Newman, 1965): 28. There is currently a debate surrounding Thomas Jefferson's dependence upon Locke and/or Montesquieu. Much of it focuses on the apparent change in Jefferson's thought in his writings about Montesquieu after 1800, Thomas Jefferson. *Jefferson: Political Writings*, Joyce Appleby and Terence Ball, eds. (Cambridge: Cambridge University, 1999.) cf. "Introduction."

93. See the exchange between William L. Portier, "Americanism and Inculturation," and Michael Baxter, "The Unsettling of Americanism: A Response to William Portier," *Communio*, 27(2000), 139-170. Portier has much the best of the exchange, yet, the genius of the "Americanists" (as he would describe them) is discovered best in their pastoral responses in their ministry. Unfortunately the exchange places the focus upon documents as solely theological statements with little attention to hermeneutical principles derived from literary or linguistic analysis. Consequently, the exchanges appear too static and simply appear to float above pastoral ambiguities that both Rome and the bishop appreciated so well that they needed not always be stated. Portier senses this but does not apply explicit hermeneutical or literary analyses to

historical events as he might have. Baxter simply reiterates a recurrent theme, "I am no reactionary, but more radical than you," in my opposition to *laizzez faire* capitalist functionalism, but he never wrestles with nor appears to appreciate the art of pastoral complexity. The "Americanist" narrative is far richer and more complex than Baxter understands it.

94. See Kenrick, *Brownson's Quarterly,* 7(1850): 186; *Records,* 7 (1896) 293.

95. In this regard see England's own treatment, *Works,* IV, 227-232; also "Montesquieu," *Encylopedia of Philosophy,* vol. 5, 368-371.

96. For an understanding of practical theology as opposed to pastoral theology, see James Woodward and Stephen Pattison, *The Blackwell Reader in Pastoral and Practical Theology,* (Oxford: Blackwell, 2000), esp., 49-58.

Chapter Five

Dimensions and Directions in the Ecclesial Response

> It is of great importance in a republic not only to guard against the oppression of its rulers, but to guard one part of society against the injustice of the other part.
>
> Alexander Hamilton

The Convention

The constitution was developed by Bishop England to govern in an orderly and acceptable fashion his new diocese. The mechanisms by which the document was made effective were the annual conventions. They implemented the constitution and, as the activities of the government of the United States interpret the ambiguities of the national constitution, so the conventions clarified the meaning and significance of the Diocesan Constitution.

Ecclesiology: Theory and Practice

Authority and Law
Some ambiguities in the constitution grew from its intention to be a document that sought to mediate the conflicting claims of hierarchy and

lay trustees; therefore, some clarity might be found in its implementation. Heavily hierarchical presuppositions about the Church, reflective of post-Tridentine ecclesiology, for example, were spelled out in the document. John England's desire to explicitate them grew from the need to answer the challenge raised by the basic principles of trusteeism. The trustees essentially asserted that 1) the government of the church should be adapted to the national traditions in which it found itself, 2) the people, members of the church, were sovereign, 3) church competency was divided into spiritual and temporal affairs with the laity administering the latter, and 4) the lay members of the congregation held the *jus patronus* in pastoral appointments, though the clergy were free and independent in the exercise of their spiritual office.[1] The constitution in principle denied each of these in the constitution, yet in practice seemed to accede, to some degree, to each with the exception of the last, the *jus patronus*. Since this last right was stressed wholly within the congregational context, namely Irish parishioners objecting to French-born pastors, England was able to defuse it quite easily inasmuch as his clergy were almost totally Irish or American-born.

Bishop Kenrick's analysis seemed to recognize this practical or moral accord between England and the role assumed by the layperson as a result of the constitution, as Kendrick noted, "which if it gave them no real authority, must prove dissatisfactory."[2] Kenrick's remark is assuredly correct. If the constitution proved satisfactory to the lay people of the diocese, it must have given them some real authority. The notion of "real" authority for Kenrick can be best understood that he did not approve of any equivalency of authority, moral or otherwise, between clergy and laity. Authority, to Kendrick's mind, whether it be moral, delegated or sovereign was not proper to the laity in the administration of the Catholic Church.

England's theoretical notions of Church tended to concentrate upon those aspects of Church that were external and juridical, such as infallibility and doctrine, office and succession. His definition of the Church as "a society established by God himself for spiritual purposes" was a case in point.[3] He focused his attention on the first part of the definition. The Church was a divinely constituted society because of 1) the natural law, 2) the divine negative law—the Mosaic Law, 3) the positive ordinances of the Scriptures which bind us to do certain acts, and 4) the divinely established legislative, judicial and executive power together with a supreme administrator.[4] A concrete and somewhat static reality was associated, therefore, with the core of his notion of the Church. England was quite aware, however, that the Church was not solely or simply the visible, static, constituent parts mentioned. It was also "the congregation of the faithful." This congregation was an undying, perpetual and living body. The Church was not the hierarchy, nor for that matter any single part of the whole. The Church was the whole body.[5] Bishop England often used a somewhat Pauline image of "body" in reference to the Church. Carey cites a religious vows ceremony at which the bishop spoke, "The Habiting of a Nun," and quotes the bishop, "As in forming the mystic body of his church, he diversified the gifts and the functions of the several members."[6] The bishop's reference here was to the differentiation between religious orders of women. Generally, it appears to me, the term was not used in the full Pauline sense by England. He never used it to differentiate the role of the laity, for example, in the ministry of the Church or even the various ministries within the ranks of the laity. Such a position is consistent with the earlier theological understanding in Catholicism of the "lay apostolate." In this case the laity's contribution to the ministry of the Church is not performed as a consequence of their baptismal character, but as delegates of the hierarchy. When John England used the term it was most often in reference to the body as the total group—that is, "The body mentioned in the little book is the Church of Rome."[7] The term in this case has little theological application beyond being a synonym for the church as a whole unit, as can be seen consistently in his *Works*—I, 196; IV, 70, 383; II, 292; V, 422. In the last case the argument is about the juridical body and his concern is the manner by which a local church affects the entire universal Church. He stressed this, for example, at the fifth convention of South Carolina: "Upon this head [point] each church or congregation is supposed to be interested in its own particular concerns, but as in the natural, so in the mystic body, the affliction or suffering of one member affects the whole."[8] England did not abandon the notion that all authority is derived from the head. When he approaches the "body of Christ" metaphor in a Pauline manner, it is in a highly clericalized way, "The Church is not merely its head or chief, but it is the head and other pastors united."[9] The hierarchy was the living tribunal that protects and directs the faithful. So too, he understood the marks of the true church in a traditional sense. "Unity" was the oneness in doctrinal belief. "Holy" was the trait of the saintly membership that characterized the Church. It was also the sign of the holiness of both the doctrines and the miracles associated with the Church. "Catholic" referenced the numerical and geographical reality of the visible Church, rather than the catholicity of its message and mission.[10] "Apostolic" was ascribed to the Church because of the unbroken succession in the episcopacy from the apostles, rather than the origin of mission and message.

Advice and Cooperation: The Practice

Little in these particular ecclesiological aspects of Bishop England's theology was unusual for his period. Yet, he was an exceptional man. His actions were themselves an extraordinarily healthy complement to his theory. For example, he constantly urged corporate action on the American Church whether it was the bishops or the local pastors and their congregations. He wrote to Rome that one of the principal impediments in the development of the Church in the United States was "the absolute want of any sort of co-operation or of common *modus agendi* among the bishops who for the most part held themselves apart and aloof from one another."[11]

The political currents and the winds of change during the period strongly influenced John England. We saw this in his role in the Anti-Vetoist movement in Ireland as well as in his apologetics *vis-á-vis* the "No Popery" folks in both Ireland and the United States. These currents led him increasingly to positions favorable to republicanism and universal suffrage. The bishop put it this way, "Since I prefer the collected experience and reasoning of the bulk of society to the results of my own weak efforts, I believe it the suggestion of reason, and the duty of an individual, to admit that he is not as wise as is the collective body of his fellow men."[12] His adaptation to "liberal" democratic processes for discernment purposes, as we recognize in this statement, hardly warrants what some suggest constitutes an unwitting accommodation or Catholic assimilation into a cultural relativism and autonomous individualism. Bishop England linked his politico-philosophical and theological notions about discernment processes very differently than critics would suppose. This is clear in his address, "On Charity," in 1841. "Religion teaches man to love his neighbor as himself, and, consequently, to uphold himself those institutions which confer the most happiness on the whole. This then is the great conservative principle of republicanism."[13] An autonomous, rationalist individual was not the determinant in the meaning of republicanism for John England. As was the case for the early republicans, "the whole" is the determinant and concern because the whole gives expression to its experience in evidential reasoning as E. Brooks Holifield observed.[14] It was both the intellectual and the affective that came into play in evidential reasoning. The early republicans look not only for the rational good of society, but for its happiness and wholeness as a community as well. England was at pains to relate the communal dimensions implicit in both the republican and the religious spirits. In his mind their relationship was far more than simply compatible; they were intimately associated in popular sovereignty and universal suffrage. As we have seen, an array of contemporary political scientists reiterate the early republican view that republican societies offer a "freedom from." Pettit says it more adequately as "non-domination" in clear counter-distinction to libertarian non-interference. This alone provided the social protection necessary from the coercive tyranny of a majority or passing social whims. Individual rights must be protected but the motivation and rationale is conservation of social equity and accountability that eventuates in the happiness, tranquility, and good of the whole.

John England shares the American republican tradition in which John Courtney Murray was later situated. It was non-ideological and arose from the bishop's experiences first, as a member of a minority in South Carolina and secondly, as a member of a marginalized colonial majority earlier in Ireland. Civic responsibility would always trump private rights in the mind of one so marginalized by social and political structures, as was England. The bishop's republicanism was rooted in the Catholic tradition to which he frequently alluded—synodal government, but also the pragmatics of the pastoral situation. The commitments he made grew from these experiences and were directed to the people whom he often saw unjustly bent to the will of a dominant majority or colonial oligarchy. From practical and pastoral experience he was adamant. Such injustice and infringement upon individual's conscience was unacceptable. Virtue, whether republican or Catholic, demanded more. It required freedom from coercion. Furthermore, only free consciences could be morally accountable. Wisdom is elicited in the practical reasoning of the virtue-driven individual. As contemporary critics of Catholic inculturation into the American experience might recognize, the bishop's rationale was that of virtue ethics and not rationalism.[15] People at the margins, whose opportunities at success have oftentimes been forfeited *for* them may seek "the good" prior to any abstract hopes about material advantage. Their agenda can oftentimes be more innocent, because of context—pursuit of "the good" rather than material advantage may be recognized as more personally available and issue in greater sensitivity to the balance between human dignity, respect and the community's well-being.

It is this republican vision that was at work in Bishop England. It was the motivating factor when he constantly urged the archbishops of Baltimore, first Marechal and later Whitfield, to convoke a provincial council. It was the same spirit that animated the decision to delineate the authority of the annual conventions in the Diocesan Constitution. The very nature of the delegations present at the conventions indicated his commitment to the notion of representative and democratic processes. The same concern was present in his efforts to introduce wider participation of the laity at the provincial councils.[16] The bitter frustration he experienced, when he saw the consultative process short-circuited, surfaced in one of his letters to Paul Cullen, a close friend and later Cardinal of Dublin:

> This faction [the bishops under the sway of the Baltimore Sulpicians]. . .instead of sustaining itself by the force and by the provisions of the law, and thus standing upon firm ground [*vis-à-vis* the trustees] as they were repeatedly advised by the present Secretary of the Treasury, the late Attorney General, and several others of our best Catholic lawyers, prefer a miserable course of evasion and chicane. . . which keeps up the impression that the Catholic religion is hostile to our political and legal institutions.[17]

The myopia of a position arrived at by the bishops, without heeding the consultation offered, he argued, provided evidence to the Church's critics that it was substantively and procedurally out of step with its American milieu. The clarity of his argument was that consultation serves mutuality and good will. It was offered not in the service of the autonomous individual, in which case it would have undermined the very values sought.

John England's creativity is seen in his ability to integrate republicanism and constitutionalism with notions of the Church. While the call or mission received by the members of the clergy and the laity differed, John England held they were of equal dignity. As we have seen, some ambiguity existed in England's ability, however, to place the equity of these values into clear relationship. There was little of the monarchical in his mind about the nature of ecclesiastical office. No ecclesiastical offices, he argued, were hereditary and, therefore, none was beyond the pale of republicanism. All had representational rights in Church bodies. Laws, not whim, were the rule, and accountability to one another was the norm of administration.[18] Nonetheless, traditional Catholic understanding about the sacramental character of Orders constituting a difference of substance, not degree, between clergy and laity remained. Surely, later theologians will move the discussion forward regarding a fuller understanding of Orders (structure and leadership) and sacrament (liturgical encounter with God) and their relationships to accountability. His practice demonstrated, but in this case did not articulate, that the call to "Orders" was a difference in function, not dignity. His experience expressed the relational appreciation that issues from their immediacy and presses on the participants the dignity they encounter in the relationship. It sets aside and cannot return to notions of "the other" that are intellectualized or reduced to ontological categories.

Importance of the Conventions

The annual conventions were the embodiment of England's constitutionalism. He saw them in much the same light as he saw a council of bishops. They were ecclesial events. He opened them with the liturgy, during which there was a bestowal of sacramental Orders. The conventions were also ecclesial events at which the Church acted as an entity. Bishop England overlaid them with the same significance as a chapter of affairs in a religious community. The sticking issue for those who opposed his vision was not republicanism, as such, but the inability of the non-ordained to have ecclesial authority over the ordained. This remains an issue in current Church law as well. The convention was seen clearly as the meeting of the Church and he addressed them as such. England wrote in this regard, "This convention is as it were the head for consultation, and the several congregations the members."[19] Because of the importance in his mind of the ecclesial dimension of the convention, it will be necessary and helpful to examine the issues he raised in his addresses to the conventions.

There is, unfortunately, no record either of the proceedings of the first convention of South Carolina or of the address, if any, given by the bishop. We do know that the gathered delegates approved the constitution for their district. In his journal on the day of the first convention, November 24, 1823, England simply recorded the occasion and the unanimity of the approval given the document. The second convention was held in Charleston in 1824. There were eight laypersons and five priests in attendance when the bishop delivered the first of twenty-five convention addresses still extant.[20]

Issues at the Conventions

A Seminary

The pastoral urgency of a constitution and the conventions was expressed well in the address to the first Georgia convention in 1826. "If you confine your views to the individual wants and interests of separate and single congregations, you will do little in your district churches and nothing as a body . . . [it is] in your co-operation [that] you will prosper."[21] It was in light of this that the bishop's addresses are best appreciated. The fullness of the Church's ministry simply could not be undertaken from a congregational base. The most obvious instance of this was the fact that mission congregations could not provide for the continuity of pastoral leadership from their own membership, let alone address either the larger issues of Church and broader community needs.

At the thirteenth convention of South Carolina, the same theme was stressed again, as it had been almost annually. The bishop described the seminary as a "school of preparation for the missions; its object is to furnish a body of clergy qualified to break the bread of life to the hungering multitudes" through the varied ministries entrusted to the Church.[22] John England's insistent reminder at each convention of the shortage of priests and the need for a seminary gives testimony to his concern for ministry. As the bishop saw it, it was only as a body that the congregations of the diocese could hope to deal with this question.

Missionary zeal

There were other supra-parochial themes and projects recurrent in the convention addresses. One such was the evangelical or missiological concern. This was expressed in the effort to make Catholicism present to the scattered Catholics of the three overwhelming Protestant states. At the 1835 South Carolina convention the bishop observed that nine-tenths (9/10) of the losses from Catholicism were due "from the want of missionary attention." The ministry that was lacking was "visiting, confirming, consoling, encouraging, instructing and preserving the faith."[23] England himself was the model of a rural pastor as evidenced by his journal for the years 1821-1823. Scarcely had the bishop arrived in his see city when, two weeks later, he began the first of his extensive journeys through the towns of the three states which composed his diocese. In each town he sought out known Catholics (and any others who might be interested), preached in a local hall or Protestant church, administered the sacraments and departed having appointed a lay reader pending the next visit of an ordained minister.[24] What is particularly interesting in his pastoral visits to the scattered flock is that when he departed he had in place appointed leaders to provide prayer services in the absence of priests.

In writing to the Society for the Propagation of the Faith at Lyons, France, the Charleston prelate estimated in 1836 that there had been a loss of over three million Catholics in the United States since its founding in 1776. His critics object that his statistics were faulty and exaggerated, but the urgency he gave to the question, which was evident in both his addresses and activity, was indisputably valid. While his data is inflated in all likelihood, his point is to balance what is often claimed —that the American South's original settlers had few Catholics among them. This may not be as likely as has been previously believed. If it is true that with the exceptions of the French settlements in Louisiana and east along the Gulf Coast to Mobile (and a smattering of Irish in a few urban areas), the Southern quarter of the United States historically has been less than one percent Catholic. This has led to the widespread and continuously repeated assumption that the original European settlers of the Southern United States were almost uniformly Protestant. While there certainly is truth to the fact that the large portion of Southern settlers came as Protestants, a closer study of this question is warranted. It has too long been an unchallenged truism. Although accurate appraisals are not possible, it is interesting to note the composition of the Scottish settlers in Nova Scotia and Upper Canada during the same period of settlement. In Cape Breton, Nova Scotia, the Catholics among the Scottish settlers were a quite large minority, composed mostly of

Highlanders and Islanders from the west of Scotland. Yet the conventional wisdom has held that virtually no Catholics were among the Scottish settlers in the Carolinas. A casual survey of the surnames and places of origin of the settlers in these two regions (Eastern Canada and the American South) during the period following 1754, raises questions whether their religious affiliations were as starkly different as supposed. The history of St. Barra's parish at Christmas Island, Cape Breton, Nova Scotia (and this may or may not be an isolated example) makes explicit reference to a settler in 1802 who noted the flow from the Western Highlands and the Hebrides during the period went in four directions: Cape Breton, Prince Edward Island, the Ottawa Valley and North Carolina. The account laments the memories of relatives, siblings, and friends at the same port and time who had boarded ships for Wilmington and Fayetteville, North Carolina. These Scots apparently found themselves willy-nilly on boats headed to various ports in North America.[25] It is doubtful that they would or could have sorted themselves according to religious affiliation. Such heterogeneity within families, clans, and among friends would have been highly unlikely. It is quite unlikely that the Highland Clearances that began in the 1750s permitted much discretion to the émigrés headed out of Scotland. Also as we have seen in numerous instances in Appalachia, in John England's experience, and in Cape Breton, small-town and rural Scots (or anyone for that matter) related to one another more on the face-to-face level than as members of a given denomination. Scottishness, as much as Catholicity, seared the identity of frightened exiles in an unknown new world. Conventional assumptions about the Protestantism of the original European settlers of the American South, I believe, need further examination. There are also numerous stories current in the Appalachians of families with "ancient" Christian devotionals consistent with the Catholic tradition that have been handed down in religious artifacts, such as pictures of the Sacred Heart of Jesus and/or Mary. Mary Lee Daugherty, founder of the Appalachian Ministry and Educational Resource Center, shared some of these stories with me.[26] In any case, it appears likely that the new bishop was aware of and concern with evangelizing the people with an aplomb not equaled by either his predecessors or successors in the U. S. hierarchy.

The oversight of a rapidly expanding urban church in this period (and throughout the remainder of the nineteenth century) was highlighted by England at the thirteenth convention of South Carolina.

> My brothers, I consider it to be one of the mistakes which has been hitherto greatly detrimental to our missions, to imagine that a diocese was sufficiently supplied with priests when one was located in every place where a congregation existed sufficiently numerous and sufficiently able to maintain a regular church and to give a competency to its pastor. How many of those desirous to hear the Word of God are scattered widely distant from such places?[27]

Objection could be made to what appears to be England's exaggerated identification of Catholic ministry with ordained priesthood. As we have already seen, in this respect he was a man of his times, because the ordained priest was, at that time, what singularly "made the church present" in a locale. The Charleston prelate's vision as a shepherd and missioner, however, must be placed among the best. More than most bishops and priests, he was aware and concerned about the "scattered Catholics" throughout his diocese and even the nation. England often made reference in his convention addresses (at least nine times) to the scattered Catholics who desired and needed ministry. He also urged mission activity among blacks, slaves and native peoples during the Councils of Baltimore. He was also intensely interested in the development of the church in the West, making reference to the frontier on several occasions. He was driven, in a very practical way, to render present the mediating and sacramental presence of the church, and this instinctively led him to creative measures to fulfill this priority.

Education

Other ministries which absorbed his interest and which he offered to the attention of his diocese covered a broad spectrum. He urged the diocese to develop religious education programs. He promoted the establishment of schools of both a classical and non-classical nature.[28] He started a school for "free" blacks, but the school was closed not long afterward by a Charleston citizenry fearful of educated blacks.[29] On several occasions he attempted to spur the conventions to establish an orphanage.[30] Another major project in which he engaged the conventions was *The United States Catholic Miscellany*. It was the first continuing Catholic newspaper in the United States, which after a faltering start, continued until the start of the American Civil War in 1861.[31] The *Miscellany* published news of Catholic interest as well as pedagogical and polemical articles on the doctrine of the Catholic Church. The bishop saw it as an instrument for instruction of his flock and a defense from the misconceptions of those who attacked it.

Episcopal Leadership

On several occasions during the conventions, John England thought it incumbent to describe the episcopal ministry. The first notable instance was a lengthy series of allusions to the Pauline letters at the eighth convention of South Carolina.[32] Heavily salted with biblical references, he saw his role as that of a shepherd in service to the flock. The flock thirsted for comfort, direction and strength. At the fourteenth convention of South Carolina, he was less theological but more graphic. The bishop was the one charged as "overseer of all churches, pastors and other clergy; shepherd to those who wander, [to make] provision for succession in ministry, [and to] superintend different religious establishments."[33]

While he appeared to set himself and the clergy apart from the laity in the conduct of the diocese and parishes, he stressed, nonetheless, the need of the divinely commissioned clergy to consult with and even accede to the laity in the conduct of Church affairs, especially those of a temporal nature. In these, he was quick to note, neither the clergy nor he could often make claim to equivalent competency.[34] A striking example of England's willingness to depend on the advice of the laity was his frequent consultation with William Gaston and William Read on legal matters surrounding the incorporation of Church properties. An example of responsible stewardship was his accountability to the conventions on the funds that he received from Europe. At the conventions he rendered an accounting of these extra-diocesan funds given for use at his discretion. At the fourteenth convention of South Carolina, he noted that he would continue to give account even though it was not a matter of obligation.[35] If any obligation existed it arose solely from the freely created bonds of mutuality among a covenanted people and their bishop. This, it seems fair to say, was what he tried to articulate to the convention as the foundation of his own understanding of episcopal leadership.

Finances

The central item that demanded attention at the conventions over the years was finances. Charleston was the poorest diocese in the nation, as the bishop himself wrote. He was strapped financially to conduct the work of the diocese on every front. This is clear in the convention addresses. The seminary, the newspaper, the support for the clergy, and other financial obligations were all either in debt, underpaid or floundering on the brink of bankruptcy. The general fund was so poorly supported by the handful Catholics of the diocese that the bishop, after years of dogged optimism, finally admitted, "(A)nd latterly there has been nothing contributed. It lies with you to say whether you will altogether abolish its name or take measures to have it more than an empty and delusive sound."[36] This was October 1837. The general fund delineated in the constitution never worked. For a great deal of financial support for the seminary and mission congregations, England founded the Society of St. John the Baptist in January 1835. This fundraising method was more effective.[37] If anything, however, was singularly unsuccessful, it was the general fund. It is remarkable that the constitution allocated the greatest degree of authority to the laity in respect to the very fund that proved to win so little support. It may have been a strategy of the bishop that simply did not result in the increased giving he hoped. Yet, we must not forget the paucity of Catholics and their relatively modest incomes as, perhaps, the most significant factor.

Inculturation and Missiological Adaptation

Other convention issues also gave insight into the prelate's vision of the Church. Several such items underscored larger diocesan questions. To deal with the need of a local seminary, the bishop presented a twofold argument: 1) the clergy needed to be native or at least sympathetic to the people's dispositions and traditions which varied even from state to state and 2) that he, as bishop, needed to be personally aware of each student's competency for ministry.[38] England had, on the "national stage," espoused in principle the idea of a national seminary. Nevertheless, he refused to send his diocesan students to the Sulpician Seminary (later St. Mary's Seminary and University) in Baltimore. As we have seen, an obvious reason for this was his opposition to the French predispositions found there. However, in this address he argued a point of regionalism, which having been in the United States by this time for a period, he must have become more appreciative of the broad differences between his diocese, Baltimore and the other dioceses and, more assuredly, of the French cultural traditions that characterized the Sulpician approach.[39] From the larger context of his writings it became clear that the real issue was the creation of a clergy that was thoroughly sympathetic to American institutions and customs. In this regard England was not fully consistent. At the tenth convention of South Carolina and at the Second Provincial Council of Baltimore, he proposed a provision for obtaining Irish clerics from an Irish seminary for the church in the United States. He even negotiated the provisions to bring Irish-born priests to the United States only to be rebuffed at the Council of Baltimore. It appears that England did have a bias as regards the Irish, believing that they would be more open and welcoming to American republicanism and rural ministry. He found it easy to see the French, German and English immigrants as not fully American and republican in spirit, but he felt the Irish to be thoroughly American in spirit. Much of this was a projection of his own very strong predisposition to American ways as well as to the simple national prejudice against other immigrants.[40] The only seminary in the nation, St. Mary's, Baltimore, did not meet his basic missiological standard either since, as we saw, the archbishops in Baltimore restricted the distance from the see city that the clergy could live.[41] It was urban in bias.

Nativism and Its Effects

A final revealing point of John England's concept of the Church is in his address to the last of the conventions. By 1840 the religious revivalism of the Second Great Awakening had inundated the nation. It made its impact in several ways. The most negative was the anti-Catholicism that permeated much of the movement. Concern about this development was a central motive of the bishop's activities during this period.

Now late in his life, Bishop England was witnessing renewed momentum among those who would have pushed Catholicism into a more defensive position than it had been for decades in the United States. One aspect in the defensive posture taken by the Catholic Church as a result of the renewed nativist aggressiveness was the reaction of the bishops to the Temperance Movement. As Catholics became more involved with the temperance societies, the bishop took exception. At the second South Carolina convention, he had criticized the "purely moral or civic" dimensions of the movement. What precisely his motivation was eludes us, but he urged a sacramental and religious foundation for the movement. It was true, he allowed, that should such a foundation not be laid, "imperfect restraint" was preferred to "total inactivity." One can suspect that the tendency of the American Catholic Church at the time, and for years afterward, to seclude itself from the mainstream of the United States' social, civic and moral societies can be found here. Yet, such a ghettoizing mentality does not fit John England's overall attitude. What may be operative here is Niebuhrian pragmatism about religion and public policy. Some years earlier in 1831, England in one of his public letters, "The Republic in Danger," mentioned that Catholics did not often associate themselves with the temperance societies because these groups frequently appeared to be "religious" parties of a political bent.[42] It is much the same impetus we see in the dynamic currently among social moralists and sectarian pacifists aligned with political policies of the Right and an anti-intellectual tone masquerading in anti-Enlightenment, anti-secularist rhetoric. In John England's time it as anti-immigrant nativism (anti-Catholic) in alliance with social reformers (abolitionists, temperance and suffragettes) with a rhetoric that cast communities into either the camp of the righteous or the unrighteous. Catholics found themselves, of course, among the unrighteous. They had no choice in the matter of their religion; in the case of temperance they did, but habit and culture constricted it. As in the case of Reinhold Niebuhr, the bishop analyzed the data and conditions prior to judgment. While his reasonings may elude us, his socio-cultural ones appear to have been decidedly Irish Catholic.

As often as England embraced bringing Catholicism into the warp and woof of the United States, like so many of his successors, he situated the immigrant church frequently at the cultural periphery of the national and local communities. He sought to establish separate schools and separate charitable organizations, such as the San Marino Society and so on. Such religio-cultural separatism resulted in both good and bad effects. It surely could be argued that such an approach strengthened Catholic identity and a sense of corporate responsibility within the Church. On the other hand, it may reflect simply a fear of assimilation into American society.[43] It was a tendency that quickened with the real or perceived hostility of nativists.

Conclusion

The delegates gathered in convention were treated as "the church" by their bishop. He kept them informed of his activities and those of the diocese at large. All plans for the development of the Church were shared. Even national concerns that surfaced at the Provincial Councils were brought back for their reaction. The bishop, at the very least, raised the consciousness of the delegates to the fact that they were an integral part of the Church's life and activity, no mean accomplishment in that era.

Constitutionalism was England's way to enliven the members of the Church awareness as active participants. Not only at the diocesan level, but also at the congregational level, the vestries within the diocese and, even at his Cathedral parish, were incorporated under the laws of the states with constitutions that distributed authority and responsibility.[44] England's logic is not difficult to fathom. He held that while the clergy did not have to do as the laity advised, nor even seek their advice, it simply was imprudent and foolish not to do so. His activities demonstrate this very clearly. His criticism of fellow bishops about the way they handled the trustee question, his desire to increase lay expertise at the provincial councils, and his advice to the clergy to seek the counsel of the laity, all indicate his commitment to lay leadership.[45] This may not be a contemporary frame for the issue, but it represented a very clear and singularly progressive thrust in the Catholicism of the early nineteenth century.

Neither simply a theologian nor an administrator, the bishop projected much more the image of the shepherd. In the early years of his episcopate, he was frequently found in the homes and towns of his people spread as they were through three Southern states. As time passed the conventions also became a symbol of the bishop's relationship to the people of the diocese. It was at the conventions that he was most closely in touch with their concerns. He also turned to Pastoral Letters as well, a creative and unusual instrument for a diocesan bishop of his day. They too came to reflect the concrete pastoral relationships Bishop England had in his diocese. His pastoral sensitivity is seen in them. The occasion for most of the letters was either the Advent, Lenten, or Easter seasons. They were usually pious exhortations related to the liturgical seasons and urged the members of the Church to a devotional life, the frequenting of the sacraments and the performance of the Easter duty. Yet, one letter differed significantly from others in that it addressed the people as voters and citizens. It urged upon them the virtues of patience, charity and honesty in the exercise of the franchise. He was particularly disturbed on this occasion by the "party spirit" that had arisen in the city and the nation. He was acutely aware of the passion that could drive a "party spirit" whether that party be religious or not.[46]

The Church and Its Mission

Necessity of the Church

Although John England clearly placed great importance upon the testimony and mediation of the church regarding divine revelation, in the end it was faith that saved, not the Church. The Church may mediate revelation, but it was the individual who had to respond in faith. The principle assuring the primacy of faith was his conviction that freedom of conscience must be respected. Carey cites the example of England's support of the French Huguenots while he was still a priest in Cork and later of his support for Protestants in Spain.[47] Faith rests on a person's freedom to believe and while the bishop held a strong propositional stance *vis-à-vis* revelation, in the final consideration the principle of charity and unity always prevailed.

> Believing as I do that truth is single and indivisible and that two contradictory principles cannot at the same time be true, that religion consists in the worship of God in spirit and truth. . . . I am forced to believe that there cannot be two religions. . . . But where people are seeking for truth, they are not always capable of seeing it; and where men honestly differ in opinion, it would

be uncharitable, it would be irreligious for anyone to condemn his fellow. . . . Hence the spirit which would denounce those who differ from us is one destructive of Christian charity and inimical to the principle of good.[48]

As with the footnote he inserted in the constitution elaborating on the notion of *extra ecclesiam nulla salus* ("outside the church there is no salvation"), John England extended membership in the Church to all sincere seekers of the truth. Freedom could not be freedom unless it recognized a plethora of physical, psychological, geographical, historical, educational and cultural factors that conditioned it and ameliorated it.

The bishop was unalterably opposed to and would never have perceived any legitimacy to criticisms of his positions that many, then and later, termed indifferentism. He wrote, "To deny known truth is not liberality, it is criminal falsehood."[49] Note especially here his nuance, "known truth." The freedom that serves as the foundation for accountability has traditionally also included the expectation that one clearly both know and understand. To the extent such is not the case and one does not have full freedom to inquire, embrace or experience, one's responsibility is diminished. Nor did his concept of liberality imply that all groups, institutions or individuals could make equal claims upon a person's faith or loyalty. The Catholic Church had a prior claim since her doctrines were the revealed truths of God. Yet, he was equally adamant that people's consciences must be respected (Pettit's "freedom from coercion") precedes any claim based upon a "freedom for" in the world of actual experience. He denied that the Catholic Church taught that whoever was not among her number was damned. "But she teaches that 'faith is necessary to salvation,' that 'without the true faith no person can be saved'. . . . Therefore the Roman Catholic Church extends the capacity for salvation to all who are sincerely disposed to believe all that God has taught."[50] The ecclesiological framework within which Bishop England operated held that the revelation of God was received with certainty because of the testimony of the Church throughout the ages. Furthermore, it was only through this testimony that true faith was called forth. To avoid the label "indifferentist" and blunt at the same time his opponents' arguments, he staked out a position, not uncommon, that all God's revelation, insofar as people hear or see it, was received through the Catholic Church's mediation disposing people, nations and the other religious bodies to this truth. England made the point clear in the letter to his friend, Daniel O'Connell. Faith in this truth transcends the Catholic Church since this catholic truth inhabits the religious response of all faithful people to Catholic evangelization and presence whether it is explicit or not.[51] England is the eighteenth and nineteenth century Romantic theologian in this case. The *volk* or community of faith is one through the ages in its experience of God, if not in the expression given to it. This point is particularly salient to Michael Baxter's objection regarding the "Americanists" (among whom it would be difficult not to place John England) since one of Baxter's primary points is that "Americanist" pragmatism divorces philosophy from theology, nature from grace in a manner inconsistent with Vatican II theology derived from Henri DeLubac and Karl Rahner. Quite clearly, however, what we find in Bishop England, as Suarez and others before him, all of whom stand solidly in the Catholic theological and Thomistic tradition, is an articulation of God's lively presence, God's grace and energy in the world because of *gratia preveniens,* the innate, essential goodness of humankind grounded in the abiding presence of the Spirit recognized in even an inchoate Trinitarian theology.[52] The theological anthropology may be philosophically and classically Romantic, but Catholic and Thomistic as well. There is no world from which God is absent and "the God in the world" is encountered in the ongoing community of interpreters, in our case the community of faith.

Ecumenical Influences

While England saw the Church as the central issue in coming to an understanding of God's plan of salvation, he did not exclude learning from other sources as well. It is a bit speculative since he did not explicitate the sources or influences that bore upon him, yet one cannot avoid the impression that his socio-political milieu played a larger than normal role in his case. Constitutionalism and republicanism were two striking examples. Another influence that shaped England's thinking was evident in the structure given the convention that consisted of three branches: the bishop, the houses of clergy and the laity. Thus as frequently as the bishop had railed against the established churches of England and Ireland while a priest in the Cork diocese, he was not so stubborn as to fail to discover and appropriate ideas from them. The structure of the convention was received almost undiluted from the Anglican communion. This was so patently clear to his fellow bishops that they did not hesitate to include this among their criticisms of his "heterodox" system of diocesan government. On this point, Carey notes rightly that the Protestant Episcopal Church structure derives from earlier Catholic synodal forms. Carey further underscores the Catholic nature of this form when he notes the argument in a pamphlet printed by the Philadelphia trustees which suggested this bi-cameral type government.[53] At first glance one may not have expected such openness by the bishop because he resorted to polemics often when speaking of Protestants. A certain reserve may have been expected about a rival ecclesiastical institution. Indeed, England penned some of his sharpest words for some of the evangelicals of his time:

> Besides having left us [Catholics] to damnation for our corruption of God's pure religion, they put us into very bad company (infidels, idolaters, such as are notoriously wicked in their lives) and called us very unbecoming names; and then tell the world that our doctrine of exclusive salvation is really too shocking.[54]

Other than for the leadership of a few divines at the divinity schools at Harvard and Yale, American Protestantism in that period was quite "evangelical" and vehemently opposed to Catholicism. The Catholic Church was not widely appreciated in the American context and the bishop did not shrink from highlighting this very un-republican attitude among a considerable number of his fellow citizens. We also note, however, the irony and the beauty of that era characterized both by polemics at the one level and a lively ecumenism in its face-to-face relationships at another.[55] But Bishop England, who in the absence of a Catholic facility and given a choice between the use of a Protestant facility or a public one, preferred without hesitation the public one.[56] None of these instances alone, however, reveal the entirety of the man. We should recall that it was a Presbyterian pastor who presided at the farewell testimonial in Brandon, Ireland, shortly before England's departure for Charleston. Bishop England also frequently preached to Protestant congregations throughout his diocese and once even presided at a Sunday morning worship service at a Protestant congregation. These recollections make it quite easy to grasp his freedom to adopt Protestant structures and to posit saving faith among his separated brethren. He knew the boundaries between people and traditions and traversed them carefully without blurring their reality. When England was asked by a local Presbyterian pastor to take his place in the Presbyterian pulpit one Sunday morning, the bishop's response was yes, "But you are aware we can have no [ongoing] partnership." [57]

While the structures of the convention were undoubtedly modeled on the Protestant-Episcopal Church, another stimulus was also present. The Baptist Convention of South Carolina had met in 1821. (The Protestant-Episcopal Church of South Carolina did not itself meet until 1829.) Though the Episcopal Church structure existed elsewhere, it was the Baptists who may have served as the most immediate, but not necessarily the most important, model of a democratic/republican communion to the Charleston diocese in the formative period of its own constitutionalism. The strength in Carey's position that it was Catholic conciliar thought that influenced John England is the fact that it surely is the confluence of many factors that ultimately moves a person to act. Surely the Anglican structure appealed to England, but there is much to be said that the trustees and the Baptist Church provided some additional impetus to his decision. The synodal or conciliar traditions may have been the historical argument retrieved for support. Immediate influences in his life in Ireland and South Carolina were the Anglicans and the Baptists. The synodal and conciliar movements allowed the bishop to understand the possible compatibility of these structures with his own tradition.[58]

Inculturation of the Church

Religious Liberty

If Lord Baltimore, Cecil Calvert, at the founding of the Maryland colony, believed a low profile was necessary on the part of Catholics to avoid arousing the antipathy of their Protestant neighbors, the situation only intensified during the later years of John England's episcopacy. The revivalism that spread across the nation during the Jacksonian period and afterwards enflamed the intolerance of Catholicism that had lain in the English Free-Church tradition. Samuel Morse, of telegraph fame, represented a sizable portion of the populace in his claim that "Popery is utterly opposed to republican liberty."[59] Since opposition to Catholicism mounted throughout the years of his episcopate (there was, of course, no causal relationship), there is reason to examine closely the charge that England's own position regarding religious pluralism was simply based on expediency.

The Charleston prelate espoused the notion of freedom of conscience. He saw it as the great principle of the United States' founding fathers.[60] To his mind, the American political principle of religious pluralism was not at variance with the profound command to charity that Jesus left his followers. If Catholicism itself had failed to abide by that command, it was unfortunately not alone in its failure and sin. Regarding persecution and intolerance, he wrote, "I would say this, it was taught by no church; it has been practiced by all."[61] If we are to judge his position as one of sincere belief in the principle of religious liberty and not one of expediency or opportunism, we may rely upon the sincerity of the words he expressed and the practice of his life. In the latter instance there is no question of his commitment to religious freedom.

To demonstrate the strength and sincerity of his position on religious liberty, therefore, his statements can be contrasted with those of John A. Ryan, a noted American Catholic theologian during the first half of the twentieth century. Bishop England, writing to the Society for the Propagation of the Faith at Lyons, held the following:

> I do not know any system more favorable to the security of religious rights and of church property than that of American Law. I have consulted eminent jurists upon the subject. I have closely studied it, and have acted according to its provisions in various circumstances, favorable and unfavorable, during several years, and in many of the details and as a whole, I prefer it to the law of almost every other country with which I am acquainted. Like any other system, it is liable to be abused, and sometimes the prejudices of the individual will accompany him to the bench or to the jury box; but this is not the fault of the system.
>
> [B]y this process of American Law, no person is obligated to belong to any religious society except he desire it himself, and he cannot obtrude himself upon any religious society which is not willing to receive him.[62]

It was unquestionably a principle with England that religious liberty must be protected from any coercion by the government. Such protection from coercion precedes any positive freedom to act. This has been part of the Catholic ethical tradition's classic argument that virtue cannot be legislated, but that the role of law is to set the minimum required for the commonweal.

> Nor can a government. . . . interfere with the conscientious rights of individuals, nor can it restrain their profession or acts, except it be specifically charged with this duty by that power whence it derives its authority, save so far as to preserve the peace and temporal well-being of the community.
> In the establishment of the Christian revelation, its author never gave to any temporal or civil government any such power, by delegation special or general.[63]

Bishop England did not live in a theological ghetto. He grasped well the practical political importance of the republican "freedom from coercion" as not only fundamental, but fully consistent with Catholic teaching about law. He had also written, "Neither was the exercise of temporal power included in the commission given to Peter by him who said his Kingdom was not of this world." [64] However, on one occasion in stark contrast to this larger context in his writings, he did write, "I am convinced that a total separation from the temporal government is the most natural and safest state for the church in any place where it is not, as it is in the Papal territory, a complete government of churchmen." [65] Perhaps, we need leave such inconsistency to the pastoral and practical nature of the Charleston prelate's theology. England proceeded to base his principle upon the parable of the wheat and the tares in the Scriptures. "We must leave the time of separation to his own harvest." John A. Ryan, the social justice Catholic leader of the 1920s and 1930s, in contrast, wrote a hundred years after John England a much more restrictive principle of religious liberty. "In a genuinely Catholic State, public authority should not permit the introduction of new forms of religion," though already existent ones should be permitted.[66] The impact of Ryan's position is appreciated when one appreciates the context. He defended Leo XIII's condemnation of the view "that princes are nothing more than delegates to carry out the will of the people." Ryan takes, with Leo, a stand in opposition to popular sovereignty. Ryan's position a century after England helps us appreciate more the clear-sightedness of Bishop England.[67] England's position was, unless we assert that he was unconscionable in his rhetoric, one that in principle and spirit is quite different than Ryan's that quite unabashedly appeals to expediency. Bishop England's position was grounded in his notion that it was a person's faith that saved, not formal membership in a church group.[68] Just as the state had no authority to restrict religious liberty, neither did the Church have such rights. In his letter to Daniel O'Connell, "On Liberality," the bishop flatly denied that the Catholic Church taught that dissenters should be persecuted. The Church, he wrote, "anathematizes, that is rejects, detests, condemns, and reprobates heresy, and not heretics." Not all those who professed heresy, he quickly added, were heretics themselves. Therefore the principle for a Catholic to follow in this as in other respects was Christian charity. "[I]t exhibits the practical love of every individual of the human race, without excluding sect or nation from benevolence of feeling and exertion for their welfare."[69] The generations that followed upon the Reformation of the sixteenth century could not be coerced against their good conscience. This, at a minimum, was John England's conception: conscience cannot be coerced.

Republicanism/Constitutionalism and Church Administration

A major ecclesiological issue for John England was the inculturation (This usage is obviously anachronistic; the bishop would not have known the term.) of the Catholic tradition in American society.[70] This appears to be the underlying issue in so many cases: his anti-French prejudices, his republicanism, his ideology in defense of the diocesan constitution, his notions of religious liberty and freedom of conscience and certainly his ringing defense of the separation of Church and State. While he espoused several of these issues prior to leaving Ireland, without exception they certainly sharpened with his experiences in the United States through the course of some twenty years. Collectively they epitomize a hope of a "new beginning" that many people projected onto North America and the United States. He certainly saw, quite rightly, new beginnings in the United States but this was not an uncritical vision. The criticisms that the Americanists characteristically understood America as a "New Israel," a "city of the hill," or a "Chosen People" is not applicable to John England and likely to none, if any, of the people with whom he is commonly associated in American Catholic leadership. John England experienced numerous hardships as a Southern bishop with a small ethnic minority membership. He was neither a-critical nor naïve about the American experience and clearly not consciously or unconsciously given to an assimilationist's or sycophant's attraction to it.

Just how sensitive Bishop England was to his version of what inculturation entailed is seen in his letter to the missionary society at Lyons—the local Society for the Propagation of the Faith. His anguished desire to inculturate Catholicism in America ran through the entire letter. A version of this letter was published in The *Miscellany* that ran twice the length of the original sent to Lyons. The letter was summarized well by Peter Guilday.

> Dr. England hints at the crux of the situation: the first members of the American hierarchy from Carroll's time almost to the time he was writing were not fully cognizant of the numerous social and political forces at work around them. They tried to keep the faith alive in this country by organizing the church partly on the European system. . . . Thus they stressed parochial and institutional life, and neglected to seek a substitute for public opinion. The hierarchy of the church was, with few exceptions, composed of prelates who had no contact with the formation of a Catholic public opinion. They were for the most part devoted to a short-sighted policy of measuring our needs by European standards. The memory of Europe hung like a pall over a fast-growing group of newcomers who remained at heart exiles from their own lands. The Catholic future of America was fashioned at a time when that future should have been alive with the larger life America had brought into being and not influenced by leaders who watched over the republicanism of the New World with anxious, if not troubled, eyes.[71]

This principle of "redoing" Catholicism in the New World was to reshape the Charleston church after a republican model insofar as this was reconcilable with the divine commission received by the Church. The confrontation between the trustees and the American Catholic hierarchy highlighted the problem of adaptation.

From a sympathetic point of view, the trustees were, among other things, pressing essentially for a greater degree of democracy or republicanism in the administration of their churches. The constant appeals by both trustees and priest-pastors over the heads of local ordinaries demonstrated their concern for procedures such as due process.[72] What finally must be understood as the most defensible of the trustees' causes was an appeal for an increase in republican forms in the administrative style of Catholicism. England's response was the constitution. It was a most positive one in this regard that came from the hierarchy. It was in this that the bishop most obviously parted company with his contemporaries in the hierarchy. It would be incorrect, however, to conclude that his episcopal confreres were simply opposed to republicanism and all that it implied in the American experience—church voluntarism, religious liberty, and so forth. John England was not the first to support these ideas in the American Catholic Church. John Carroll and the Maryland Catholics were very much in this tradition also. Nonetheless, England moved farther along, particularly as regards those ideas that became associated with Jacksonian democracy and consequently popular democracy and universal suffrage. Carey in *People, Priests, and Prelates* stresses England's insight into the trustee question was the recognition that a good Church constitution would make clear and effective distribution of rights and responsibilities proper to people, priests and episcopacy. Whether the other bishops thought and/or felt as deeply and positively about these issues is known in only several cases. Bishop England alone, however, was to apply the implications of the American socio-political environment to Church administration. Because of this he frightened some of his confreres, while at the same time he himself became increasingly frustrated with them for their failure to put aside old and archaic ways. He, like so many of the immigrants, brought a "European dream" to North America and thought it could and would flourish in the new context. He thought it could be and would be a "new beginning" for the Church as well as for social and political institutions. Yet, there is nuance to be added. "The American dream" is surely something of a misnomer. American political institutions were in part the consequence of the dreams of Locke and Montesquieu and others. So too Bishop England's dream of a republican-styled Catholic Church was Chateaubriand's before it was the bishop's of Charleston, although the bishop of Charleston modified the earlier dream, just had Jefferson and Madison.[73]

John England frequently used political analogies when he spoke of the Church and this propensity to the political sphere drove his interests as a reformer. When he was offered leadership in Charleston, these surfaced and blended into a fully recognizable consultative-style of leadership. The bishop's ideas regarding a General Council of the Church as the supreme legislative body underscore well the republican bias in his thinking. The *Miscellany* of March 13, 1830, emphasized the fact that a church council was a blend of republican freedom and religious obedience. It was another instance of the broad sympathy he held for a consultative or collegial church polity; at the same time, he placed great value on the inherited tradition of religious obedience as central to effective community life.[74] He understood the dialectic and we in later generations must as well.

Bishop England has frequently been accused of Gallicanism, because of his views on General Councils. He believed that such councils with the pope and not the pope alone were the infallible teaching organ of the Church. He wrote, "Authority to give infallibly correct decisions was given to an aggregate body, not to the separate members who compose that body."[75] In any case Bishop Gabriels, and even England's friend, Bishop Francis Kenrick, among others, attributed differing degrees of Gallicanism to him. Bishop Kenrick observed "that, whilst scrupulously tenacious of the defined doctrines, the illustrious prelate, in the early part of his career, was tinged with those theological opinions which pass under the name Gallican."[76] Just how Gallican were the influences upon his principles was discussed earlier. It may have been a factor in shaping his understanding of infallibility, but certainly only one among others, many of which would have been far more important. Carey, for example, largely dismisses the Gallican charge.[77] If a key factor in England's thought and action is found, it is not so much theological Gallicanism as it is a simple response to the socio-political realities in which he lived. Yet, the role of Gallicanism among the early American Catholic bishops remains disputed. Kauffman and others assume its influence because of the presence of the French Sulpicians in Baltimore who had been trained in France in the latter part of the eighteenth century.[78]

In Ireland the feelings of the people were stirred by the liberating ideas of the emancipation movement. They had in many ways distanced themselves from English symbols. In the United States much the same dynamic and distancing had begun to flourish in the period following independence. It was with such ideas that England closely associated himself. His political involvement in Ireland, his close relationship with the emancipationist Daniel O'Connell and the notions found in his writings from the very beginning, make clear the progressive nature of his thinking. The term "liberal" could be used to characterize his attitudes if we understand it to mean "open to change," "the willingness to advocate adjustment and renewal," and "open to fresh approaches" but not as an ideological term in reference to the French *philosophe* or autonomous individuality.[79]

The American biblical and classical Greco-Roman symbol system was a conscious rejection of the British symbol system for our democracy and society and one with which John England could resonate. It was continuous with the Anglo-Saxon socio-political tradition while symbolically freeing itself from indebtedness to the English.[80] With a diocesan constitutional form England reflected a spirit on the ascendancy at the time. It was the spirit of Locke and Montesquieu among others. They and the American experiment differed from other visionaries and revolutions in the degree of pragmatism they evidenced. Although Locke was a very religious man, his understanding of the social compact was not a contradiction of, but neither was it based upon, divine justice and right, but upon self-interest. Individuals entered into a social compact and established a government because it protected them from the inclination in humankind toward self-aggrandizement. The American Constitution reflected the same suspicion of people in a state of unchecked freedom. The argument mounted was not individual rights, as often heard and held today, but natural law argument about human freedom and dignity. Contracts that advantage the domination by any one party or group were opposed as contrary to the nature of humankind and immoral. Pettit writes,

> My inclination is to think that when the republicans spoke of natural rights, however, they generally meant to argue that certain legal rights were essential means of achieving freedom as non-domination, and the description of such rights did not have more than rhetorical significance for them. In particular, it did not imply that the rights were fundamental norms that called to be honoured [sic] in deontological fashion.[81]

The founding fathers reflected this same concern to protect citizens from the domination of the powerful or the majority when they wrote the

American Constitution. It was written with an emphasis on the separation of powers with checks and balances, a concept developed by Montesquieu and amplified by John Locke and John Adams. If ever a philosophical system undergirded a form of government, the idea of the social compact did in the American system. Bishop England, Montesquieu, and the American republicans, as we have seen however, believed that the authority of the social contract arose from the human dignity that God endowed upon the contracting individuals according to the natural law. Individual rights were not understood or promoted as deontological. They were natural insofar as they were meant to assure individual dignity in relation to a person's freedom of conscience.

Pettit suggests that the forebears of the American tradition were republicans who have "always taken a pessimistic view of the corruptibility of human beings in positions of power, while being relatively optimistic about human nature as such."[82] The American social theologian, H. Reinhold Niebuhr, made this point strongly in *Moral Man and Immoral Society*. "All social co-operation on a larger scale than the most intimate social group requires a measure of coercion." His basic assumptions were quite clearly American in the very sense we have just seen. "As individuals, men believe that they ought to love and serve each other and establish justice between each other. As racial, economic and national groups they take for themselves whatever their power can command."[83]

Freedom for the individual necessarily requires laws that limit or regulate both the government and the citizen. As Locke wrote, such law "ill deserves the name of confinement which serves to hedge us in only from bogs and precipices."[84] Robert Bellah described the impetus of this philosophical mood. "(A) revolution that does not move toward a constitution quickly becomes a new despotism."[85] The Lockean social contract was increasingly envisaged as something that must be written and became the *sine qua non* in the new American society. An assumption in this Lockean notion, of course, was a profound sense of the individual's importance and a degree to which the principle of self-interest makes eminent sense in a sin-flawed world. It would be sheer nonsense to dismiss Locke, Niebuhr, Paul, Augustine or Luther on this point. On the other hand, the epigons of American constitutionalism and, in particular the Bill of Rights, do open to question the use of coercion by a nation or community in their attempt to balance the claims of the common and private good. Locke, however, did not promote "rugged individualism." He wrote, "We do deny that each person is at liberty to do what he himself, according to circumstances, judges to be of advantage to him. You certainly have no reason for holding that each person's own interest is the standard of what is just and right."[86] He understood the individual was a social being and believed individual behavior was rooted within a community that served to reign in individual excess.[87] A close reading of Adam Smith reveals the same assumption that the community with its religious-ethical standards served as the rein upon the capitalist.

The idea that society or government was founded on the principle of self-interest, as held by some contemporary critics of this earlier era, was equivalent for most of the eighteenth and nineteenth century republicans to the adoption of the maxim of outlaws. John Locke had never proposed such a concept of self-interest. Serious questions arose whether the common good could ever prevail in an individuality-centered political society but this arose much later with the ideology of many Americans in the era of *laissez faire* economic growth and persists incorrectly among many today as an unquestioned assumption about the original thinkers. The emphasis in Niebuhr, Luther, and Calvin, perhaps, more than in Locke or Montesquieu, was the utterly fallen or depraved nature of the individual that required Niebuhr's regulation of individual behavior in order to assure the commonweal. In either case, to the founding fathers and thinkers along their lines of the Protestant ethic which characterized the remainder of that American era, civic responsibility was a republican priority and the republican tradition of John England can safely be said to be "non-coercion" and not the "non-inference" notion of the later *laissez faire* capitalists or libertarians.[88]

John England settled decisively on the validity of constitutionalism. It was "the American way," as he pointed out to the Vatican in a letter explaining his own diocesan government. In this sense, the bishop was indisputably Lockean. The bishop wrote, "In entering onto society, everyman parts with a large portion of his natural rights as the price for social happiness and protection."[89] This makes crystal clear that he saw government much in the same terms as Locke, if we understand Locke's position that the common good is the context of individual well-being. But it is striking that in his defense of republicanism John England explicitly turned, as might have been expected of a churchman, to Christian moral/ethical values and not to Locke. This should be seen in contra-distinction to the relationship Bellah attributes to the eventual

American synthesis in the latter nineteenth and twentieth centuries around the principle of self-interest. This was not the position of the founders or the early Catholic "Americanists." England asserted that republicanism was sure to fail "if we forget our gratitude to God and the republic at large and substitute for a sense of duty, a looking after private interest."[90] It appears also that these ideas explain better the bishop's ecclesiological preferences than the Gallicanism some have attributed to him. They also attest to his ability to graft new ways of speaking onto old ideas, if not new ideas grafted onto old values. If others later forgot this, however, it diminishes him little since his thought is clear. It appears his critics and some epigons may well have encrusted onto his era values more appropriately associated with "robber barons" and the Gilded Age.

Social and Cultural Dimensions

Awareness of *missiological* adaptation helps to comprehend the bishop's style. This is seen in the criticism Bishop England leveled at his episcopal confreres. He maintained that they projected European patterns upon the North American reality.[91] It is seen also in the blistering criticisms he directed at French priests who arrived in the United States after the French Revolution. He believed that they severely afflicted Catholic ministry in the United States with their cavalier European attitude toward American institutions. He observed, "So far as religion, and especially the ministry, is concerned, this mistake [to underestimate American institutions and society] has not seldom led to very pernicious results."[92] The high value that the bishop placed upon American "legislation, manufactures, literature and the polish of society" compelled him to turn to that society as a teacher and aid in his own life's work. He thought it horrendous that ministers of the Gospel would hope to bring that Gospel to a people of whose British-American history they were ignorant and of whose literature they knew nothing. The clergy had to be part of the people and the history in which they found themselves. So too had the Church to be a part of its culture if it expected to communicate and thrive effectively within it. It would be, as he wrote Pope Gregory XVI, "as if one would think it possible to place an Italian cleric in France and put a French cleric to preside over the Church of Rome."[93]

Personal and Individualist Dimensions in the Challenge to Adapt

Immersed in the spirit of republicanism, Bishop England strove to demonstrate the compatibility of these new ideas with the Catholic tradition. As a Catholic churchman, the Charleston prelate placed significant emphasis and nuance on Locke's motivational principle (which can somewhat fairly be described as self-interest) that some later followers of Locke could not and did not keep in proper balance, such as Locke's stress on the common good. The same occurred in the other instance of an underlying principle of democratic-republicanism. The liberalism that begins to emerge in the late eighteenth century and early nineteenth was related to, if not an outgrowth of, a romanticism, unlike Drey's natural law theory, that envisioned a world of pristine innocence, untied to the Divine Law, that had currency from the time of J.J. Rousseau to developments seen in H.D. Thoreau's and H.W. Emerson's emphasis on individual rights with deontological overtones. Some of these later Romantics came to exalt individual reasoning as the foundation of and sole legitimate tribunal of judgment. As DeTocqueville noted, even religion in America became democratic and republican and, oftentimes, each individual's opinion was considered as of equal weight.[94]

As with most Catholics, England discovered that even in his attraction to republican notions there were boundaries that instinctively became difficult, if not impossible, to cross. The engrained alienation within a Catholic consciousness to "private interpretation of the Bible" or the "Bible alone" was an example of the social, communal emphasis upon an ongoing tradition or culture that could not be left behind and continues to play a role in any Catholic integration of Protestant theological values. It reminds the Catholic how different George Lindbeck's cultural-linguistic model is from the Catholic experience of the Tradition as the cultural vehicle overseeing the interpretative and growth processes in the comprehension of Divine Revelation. For the Catholic, Christian discourse cannot be confined solely to the biblical but necessarily is and has been enriched in its exchanges with the world around it as seen in the Capadocians, the Greek Fathers, Aquinas and, of course, even contemporarily in Rahner and others.

For Bishop England, as it was for Locke, the crucial difference was found in the proper understanding of the individual on the one hand and claims regarding private rights that would constitute "privatization" on the other. If Catholics could have unthinkingly drifted into such a philosophical laziness and assimilation as to obfuscate the two, the second Great Awakening in full bloom by the 1830s assured that they would not. The slogans and shibboleths of the Great Awakening, "private interpretation of Scriptures" and "No Popery" more than made a sensitive Catholic minority wary. Catholic practice and "Catholic cultural" experience necessitated the fragile minority's recommitment to the communal dimension in its life. A driving force, for example, in the second Great Awakening was an evangelistic Protestant view that individuals "establish and transform institutions."[95] Based as this was on a concept that society began with the individual, a concept even stranger to the Catholics of the nineteenth century than today, and that it was a concept promoted by a movement with a strong anti-Catholic bias, an apologist such as England lost little time. He stressed precisely those things most opposed by such religious individualism: the centrality of the Church and the social dimension of humankind. He argued strongly that Church infallibility was not given to an individual, but to a church body.[96] The consultative process was defended by the simple argument that people were most effective when they worked together and when leadership acted upon broadly sought advice. The communal dimension he stood within, the Catholic notions of grace, salvation and Church was accentuated by Bishop England as precisely the reasons to adapt a republican-democratic style.

Separation of Church and State

There were several presuppositions the bishop of Charleston took *vis-à-vis* Church-State relations. The first was the strict distinction between temporal and spiritual authority in the divine commission given in the Gospels. This was particularly evident in his argument regarding the loyalty of Catholics to their government. The second presupposition was the principle of freedom of conscience. It flowed from his notion of saving faith and a witnessing church. England is clear about his principle of freedom of conscience: "when some cities would not receive his [Paul's] doctrine, they asked why he did not call down fire from heaven to destroy them; but his calm and dignified rebuke was that they knew not by what spirit they were led, it was the spirit of human passion assuming the garb of heavenly zeal." He also wrote in the series "Republic in Danger," "I trust there will be no difficulty in admitting that each individual has at least one indefeasible right which no power can interfere: that right is the liberty of thought, in the most extended meaning of the expression."[97] This supports an indisputable point, namely that John England would have extended this indefeasible right to freedom of thought and the right of individuals to practice and live by their consciences. The third presupposition was a collection of ideas that included republicanism, popular suffrage and constitutionalism. All were current and, obviously, none were original to the bishop as a Catholic. They were the learned and popular positions either of theologians such as Delahogue and Bailly or philosophers such as Hooke and Montesquieu.

To grasp England's concern regarding the separation of Church and State, it is important to recognize that Gallicanism was not vital. His opposition to the trusteeism was precisely based on several principles that he believed unacceptable because they were Gallican and nationalist. The strongest objection that he had, for example, was the *jus patronus* claim and the lay supervision of the clergy to the extent that to hire and fire was vested in the trustees. In his mind lay control over the clergy was the same whether exercised by the State or a lay board of trustees. It was a lesson he learned well from the Church's history. The defeat of Lay Investiture had been a hard-earned victory in the early medieval period. In such instances John England, as much as the lower clergy of France, saw freedom from secular domination strengthened in alliances with the Holy See. It was also witnessed in the Roman See's assertion of independence from and surveillance over local bishops who often aligned themselves too closely with local government when Rome established male religious orders directly responsible to the Vatican rather than the local bishop, as the diocesan priests were. We can understand why Bishop England was unalterably opposed to any notion of popular sovereignty among the lay people in their relationship to the church.[98] John England worried that to vest so much authority locally, whether in the parish, diocese or nation, could result in xenophobia or "balkanization." Gallicanism unquestionably embodied some notions he believed inherently wrong. Above all, it would be too close a relationship between the Church and State that each one's interests could thwart or attempt to thwart the other's. This had often been experienced in earlier centuries by lay interference, usually wealthy oligarchs, in the ministry of the Church. One easily can recall the tragedy of the Avignon papacy and the Great Western Schism in the fourteenth and early fifteenth centuries or the numerous examples of monarchs' and aristocrats' manipulation of the Church to their own advantage throughout the Middle Ages. Luther, of course, understood this well.

The Gallican articles, understood politically or theologically, essentially diffused ecclesiastical authority. The state would have some considerable say in local religious affairs *viv-a-vis* the papacy. The Gallican articles did not designate authority either to lay people or to the State, but in practice and popular perception this was attached to them since it regulated the external authority, Rome's, in the internal affairs of a French institution. Gallicanism provided the French State and local bishops many rights in the ecclesiastical sphere by vacating Rome's rights in these areas. There is little reason to believe in either his writing or his actions that John England espoused such a position. He was collaborative, but he never attempts to dilute episcopal authority, let alone papal authority as such. In this regard, then, he was traditionally Catholic in opposition to any erosion in the separation of powers.

Bishop England seemed most open to popular suffrage in terms of the government, yet paradoxically denied the principle when applied to the Church and its members. Theologically the reason was clear. He maintained that we receive revelation, salvation, even creation itself from the Creator, not of ourselves. It is a consistent principle found in Paul, Augustine, Aquinas and Monotheism itself; authority does not arise "from below." We act *in loco creatoris*. The principle of delegation is the key to understand England's reasoning.[99] The hierarchical principle seemed unavoidable in the case of revealed religion, but neither did it obviate a diffusion of power in the Church.

Alexis deTocqueville observed, "In America religion is a distinct sphere, in which the priest is sovereign, but out of which he takes care never to go."[100] So thoroughly was this perceived as the operative principle in Church-State activities by Church members that political involvement of virtually any sort on the part of the (Catholic) clergyman was seen to compromise the ministry. "The body [Church] to which I belong professes to be of peace and conciliation; should its leaders unite actively with political parties mutually opposed, while each declares that it seeks only the prosperity of our republic, their capacity to promote peace and conciliation would be at an end."[101] The Charleston prelate, no doubt, was quite conscious that one must distinguish principles from the motivation that may drive programs or policy. The distinction is not an easy one, but in its absence he may well have feared the embrace of theocratic thought by a population whose emotions have been aroused. Such a reservation is not surprising for a man of his education, let alone as a Catholic bishop of a very small minority in South Atlantic states.

Church and State were two distinct sovereignties. Neither had the right to interfere in the domain of the other. In this respect the bishop differed greatly in his concerns from the Gallicans who emphasized almost solely independence from Vatican hegemony. They were far less concerned about the State or a majority's domination or interference in Catholic life. England was not sanguine in these matters. Both the Church and State needed to be free of one another. England's principle was twofold where the Gallicans' was not. If the Church could not exercise temporal power, neither could the government do so in her name and this is precisely what was to be avoided: legislation of moral values and beliefs on the basis of the civil authority's police power. His adherence to the principle of Church and State separation was testified to regularly. In a letter to Daniel O'Connell, he wrote, "One conclusion is evident, there never was a union of church and state which did not bring serious evils to religion; I shall not now examine whether those evils were counterbalanced by equal benefits. But I do know that the Founder of our faith did not unite the church and state."[102] The bishop of Charleston synthesized well the interplay of Church and State or the civil and ecclesiastical orders. He believed that coercion ought not be exercised by the Church, the pope, or any other part of the Church to punish or prevent the free profession of religious belief, otherwise the most basic principle, freedom of conscience was impaired. Nor could the Church expect the State to wield the sword for her as it did in earlier periods.[103] Thus regardless of the papal position in *Mirari Vos*, John England was both clear and emphatic that American separation was not just tolerable but "with the exception of one, perhaps two states, that it is a more fair, honest and liberal system."[104]

Difficulties with the Prophetic Role of the Church

Though the Charleston bishop was clear in the statement of principle, in practice there were some very interesting deviations. On several occasions he adamantly held to the line that the clergy were to be strictly non-political. In reading some of his works he seemed guilty of almost rendering the priest toothless *vis-à-vis* the political arena and its moral implications. Yet a more complete look at his writings indicates that he did wrestle with this difficult issue. He saw that moral comment and commitment upon those political issues that necessitated a moral evaluation could be valid, even obligatory, for the Church leader.

In 1831 he wrote a pastoral letter to the Catholics of Charleston that addressed issues in the civic arena. The struggle not to intrude into the political life of the members of the Church would always be in tension with the need to proclaim Gospel values in society. The 1831 Pastoral addressed the nullification controversy then raging in South Carolina. In his introductory remarks, the bishop noted that the Church and clergy were not particularly competent in political affairs. "I have political limits and am not more competent than you . . . . There is nothing in the present contest which directly or indirectly affects either our faith, our discipline, or our religious freedom; and therefore nothing to enlist your religious feelings either on one side or the other."[105] At this point, the question would have appeared simple. But he continued. "By your religious obligations as Christians, you are bound to adhere to and to uphold regularly constituted government."[106] He then elaborated on the obligations of the social compact that the people entered into when they chose to live within the protections of a political society. Finally, the issue of nullification, a clearly political issue and principle, was unabashedly assailed, in apparent contradiction to his earlier remarks. Nullification, he believed, derived from a selfish "party spirit" that was destructive of both republicanism and Christian charity. For these reasons, then, he did not hesitate to enter into the fracas. Thus while he sharply distinguished the two competencies, the civil and spiritual, he did not intend, at the same time, to establish an absolute and irreconcilable alienation between them. He stressed that the civic order was to be held accountable to moral assessment. The moral judgment he passed rested upon the community's obligation to recognize and acknowledge disloyalty to the common good. His appeal would not be, to be sure, Catholic teaching. Nonetheless, if the principle is truly "catholic" its reasonableness extends beyond membership in institutions or religious movements.[107] He judged the situation to be one in which the good and the just, the virtuous, were the norms by which all should be measured.

There are, however, inconsistencies in England's application of the principle of separation as illustrated in a letter he wrote during the 1840 presidential campaign. He became involved in a major political controversy with The *Baltimore Pilot and Transcript* and its editor, Duff Green. Green had written rather accusingly that most Catholics, as well as Bishop England, were aligned in the 1840 presidential campaign with the Democratic candidate, President Martin Van Buren. Specifically, Green charged England with public partisanship when a private letter of his was published exonerating the Democrats of responsibility for the country's economic recession. At the same time, the letter had none too subtly poured abuse upon the opposition Whigs. In the letter declining an invitation to a political gathering of Democrats in Georgia, England had written,

> I think, however, I may venture to say that the best remedy for our present unfortunate position is to be found in preferring industry to speculation, labor to cabal, economy to ostentation, patient and persevering frugality to dissipation. I therefore consider that a man who aids in making our lands productive, to be our most useful citizen; I regard the laborious well-conducted mechanic, as preferable to the speculator in stocks, or the usurer.[108]

Green believed the "code-words" of Democratic partisanship were clear and undeniably in the letter. The letter from the pen of a very influential Catholic bishop was an unacceptable attempt by the bishop to wield political influence in an exercise of sheer, blatant partisanship. Green finished his article in the *Pilot and Transcript* writing that he had to "regret the publication of the (bishop's) letter."

In light of the highly partisan nature of the campaign of 1840 with a Jacksonian Democrat running against the newly prospering Whigs (in the person of William Henry Harrison), the sensibilities evident in Green's editorial were more than understandable. England's own response proclaiming total innocence was either disingenuous or simply partisan blindness. The bishop's response to these objections opened him to accusations of outright cynicism in the matter and underscored England's insensitivity in the original letter. England referred to himself in the third person and wrote,

> This commentary contains an assault upon Bishop England, for an assumed partisanship against the party of Mr. Green,

which the bishop positively did not commit, unless Mr. Green will assert that his party is deservedly characterized as noted for 'speculation,' 'cabal,' 'ostentation,' 'dissipation,' for 'usury,' 'monopoly of commerce' and 'seeking to create sectional preferences and facilities by the use of the public purse.[109]

Aside from the substantive issues in this particular incident, we can observe that John England did not, for whatever reasons, always remove himself from the political issues of the day. Thus while his writings may have stated principles in such a manner as to limit severely the Church's prophetic role in the society, his practice was frequently quite otherwise. What we may learn from these instances is the bishop's consistent alliance with the social vision of the Jacksonians as opposed to the emerging liberal, entrepreneurial vision of the Whigs and the Calhounite Democrats.

Educational and Social Ministries

A multitude of other interests in the social order also testified to the fact that Bishop England was not a romantic who saw no relation between the Church and the social order. The Church extended quite clearly beyond what was too simply conceived of as the "spiritual." Though the constitution necessarily dealt with the structural aspects of the Church, the obvious concern it demonstrated to delegate authority and establish accountability presupposed principles of ministry that reached out beyond the barriers of purely "spiritual" or "other-worldly" concerns. Leadership and accountability, furthermore, demanded people who were educated, informed and experienced. Education was a high priority for Bishop England. Furthermore, since faith needed to be reasonable, a strong educational or pedagogical concern also arose from this concern. He established schools and stressed strongly their value for Christian faith and the formation of republican citizens.

A central issue in the Church's and the bishop's own message was that all persons were equal because they were children of the same Father. In his address to the United States Congress, this theme was emphasized. "Nor is any man's mind made subject to his fellow man. But we are upon this ground made originally equal."[110] A corollary to this was that people must love and respect one another. The Church itself likewise needed to witness to this fact as a corporate unity. He founded, therefore, communities of religious women within his diocese to teach, visit, nurse and otherwise assist in the Church's ministry to provide opportunity to all, since all could make equal claims upon the Church. He established a classical and philosophical academy and a school for the "freed" blacks, as well as seminaries for young women and one for students for the priesthood. For the bishop, as for the immigrant American Catholic Church generally, education became often the avenue of all solutions. It provided the possibility of equal opportunity in social and economic advancement, while at the same time it helped to make faith more personal by bringing the life of the Church into individuals' lives beyond Sunday morning. While the programs and projects drew the Church near to its people and the people of the community at large, the bishop's critics today may well question whether the energy was focused so programmatically that it failed to expend the same energy on the inner conversion to the values of God's Rule or Reign. Such a question certainly is posed legitimately, but it is one that hangs over, perhaps, all religious leaders through the centuries. The goal of education in the American context has often been professional and/or economic advancement ("Get an education to get ahead.") more than human integration and development.

The Slave Trade Dispute and Immigrant Laborers: A Conflict

There was much the same ambivalence in the bishop's outlook with regard to some social issues as we have seen in his vision and practice elsewhere, such as his involvement in party politics. An example of such ambivalence in Bishop England's efforts in social ministry was the San Marino Society. Established at Charleston, this group had as its primary purpose the operation of a hospital for the needs of working persons. The *Miscellany* in August 25, 1838, announced that members of the San Marino Society were to avoid conversations about politics, elections, religious disputes and other divisive matters when they met.[111] The article, however, continued with a lengthy report by the society regarding the social welfare concerns of immigrant workers. It described vividly the living and health conditions of such immigrants.[112] Poverty, social isolation, as well as broken health were described as the lot of the immigrant working person. The Church, if she was to live the Gospel, was responsible to assist these men and their families. The equivocation in the bishop's rhetoric is striking. Highly political issues such as working conditions, health problems, and economic oppression were concerns of the Church's ministry. Such issues were addressed, as we have seen, by the bishop in the 1840 presidential campaign just as they were in this article in the *Miscellany*, but the reader was, on the other hand, if a member of the San Marino Society, cautioned not to talk about such things. A clear statement of principle for the application of social justice principles and the principles of the separation of Church and State were not articulated. In the caldron of conflicting social and economic interests, and his own personal loyalties to his ecclesial constituency, the bishop appears often less the systematician than the pastor. He often responded to the needs within his community of faith and its social-political alliances rather than hew strictly to the responsibilities of a theologian or academic. At the same time, it must be remembered that he was also often the polemicist and partisan.

As a consequence, a tragedy did develop from the identification of Bishop England with the immigrant working people. This became clearer with the passing years. When the abolitionist movement gained momentum in the 1830s, Catholic leadership, and Bishop England in particular, felt immense pressure from conflicting interests and practices. The economic interests of groups such as the essentially Catholic immigrants came into conflict with abolitionism. The result was that the Catholic Church in the popular imagination was identified with the pro-slavery bloc. If slavery were abolished, it was assumed by many immigrants, there would be a fierce contestation for jobs between the freed slaves and them. This alone was often seen as reason enough to oppose abolition. Another factor in the era was that American Catholicism was still to a great extent a Southern and border state reality. Baltimore, New Orleans, Louisville and St. Louis were among the largest dioceses. Each was either in a slave-holding state or one sympathetic to slaveholding. In the end, whatever the original justifications, the Southern moorings of many Catholics and the bitter experience in the exchange between the immigrant working poor and the abolitionists (and their allies) led to prejudice, bigotry and racism.

On a number of occasions Bishop England stated his opposition to slavery. He wrote to the Propagation Office in 1841, "But since the Vicar of Jesus Christ . . . has sent me to those regions, no matter what may be the difficulties that surround me, no matter how great may be my disgust with the condition of the slaves brought into my diocese under a system which is perhaps the greatest moral evil that can desolate any part of civilization, still I am content with my lot and with my surroundings."[113] England denies explicitly any support of slavery in the letter. He may have been driven to this, however, because others frequently reminded him that the opposite impression had become widespread because of the series of his public letters on the question of domestic slavery addressed to John Forsyth. Undeniably, the image generally of John England was that of a friend to that "peculiar Southern institution." Even more damning than his own words in the letters exchanged with John Forsyth, as we will see below, were those of Southern partisans upon his death. They indicate the certainty that Southern slaveholders had that he was one with them. An example is found in a "Memoir" written in his honor. We read, "He could control his national prejudices [England's Irish friend O'Connell had blisteringly condemned American slavery] on the subject of slavery and vindicate the institutions of his adopted country against the machinations of malice or fanaticism."[114] Madeliene Rice wrote, "Indeed, in refuting the charge of abolitionism, England went to the opposite extreme and gave ecclesiastical endorsement to slavery."[115] England, likewise, handled very poorly the request of a female of mixed race who sought admission to a Charleston convent.[116] John England was a leader and must share responsibility for what I am sure is an accurate assessment of the situation by Stephen Theobald, who lamentably notes that by 1840 Catholics were seen as a bloc aligned with slavery proponents because of its leadership's inconsistencies on slavery.[117]

This impression had been solidified in a series of letters that the bishop addressed to John Forsyth, the federal secretary of state. In them he asserted strongly that the Apostolic Letter of Gregory XVI on the slave trade (1839) did not condemn domestic slavery in the United States. Because of the timing of the Apostolic Letter, Forsyth had tried to associate Catholics with the 1840 presidential ambitions of William Harrison, a Whig. This is an ironic twist away from the accusations of Duff Green that we saw above that tied England to the Democrat, Martin VanBuren. It appears everybody would like to have associated "those Catholics" with their opponents in any political campaign. In any case, Harrison was the first genuinely pro-abolition presidential candidate. England, eager to obviate such an association with the abolitionist cause, dismissed the papal document as aimed solely at Portuguese and Spanish slave traders, not American slaveholders. In attempting to distance himself from the abolitionist position (unacceptable to his Catholic constituency of immigrants as well as the slave state of South Carolina) and from the impression that Catholics were controlled by the Vatican and not loyal to local customs and institutions, he wrote, "Whatever our own wishes respecting slavery may be, we are firmly of the opinion that in all the South there is less an injustice committed against the slave by his owner than there is committed by the American abolitionist against the American slave-holders."[118] He, of course, reflects a type of populism seen in the Southern states at the time that cried about the injustice of the federal tax system weighted in favor of the industrial North.

In what appeared to be a convoluted process of reasoning, he wrote that while voluntary slavery was moral and American domestic slavery on the whole was involuntary, yet Old Testament precedents allowed it. In this matter, however, we must concur that John England, once again, demonstrated that he was very much a person of the Church. Joseph Capizzi argues effectively that England's position mirrors that of his brother American bishops generally.[119] It was common tradition, if unfortunate error of great magnitude, among the Church's leadership to hold that the apostles had not called slavery a "state of unchristian endurance . . . nor did the apostles consider the Christian master obliged to liberate his Christian Servant."[120] Slavery was the consequence of sin, as several of the Fathers of the Church had said and Bishop England made note. Therefore, whether voluntary or involuntary, the institution of slavery was not ultimately a question the Church must decide. It was the prerogative of the state assemblies to make such decisions regarding the institution of slavery.[121] Perhaps an obvious blindness we discover in England was that he made no effort whatsoever to relate the institution of slavery with the emerging principles of republicanism and universal suffrage which he himself otherwise so enthusiastically promoted. It is the Greek tragedy. Great men possess great faults as well. Such an observation is not meant to dismiss or trivialize the tragedy. We must learn from it and three items find stark relief. First, John England was a person of his times. He lived in slave-holding South Carolina. Second, he focused so much on his obligations as a bishop of the well-being of the local Catholic Church that that priority blinded him to other more important moral obligations. We can be blunt. It is likely that he saw the issues of his own constituency, Catholic immigrant laborers, as so great a part of his world that he failed to recognize other claims even greater.

But his focus was precisely his constituency and it was white immigrants. Three, we all can be intimidated and John England had earlier almost been lynched by Charlestonians when he established a free school for blacks in Charleston.[122] He lost his prophetic voice following that incident; whether the relationship was causal we cannot be sure. In the end, in the broader scholarship, John England's interpretation of Gregory XVI's *In Supremo* as a condemnation of the slave trade, not slavery itself, was accurate. John T. Noonan, Jr. handled this matter thoroughly in his recent book, *A Church That Can and Cannot Change*. Noonan accurately notes that Catholic teaching, until Vatican II, had never clearly understood slavery as intrinsically evil, holding instead that the conscience and spirit of individuals could not be enchained so that they remained intrinsically free—that is free to be morally accountable. As Noonan observes, Catholicism now appears quite unanimous in the recognition of the intrinsic evil in any person's holding another in bondage. Yet, for all his shortcomings in the matter of abolition, John England generally and unfortunately reflected the Catholic and papal position current at the time. In this regard, he was not ahead of the curve within his tradition nor responsive to the gathering consensus in the larger world of which he was a part. Noonan noted that the Catholic theology changes quite frequently in response to settled situations rather than as an initiator of change and in this case John England was a classic churchman.[123] The Church too changed. What was, then, not intrinsically evil is taught to be so today.

Evaluation

The Question of Inculturation or Assimilation

Several explicitly espoused factors came to bear upon the bishop and led him to such an unacceptable position on slavery. He was a missioner, immigrant and disposed to adapting the good found in his new environment. He consciously sought to engraft Catholicism onto the culture of the Southern portion of the United States. This drive served him well in the instances of republicanism and lay leadership. Yet, it led him into a hopeless moral quagmire when he attempted to prove Catholics and Catholicism compatible with and loyal both to American and to Southern institutions. Nonetheless, the facility of his adaptation to local customs should not be exaggerated. He was not a-critical, as we have already seen. On another issue with much the same emotional and regional overtones as slavery, nullification, he had voiced strong opposition. Although different factors and circumstances account for the positions that he took in each case, among the more important on the abolition question was his commitment to the interests of immigrant Catholic workers, possibly more so than to adapt to Southern ways. If slavery were abolished, the "freed-men" would become competitors with these Catholic immigrants on the job market. This, along with the fact that the abolitionist leaders were also frequently nativists and anti-Catholic, obfuscated the moral vision of England and virtually all his contemporary Catholics. It muddled their and his affects and logic. In contrast to other earlier statements, he now claimed slavery and its abolition was solely a political decision and therefore the prerogative of the legislature. He was to write in 1840, "I am not [friendly to slavery], but also I see the impossibility of now abolishing it here. When it can and ought to be abolished is a question for the legislature and not for me."[124] He found himself reflexively defending Southern institutions as he associated the Church with the socio-political interests of the immigrants whose interests were not those of the Southern planters.

There should be no question that he may have consciously feared an even greater nativist reaction to Catholicism had he opposed clearly and resolutely slaveholders. Yet, he failed either in vision or courage or both. We cannot be certain. His alignment with the Jacksonian Democrats and the workingman's party placed him in the company of Southern populist attitudes both in content and rhetoric about Northern business oppression of working and small farmers in the non-industrial South. Populism in the American political tradition has often been associated with a certain xenophobia and provincialism. Whether it was Theodore Bilbo, Huey Long, Tom Watson, Ben Tillman, William Jennings Bryan or George Wallace, American populism and its attendant rhetoric often led to an anti-elitism that resolved itself into anti-intellectualism and charged emotions in the name of a solidarity that made "the others" either unimportant or unprincipled competitors. While it must be made clear that John England was never a "race-baiter" in the way some of these politicians were, his partisan alignment with white tenant farmers and immigrant laborers paralleled the myopia populist leaders and movements, for all their good, too often demonstrated. England's socio-theological instincts usually led him to a position in defense of the little person, the oppressed. The one striking exception was the question of slavery. Recent scholarship on American populism has helped us understand why this occurred so often.[125] The difficulty in political populism appears to have stemmed from two factors:

1.) The strong identification with the immediate interests of a specific segment of the marginalized (in this case, Catholic immigrants and Jacksonian populism) and

2.) The inability to balance and coordinate better the immediate and pressing needs of people (jobs and opportunity), with an analysis of the practical and longer term need for moral and structural transformation (justice for all through just structures)— the theoretical imperatives.

From the viewpoint of missiology, the challenge is rooted in the dialectical relationship in the Gospel imperative for a conversion/ *metanoia* (a "turning around" in response to the prophetic imperative) on the one hand, and the expectation for comfort and forgiveness (pastoral nurture) on the other hand. Academically, one may say these represent the dynamic tension between the use of a liberationist-social analytic and an anthropological analytic. The former critically surveys shortcomings, the latter attempts to understand though appreciation and sympathy.[126]

These same principles of analysis were applied well in the decision to draft and implement a constitution for the diocese. The constitution challenged the people to contribute to and build the community even as it nurtured hopes and dreams that may have stood at some tension with the challenge. The process, however, proved somewhat inadequate because it was not experientially integrated into the entire life of the Catholic community. It demonstrates England's keen mind and his gift for analysis. It witnesses to his pastoral abilities and empathy. But the constitution survived too few years and never had sufficient theological opportunity to mature and integrate better the outlines of what we see in it only in the rough. Why might this have been the case? It is probably that it came much too heavily from the heart, head and pen of one man. Certainly the people, perhaps intuitively, were religious republicans and longed for greater participation in the work of their Church, but an appropriate theological and educative process was not undertaken. The constitution was more a gift to them and less the fruit of their own efforts. It was effective during the bishop's lifetime, but the leadership necessary to assure its continuance under a successor in the episcopal seat was not. Gramsci's "organic intellectual" fits John England well. But such an intellectual may not fit the Weberian insight that organizations require leaders who can routinize. Gramsci's leader may well be Weber's charismatic leader without sufficient talent to institutionalize his/her charisms.

On the slavery question, John England egregiously erred. He simply did not have sufficient experience to root out the bad in the environment. He had also come as an adult to a world previously unknown to him. The African-American was a stranger to him and may well have never registered in his mind and heart in the same way personal relationships might have forged for him had he had more of them. In this sense, his Irish agenda and experience were not broad enough to alert him to what had been so absent to them. This is not an excuse. Even wise people mature and integrate their thought only in the crucible of experience and personal error. John England's years did not span the events that may have forged a deeper awareness and sensitivity.

American Political Presuppositions

The spirit of John England and the entire American experiment seems best illustrated in the importance given written law. The bishop himself made this point emphatically in a letter to the Vatican.

> I have learned by experience that the genius of this nation is to have written laws, to have the laws at hand and to direct all their affairs according to them. The people of the United States are accustomed to have all their affairs transacted in accordance with fixed laws, and not according to the dictates of the will of an individual. They observe that nothing is done by the Holy See without previous consultation and deliberation. They know that in the Catholic Church the power of legislation resides in the Pope and the Bishops and they would be greatly impressed if they would see the Church in America regulated in accordance with the laws emanating from a council of bishops with the approbation of the Holy Father. The conformity of this mode of procedure with their own principles and practices is so striking,

that it would easily gain not only their obedience but also their attachment. But they will never be reconciled to the practice of the bishop, and oftentimes of the priest alone giving orders without assigning any reason for the same."[127]

The assumption in this thinking was that consultation necessarily included written and rational statements on present and future relationships. Failure to comprehend this had been the source of many difficulties for the American Catholic Church of the time and spawned the trustee question. It was only with the aid of William Gaston that England himself came to understand the American mentality of law. "But where the society [e.g., an incorporated congregation or other church body] makes no constitution or does not adopt special regulations, but merely has persons chosen as trustees to manage its concerns, without any special restrictions; these trustees have the power to make all regulations."[128] The roles and functions of both clergy and laity needed definition; without them the commonweal could not be protected against the resources of the powerful. This had become abundantly clear in the American context of the time.[129] The conclusion for England both in practice and theory was the necessity of the adaptation of Catholic institutional forms to American political and legal presuppositions. Although he had frequently made the point that the government of the Church was divinely established and unchangeable and that lay people did not possess a divine commission to govern in the Church, Bishop England just as often spoke of new institutional forms and lay authority.

Karl Rahner more recently has examined the question of the changeable in the unchangeable constitutions of the Church and resolves the question in much the manner England had. He writes, "The *jus divinum* of the church always and wherever it exists has a concrete embodiment which itself is not *juris divinum* though, of course, this does not mean that this *jus divinum* in the church is not real." He continued, "It is impossible to draw any full or adequate distinction between the changeable and unchangeable factors solely by means of the theoretical reason."[130] John England reflected precisely the virtue Avery Dulles wrote of recently, "The greatest systematic theologians have always been, in my estimation, somewhat unsystematic. They have never been slaves to the logic of their systems."[131] Three points have emerged compellingly in the past century. 1) All reality is in a process of constant change. 2) Any law that proposes to norm behavior must be amenable to the fact that change will likely undo in some newly emergent circumstances the lawgiver's logic. 3) Neither law nor logic can be static. Law establishes the parameters for modern organizations. Law, however, can serve only social requirements through passage of the minimum norms to be exacted of members. The Church is both and simultaneously of divine and human origin. Dulles reminds us of this fact: Our theological anthropology paradoxically points us to a community with a focus on love and virtue, not law, but that, nonetheless, just as marriage requires law and norms not only for those periods in which the dryness in love exists in the place of its spontaneity, but also because of the social need to organize life, its expectations, and to forestall the insecurity of an otherwise chaotic existence. God's law and social, historical human need are distinct, if inseparable politically (in the *polis*). We are, as Rahner famously noted, "spirits in the world." As Peirce noted, everything is a sign. What is of the spirit or "substance" can be communicated and received only through the mediation of signs. The *de jure divino* is never approached except through *de jure humano*.

We must always remember that it is England's practice that mediates his thought. (Practice reveals intention and motivation. It is not that practice reveals perfectly intentionality, as we saw with the case of slaveholding; nonetheless, it does better reveal what is truly important and real. Whether explicit or implicit, conscious or unconscious, the motivation that drives practice is seen in its consequences. It is a finely tuned gauge of human preference, insight and priority. Practice is revelatory in the particular actions, but most importantly in the "flow" of activity that constitutes social or personal identities. In the range of his practice there is no question that Bishop England's thrust was strongly in the direction of change and adjustment of Church polity through avenues of lay participation. Neither of these would England have understood as change to or erosion of the core, transcendent (and unchanging) reality that was *de divino*. Change occurs only in the "signing" or mediating processes that convey the presence of the Transcendent and the Will of the Transcendent. The constitution, for example, was quite forceful when it stated that the role of the laity was simply advisory. No deliberative voice was given to the laity in the government of the diocese beyond the management of the general fund. This remained within the well-accepted patterns of contemporary Catholicism. Yet, it would be a foolish and naive error not to recognize the presence of a dynamism that made the role of the laity in Bishop England's Charleston far more vital than simply *pro-forma* consulters. It "signed" much more than any static expression given it. The major flaw of the constitution and its inherent authority was that it could bind only Bishop England. His successors were not so bound by canon law. Its authority as a result, whether moral or legal, could be of little consequence in the long run beyond its role as a model of what could be.

The Charleston prelate established a written and a moral obligation with his people to govern within a process of consultation. The arrangement endured the remainder of his life, nearly twenty years. Its endurance was testimony to the reality of the laity's moral authority, established and protected by the constitution. Illustrative of the bishop's attitude was the accounting he made annually to the conventions. He noted once that while such an accounting was not obligatory on his part, "Yet, I feel better satisfied at submitting them to your examination and having your testimony to sustain my own consciousness of rectitude in the application."[132]

Even as we note the movement to shared government in Bishop England's efforts, we must also recognize it was but movement. It was not a point of arrival. Power, whether social, political, clerical, or economic, remained securely in the bishop's hands. With goodwill the bishop obligated himself to the people of the diocese. He could not obligate his successors as we have noted. Steven Lukes has demonstrated in his analysis of groups the significance the exercise of power (authority) plays in the establishment of a group's agenda. While consultation is undeniably important, leverage to initiate policy, questions or objections are fundamental to a genuine democratic-republican experience. The Charleston constitution did not afford the people of the diocese the power to initiate. Therefore, as Lukes points out, to the degree people's wants "may themselves be a product of a system," power is in the hands of another.[133] Theologically the crunch comes here, for the revelation received from God ultimately sets the Church's agenda, as even one who appreciates Lukes might concede that the received divine revelation is non-negotiable. But must it render the laity passive and mere puppets of power placed in the hands of a hierarchy charged with the protection of the "received deposit?" Such, if it were the case, would seem to fly in the face of a larger and basic religious hermeneutical principle that Divine Revelation can and must be submitted to historical-critical evaluation, as Pius XII noted in *Divino Aflante Spiritu.*

Vatican II taught that the divine revelation is Jesus himself. The Scriptures and tradition witness to that revelation. Each witness in its turn must be submitted to interpretation (Pius XII). The *magisterium*, for its part, serves the revelation insofar as it strives to promote, as well as protect, the proper hermeneutical tools by which the community of faith can discern what is of the divine and what is of human origin. The *magisterium* itself is certainly subject to historical critical evaluation. We can certainly hold to this since the question put to us in I Peter 3:15 is to "be ready to give an explanation [*apologia/ defensio*] to anyone who asks you for a reason [*logos/ ratio*] for your hope." We must study and understand, since clearly the received revelation demands this of us. Again, the transcendent God cannot be met face-to-face, but only through mediating signs. The "deposit" is not in God's language, but ours. God's acts are in history and so mediated through the actions of humans and nature.

England did not apply the principle of popular sovereignty to the members of the Church, since the Church was a community established by and subservient to its God. The Church, in that sense, is not a creature of a covenant entered into by the initiative and will of its members. Nor is it simply a tool for governance, an outward structure or institution. As we saw, he was able to perceive the people, however, as the Church, an *ecclesia*—a gathering of the people. In this way he arrives close to a position consistent with the priesthood of the faithful, more appreciated in Lutheran than Catholic circles at the time.

Among the more important theological influences on England would have been a type of conciliar or, as we have suggested earlier, syndol governance characteristic of the Eastern Orthodox traditions and earliest Christian tradition. This tradition stressed the consultative and the collegial nature both to government and discernment of the spirit within the Church. This thought, along with the political influences already noted, shaped the bishop's perceptions of the papacy and the college of bishops. The modern era was in reaction to arbitrary power and authority, whether it was king or the church leader. They believed authority was exercised properly only when it was within both reasoned and prescribed limits.[134] England agreed with Bellarmine to the extent that the pope was similar to the doge in Venice. He was superior to all other authority figures. The doge was "over and above them all, but yet he is not greater than the assembled senate." To which England added, "The pope must act in concurrence with the other branches of government: his power is limited."[135]

Though Bishop England did not develop clearly the Pauline concept of the Church as a body with diverse members having diverse ministries, it was present in his thoughts, if only in embryo. Such a notion lay at the foundation of the bishop's insistence that the Church was a body united by mutual cooperation.[136]

There was also a consistency in England's approach to authority and decision making. Time and again as he urged Archbishop Marechal to convoke a provincial council, references were made to the need to act in concert.[137] Common counsel and advice led to more uniform and well-balanced solutions. The processes themselves were believed to be key factors that would bring matters to successful conclusions. In the matter of cooperation between leaders, England wrote to Marechal, "I know that by regular meetings of this sort, the other churchmen in this country are outstripping us, though we have more resources." Elsewhere he wrote Marechal (regarding trusteeism), "Surely there must be some remedy, and the remedy should be devised upon consultation."[138] He was also critical of the archbishop for acting improperly and individually in matters that, he held, were proper to a provincial council.[139] Although the context in these instances was the episcopal college, England's attachment to the shared decision-making process was eloquently stated in another of his letters to the Baltimore archbishop. "I would merely suggest to your own zeal and piety . . . Whether it is not necessary that we [the American bishops] should know each other, confide in each other, consult with each other and be united with each other."[140] Such was the vision England had of the workings of the national hierarchy. It cannot be considered too striking that his diocesan conventions paralleled the concept of a national or provincial synod.

Conclusion

It was only in 1840 that for the briefest of periods not long before his death, John England despaired of the usefulness of cooperative efforts within the hierarchy and with the laity. He wrote Archbishop Eccleston at Baltimore to indicate that he had no pressing matter to place on the agenda of the upcoming provincial council. He was in the minority regarding issues of substance and it would, he wrote, be best not to continue to raise the same questions. He would leave to his younger colleagues responsibility for the future. They could pick up the torch of cooperation and would "better plan and execute by reason of their mutual acquaintance and closer vivinage, whilst I, in my isolated position, shall still as far as I can co-operate."[141]

The bishop's withdrawal from leadership was short-lived. He soon rejoined the fight, urging upon his conferees the very issue of mutuality he always promoted. But he was nearing the end. He continued these final efforts during the few months before his final illness and death in April, 1842.

NOTES

1. Here I follow Carey, *England*, 156ff. These principles emerge clearly in the documents sent by the Norfolk trustees to Rome, May 31 through June 1, 1817, esp. no. 4 in the petition, cited by Guilday, *Church in Virginia*, 46, 55-56.
2. Kenrick, "Reviews," *Brownson's Quarterly* 7(1850):156.
3. *Works*, I, 195.
4. *Works*, 195-196.
5. *Works*, II, 292.
6. Carey cites "The Habiting of a Nun," *Works*, IV, 199.
7. *Works*, II, 31.
8. *Works*, IV, 326.
9. *Works*, I, 322.
10. *Works*, 329-330; 333; II, 93.
11. *Records* 8(1897): 460.
12. *Works*, V, 65.
13. *Works*, IV, 228.
14. Holifield, E. Brooks. *Theology in America: Christian Thought from the Age of the Puritans to the Civil War* (New Haven: Yale, 2003).
15. Pettit, passim, Hauerwas and Pinches, passim, MacIntyre, *Whose Rationality*, passim and consult the analyses of Komonchek, Portier and others in Kauffman, *U.S. Catholic Historian*, 1(2000) the entire issue is on the contributions of J.C. Murray to *Dignitatis Humanae*.
16. *U.S.C.M.*, October 18, 1828, 112f. and November 22, 1828, 153 as cited by Carey, *England*, 368.
17. Cited by Guilday, *Life*, I, 537. Interestingly the same letter appeared in part in *Records* 7(1896): 481-485 with the most bitter criticisms of his fellow bishops extracted.

18. See Carey, *England*, 296-305, 380-391.
19. See also note 7 above, *Works*, IV, 326.
20. Thirteen addresses were given to the South Carolina conventions; two to the district of North Carolina; eight to the conventions of Georgia and two to the diocesan-wide conventions, *Works*, IV, 316-434.
21. *Works*, IV, 383.
22. *Works*, 359.
23. *Works*, 348.
24. This is the pattern throughout the journal, for example, *Records* 6(1895): 29-55, 184-224.
25. Archibald J. MacKenzie, *History of the Christmas Island Parish* (n.d., place, photocopy found in Robards Library, University of Toronto) and "Christmas Island Parish," in *Mosgladh*, n.s. 8, n. 5, 1931, and information from Stephen Dunn, *The Highland Settler*, (Toronto, Univ. of Toronto, 1953).
26. Dr. Mary Lee Dougherty later directed an Appalachian Studies program at the University of Charleston, West Virginia.
27. *Works*, IV, 359.
28. At seventh, twelfth and fifteenth conventions of S.C., *Works*, V, 348; 419; 375.
29. *Works*, IV, 354f.
30. At the seventh, eleventh and fifteenth conventions to cite but a few, *Works*, V, 426; IV, 353, 367.
31. *Works*, V, 426; IV, 353, 367. Fr. Gabriel Richard, SS began a Catholic newspaper a decade earlier (1809) in Detroit. It did not survive long as a newspaper, becoming quickly a publishing house of various flyers and tracts.
32. *Works*, V, 422f.
33. *Works*, IV, 369.
34. *Works*, V, 423.
35. See the ninth, tenth, twelfth and fourteenth conventions of S.C., esp. *Works*, IV, 366.
36. The fourteenth convention of S.C., *Works*, IV, 366.
37. See "Addresses to the St. John the Baptist Society" in 1836 and 1837, *Works*, IV, 434ff. See also the second, fourth, seventh, eighth, eleventh, fourteenth and fifteenth convention addresses to S.C. as illustrations of the financial difficulties of the diocese. The "tax" was a customary practice in the various Protestant communions at the time. Bishop England several times referred to the much more successful Protestant efforts in voluntary support methods.
38. The second convention of S.C., *Works*, IV, 319.
39. Christopher Kaufman, *Tradition and Transformation in Catholic Culture: The History of the Priests of St. Sulpice, 1791 to the Present* (NY: MacMillan, 1988), cf. esp. 33-132, the invitation, founding and early years of St. Mary's Seminary in Baltimore.

40. *Works*, IV, 340.
41. Lou McNeil, "Catholic Mission," in Bill Leonard, ed. *Christianity in Appalachia*, (Knoxville, Tennessee, 1999), 259.
42. *Works*, IV, 432-433.
43. See the second diocesan convention, *Works*, IV, 432-433.
44. There was, for example, a constitution for St. Finbar's Cathedral, "Journal," *Records* 6(1895): 210; the St. John the Baptist Society, *Works*, IV, 434. The Cathedral parish did not for some ten years join as a signatory of the Diocesan Constitution.
45. Guilday, *Life*, I, 536f, and *Works*, V, 423.
46. The Pastoral Letters are found in *Works*, IV, 232-316.
47. Carey, *England*, 105 and 325-326.
48. *Works*, IV, 229-330.
49. *Works*, II, 354.
50. *Works*.
51. "On Liberality," *Works*, II 355-356. We must be aware of the fact that John England's concern was never raised to the point at which he handled the question of those who never came into contact with either the Catholic Church or the Christian Gospel. His context and thinking was the social milieu of Western Christendom and the American South.
52. Baxter, "Catholicism and Liberalism," 755. Baxter is an ethicist and fails to appreciate the continuity in the thought of DeLubac and Rahner on grace and nature. Their position is distorted when seen as without root in the thought we find in Suarez and others on salvation outside the Church's membership. See Sullivan, *Salvation*, 88-99. This lack of appreciation conveniently permits a stereotype of eminent leaders in the American Catholic tradition as accomodationist. He, of course, follows David Schindler who offers a more nuanced assessment which nonetheless falls short. David Schindler. *Heart of the World, Center of the Church: Communio Ecclesiology* (Grand Rapids: Eerdmans, 1996). Particularly helpful to understand Catholic thinking at this time is Holifield's *Theology*, 412 ff. where he discusses Catholic theology of grace and revelation as it shaped John England and others.

An inchoate Trinitarian theology refers to the fact that no Person of the Trinity acts without the "presence" of the Other. In this case the Word, Second Person of the Trinity, is present in the very nature of the world as the uttered Word of God that imparts existence; see the Prologue of the Gospel of John. See also Robert S. Corrington. *The Community of Interpreter*, (Macon, GA: Mercer University, 1987), 1-30.
53. Guilday, *Life*, II, 497. Carey cites Albright, *Church History*, 33 (1964): 14, 372, and on the Philadelphia trustees, 161.
54. *Works*, I, 219.

55. See McNeil, "Catholic Mission," where it is noted how frequently Catholics and Protestants met together in church services in the rural South during an era known for its "anti-Catholic" polemics.

56. For example see *Records* 6(1895): 221.

57. See Guilday, "John England: Catholic Champion," *Historical Records and Studies* 18(1928): 179; Records, 6 (1895) passim; "Memoir," *Works*, I, 17.

58. See Carey, *England*, 277-278.

59. Cited by Guilday, *Life*, I, 196.

60. See *Works*, IV, 230.

61. *Works*, IV, 230.

62. *Works*, III, 241-242.

63. *Works*, IV, 55.

64. *Works*, I, 170.

65. *Works*, III, 511.

66. John A. Ryan and F.X. Millar, *The State and the Church* (N.Y., Macmillan, 1922), 60.

67. *Works*, 54ff.

68. In this matter see also John Courtney Murray's assessment of Leo's notion of democracy, "The Problem of State Religion," *Theological Studies* 12 (1951) 163ff. Carey, *Immigrant*, on England's background and thought on religious liberty and the separation of Church and State.

69. Works, II, 357-370.

70. Patrick Carey and William L. Portier were the first, in print, (that I know) quite appropriately to describe John England's (and the other "Americanists") attempts as inculturation rather than adaptation, assimilation or accommodation.

71. Guilday, *Life*, II, 369-370.

72. See the literature of trusteeism, especially Carey, *People*, passim.

73. Francois Chateaubriand, *The Genius of Christianity,* 1st ed. (1802), 661ff. With hesitancy one might even timidly suggest that Tallyrand-Perigord and the civil construction of 1790 provided some insight into a direction of thought for Bishop England.

74. Cited in Carey, *England*, 365.

75. *Works*, I, 239.

76. Guilday, *Life*, I, 367, 509, 517. For the term "Gallicanism," *Sacramentum Mundi,* II Karl Rahner, gen. ed. (Montreal, Palm, 1974) 373-374.

77. Carey, *England*, 68ff. esp. note 26.

78. Kauffman, *Tradition*, chps. 1-4.

79. "On Liberality," *Works*, II, 351-354; "Letters to O'Connell," *Works*, III, 476-520; "Catholic Emancipation," *Works*, IV, 447-451; "To the Roman Catholic Citizens of Charleston," *Works*, IV, 303-314, and the preface to the constitution.

80. Robert Bellah, *The Broken Covenant* (N.Y.: Seabury 1975), 22ff.

81. Pettit, 101. See his footnote 4 that argues "natural rights" should not be perceived as deontological, but only as they flow from one's natural right not to be dominated by another, which requires interpretation grounded, however, in the cultural or social community.
82. Pettit, 210.
83. H. Reinhold Niebuhr, *Moral Man and Immoral* Society (NY: Scribner, 1960), 3, 9.
84. Pettit, 302.
85. Bellah, 34.
86. "Essay on the Law of Nature," in *The Selected Political Writings of John Locke*, Paul Sigmund, ed. (NY: Norton, 2005.) 180.
87. Locke, "The Second Treatise of Government," 22, 78, 140. Sigmund stresses Locke's insistence on the common good, pp. xi-xxxix.
88. Pettit, 12. Pettit does not speak of England, but of later developments around the notion of republican freedom.
89. *Works*, III, 307.
90. *Works*, IV, 228. See Bellah, 30-34.
91. Cf. note 68 above.
92. *Works*, III, 228, see also *Records*,8 (1987): 459f.
93. "...cosi si penserebbe di mandare il clero italiano in Francia e portare il clero francese ad officiar le chiese di Roma!" "what if they were to think about assigning an Italian cleric to France and place a French cleric to officiate the Church of Rome!" Cited by *Guilday*, Life, II, 374-375.
94. Steven M. Dworetz, "Locke, Liberalism and the American Revolution," in Sigmund, pp. 388-398. He argues against Pocock, Pettit and the entire school of civic republican interpretation.
95. Bellah, 47.
96. *Works*, I, 239.
97. *Works*, IV, 186 and IV, 54.
98. Bokenkotter, 89-138, esp. his argument about Roman centralization of authority and the role of an organic hierarchy, pp. 136-138, that counterbalances any romanticism the tradition may have with the principle of subsidiarity.
99. Emile Delaruelle. "Gallicanism," in *Sacramentum Mundi*, II 373-374. See also *Works,* III, 511-512; II, 461; Carey, *England,* 273.
100. DeTocqueville, Democracy in America, 154.
101. *Works*, IV, 70. The authorship of this piece is disputed. Bishop England and the editor of the *U.S.C.M.* refused to divulge which of them wrote a given editorial. Both, however, accepted responsibility for the contents, *Works,* IV, 95.
102. *Works*, I, 170; III, 311.
103. *Works*, IV, 180-182.
104. *Works*, III, 241.

214   Chapter Five

105. *Works*, IV, 304, 306.
106. *Works*, 306.
107. See the ongoing debate upon ethics, natural law and John Courtney Murray found in the bibliographical material from David Schindler, Michael Baxter, William L. Portier, and the Murray fortieth anniversary issue of the (Christopher Kauffman, ed.) *U.S. Catholic Historian*. David Schindler began the debate. It illustrates Catholic theology devolution since Vatican II back into intramural school debates between theologians based little upon experiences or reflection on the world beyond theology and/or ecclesiastical history. Too little is understood on the role of interpersonal, social, economic and political issues that impact communities of faith and their leaders. Reference to Church documents, history and theology alone narrows the scope far too much.
108. *Works*, IV, 70. Duff Green was a close associate of J.C. Calhoun. Both were originally allied with Jackson and Van Buren, but drifted into an opposing Democratic Party camp that was far less populist and pro-Nullification. Clearly Bishop England did not go in the same direction. This should be considered as a clarifying factor in England's letters to John Forsyth on the slave trade. See Wilentz, *American Democracy*, 318, 359.
109. *Works*, IV, 71.
110. *Works*, IV, 175.
111. Guilday, *Life*, II, 160.
112. See *The U.S.C.M.*, 18, 318-319, cited by Guilday, *Life*, II, 163ff.
113. "Report to Propagation Office," *Records* 8 (1897): 328ff. See also *U.S.C.M.*, Feb 17, 1841, cited in *Works*, III, 191.
114. See "Tribute of Respect," *Works*, I, 10; "Memoir," *Works*, I, 14., III, 106 .
115. Madeliene Rice, *American Catholic Opinion in the Slavery Controversy* (N.Y., Columbia, 1944). 69.
116. *Records* 23 (1917); 232.
117. Stephen Theobald, "Catholic Missionary Work Among the Colored People of the U.S.," *Records* 35 (1924): 334.
118. *Works*, III, 112.
119. *Works*, 117-118. Joseph Capizzi, "For What Shall We Repent? Reflections on the American Bishops: Their Teaching and Slavery in the United States, 1839-1861," *Theological Studies*, 65(2004) 767-791, particularly the second half of the essay.
120. *Works*, 120-125, esp. 125.
121. Maria Caravaglios, *The American Catholic Church and the Negro Problem in the Eighteenth and Nineteenth Centuries* (Roma: Gregorianum, 1974) treats of the immense pressures England was submitted to on the slavery question, p. 33ff, 132f and finally his assertion that the issue was not a moral one, 134. See also Theobald, 335-336.

122. Janet Duitsman Cornelius, *When I Can Read My Title Clear: Literacy, Slavery and Religion in the Antebellum South Columbia* (SC: Univ. of South Carolina Press, 1991).

123. John T. Noonan, Jr. *A Church That Can and Cannot Change* (Notre Dame, 2005), esp. 258.

124. *U.S.C.M.*, Oct. 10, 1840 cited by Guilday, *Life*, 134.

125. See the rich material on populism and the progressive movements and the not infrequent relationship to racism. Among the best studies are Lawrence Goodwyn, *The Populist Moment* (NY: Oxford, 1978) and C. Vann Woodward, *The Burden of Southern History* (Baton Rouge, LA: Louisiana State University, 1993) and *Tom Watson: Agrarian Reformer* (NY: Oxford, 1972). *Inherit the Wind*, the play and movie, told the sad tale of an otherwise great populist, William Jennings Bryan, c,aught in the "Scopes Monkey Trial" in Dayton, Tennessee.

126. Robert Schreiter, *Constructing Local Theologies* (Maryknoll: Orbis, 1985), 42-44 and 92-95.

127. *Records* 8(1897): 458, 462.

128. *Works*, III, 242.

129. *Works*, 243.

130. "Basic Observations on the Subject of Changeable and Unchangeable Factors in the Church," *Theological Investigations, XIV* (N.Y., Seabury, 1975) 20, 23. This writer does not mean to imply that John England drew the same conclusions with the same theological sophistication.

131. Avery Dulles, *The Craft of Theology* (Mahwah: Paulist, 1992).

132. *Works*, IV, 366.

133 Steven Lukes, *Power* (London: MacMillan, 1991), 21-25, esp. 34f.

134. LeBuffe, 93ff. pin-points England's intellectual response to authority.

135. *Works*, II, 285. We cannot, of course, speculate how Bishop England would have understood Vatican I's position on papal infallibility as regards the *ex sese* clause, i.e. the pope's infallible statement is not subject to review by the college of bishops clause.

136. *Works*, I, 322, 329-330.

137. The bulk of these letters are cited in Guilday, *Life*, II, 68-110, esp. 77, 92.

138. *Works*, 77, 90, 92.

139. *Works*, 105.

140. *Works*, 106.

141. Cited by Guilday, *Life*, II, 505-507. In this letter he also urged the bishops to join the clergy and laity in a mutual effort in Catholic publishing.

Chapter Six

Conclusion

> It is the prerogative of great men
> Only to have great defects.
>
> LaRochefoucald

It may be well to conclude in summary fashion with a look again at some of the conclusions that have been drawn throughout this study. We can do this by drawing a general assessment 1) of the thought and activity of Bishop England insofar as it relates to his being an effective model of inculturation and 2) of the situation or context of the Church as an effective one for a practical theology reflective of Fr. Arrupe's notion of inculturation. The latter case also involves an assessment of the esthetics that complement the rational in England's pragmatic approach to ministry. England's pragmatic theology reflects the influences both of romanticism (we suggested, perhaps, J.S. Drey or, at least the Tubingen school) and a communal sense that culture constitutes a central factor in the development of knowledge or, in our case, doctrine. In both England's leadership and the context of which he was a part, we note positive and negative impacts that were made on his ministerial efforts. This was not to be unexpected. It reflects the debates at Vatican II surrounding the notion of ongoing revelation enunciated by Cardinal Leger (Montreal) on the one hand and Cardinal Meyer (Chicago) on the other. In the first case the insight was, indeed, development, in the second that such development was not always progression, but at times, regression. Events and developments cannot avoid the very flawedness that embraces any human endeavor. The presupposition, of course, of our evaluation of John England, is that inculturation and dialogue with the culture in which the Church finds itself rest firmly on a traditional Catholic theological anthropology of nature and grace most recently well articulated by Henri DeLubac that faithfully reflects the Tridentine theology of grace. This is in contradistinction to the imputation of the Reformers that humankind is "essentially sinned." Catholicism holds a more optimistic position that while humankind is flawed, grace is not totally absent from nature. It is such a theological anthropology that distinguishes Catholic positions today so clearly from the post-liberal positions taken by even the Catholic critics we addressed in this study.[1] Nature cannot exist apart from God in the Catholic and Orthodox Christian traditions.

Inculturated Ministry

1.) John England was keenly aware of the fact that pluralism in belief (and, of course, discourses) among sincere Christians made a clear and persuasive argument for religious liberty on the grounds of freedom of conscience that ran counter to the Catholic position of the time that "error had no rights." The bishop found himself in a heterogeneous nation and chose not to live in isolation but in daily and constant relationship with the larger pluralist community. The choice was clearly a theological one as much as a pragmatic one. He understood the church as church and not as sect and ministry as mission and not simply pastoral nurture. He stood on the texts of Matthew 13 and 25: the city on the hill does not hide its light but indeed reaches out to all nations proclaiming its good news. To be such a church—that is, one that stands clearly in the midst of the people, is to mirror the ministry of Jesus who went out to the people and did not withdraw. Effective outreach cannot have the air of satisfied smugness, but the wonder and curiosity of the one who shares discovery and conviction as indicated in the age-old aphorism, *ecclesia dicens, ecclesia discens,* loosely "the church speaks, but also learns." John England highlights inculturation in precisely this retrieval of the tradition. To place oneself in the midst requires a willingness to dialogue. Dialogue, of course, necessitates an honest engagement and exchange.

While this position is fully in accord with the long tradition of Catholicism's positive response to culture, it was, nonetheless, not the common one during Bishop England's lifetime. John England's context as a member of a minority, political or numerical, goes a long way toward understanding his insight regarding the multiple discourses in society.

2.) He promoted episcopal collegiality as witnessed in the national council he urged and in the national Pastorals he penned for the American bishops over the years. Here again he retrieves the synodal tradition in governance of the Eastern Church and the lost custom of regional councils in the Western Church. Yet, we cannot overlook the influence of the federal vision of the American republic, especially in its Jacksonian expression. The national councils and the Pastorals of the national bishops along with his Diocesan Constitution were instruments surely designed, at least in part, by England's interest in and admiration for democratic-republican ideals. Together these two tools would form his vision of a well-governed local and regional church. His vision certainly was prescient since the exponential nature of the developments in travel and communication underscore the need that developed over the following decades for effective coordination of policy between the local, regional and international ecclesiastical bodies. Yet, in this regard, Bishop England's efforts hewed well to the Catholic principle of subsidiarity, the American principle of federalism, and current global awareness of the need for the international standards or norms. The Diocesan Constitution, the national body of bishops, and the international role the Vatican offered, paralleled the political structure that he saw on the other hand in South Carolina, Washington, and an international body such as would be illustrated in the UN today.

3.) Bishop England, however, reflected his time in other ways. He had a theologically narrow concept of the Church's ministry because he identified ministry with the ministry of the ordained. This did somewhat inhibit his pastoral sensitivity and sensible approach to lay ministry and leadership. He was, in this case, a person of his times and lay ministry was perceived as an "apostolate,"—that is, lay people were delegated by the clergy to perform those services that the clergy themselves were unable to do because of circumstances (distance, time, etc.). While we see creative breakthroughs in his episcopal leadership, such as to provide for services led by lay people in the absence of a priest, the breakthrough is a practical and pastoral one, not a theological insight. In another sense, however, the bishop's vision of ministry was quite broad. He shunned other-worldly or exclusively spiritual tendencies so prominent, particularly in Catholicism, during his lifetime and engaged himself and his church in a broad range of social and educational ministries. This active response to the pastoral, but "secular" interests of his flock highlights his passion for ministry and his ability to move beyond the boundaries more normally established in the pastoral practice of the Church. This stretch into new areas of ministry, such as Catholic schools, engagement of laity in leadership roles, and economic interests reflected in his vocal support of Jacksonian reform reflects an impetus that quite naturally appears to be concomitant with inculturation as would be seen when the American episcopal leadership, following Bishop England's lead, typically adopted some of the same new forms of ministry during the rapid growth of Catholic immigration in the 1840s on. Bishops and priests in increasing measure placed their energy into Catholic school systems and an array of social service agencies. Previously, Catholic-sponsored schools had largely served a small core of Catholic families that could afford education for their children. The American ideal of universal education found impetus in the Catholic community as well when the bishop's efforts in Charleston turned not only to the immigrant Catholic community but also to the African-American community.

4.) While his theological notions would not have led one to expect it, Bishop England, in fact, introduced a high level of interaction between lay and clerical leadership. He stressed the importance for a wise leader to seek a wide spectrum of advice before action was taken on any matter of consequence. Not only did he advise his clergy to work in concert with the laity, especially in those fields in which the laity were far better qualified than the clergy, but he did the same himself. His wisdom did not stop with advice; he also created structures that facilitated such advisement. Success was witnessed in the resolution, among others, of the lay trustee controversies that had convulsed parishes in his diocese.

5.) John England stands out as an early partisan of Catholic evangelization. He frequently expressed his concern for the "scattered Catholics" with whom he wished to put the Catholic Church in contact. He was also interested to work among African-Americans and Native Americans as well as the arriving immigrants. His Catholic imagination as regards evangelization was not restricted to evangelizing and pastoral nurture. He ventured always outward seeking to engage ecumenically other Christians and the "secular" world around him. His efforts at evangelization among those not committed to a church were certainly social in orientation. He sought contact with unaffiliated people through offers of an education in church-run schools, home visitation nurses and other services for families under the auspices of women religious. It should be remembered that the expected role of the diocesan bishop during this period was to minister to the pastoral needs of the Catholic flock. England went far beyond that in part because of circumstance. He surely had a small flock that allowed him to look about more broadly. But he also reflected somewhat the American Baptist and Methodist leadership that surrounded him. Unlike the established churches, they ventured beyond the circles of the established cities on the coast evangelizing the hinterland. John England was explicit, for example, in his criticism of the Sulpicians and archbishops in Baltimore who, like their counterparts in the established historical churches of European origin, neglected their membership in the rural and distant regions. The Charleston bishop believed millions of Catholics were neglected in the Carolinas for want of a missionary or pioneering vision. He believed the elitism of a satisfied hierarchy and educated clergy could not see much beyond the borders of their see cities and the satisfactions found in the social and literary opportunities there.

6.) England's sense of the missiological extended also to the regional peculiarities of the ante-bellum South. In this instance the man at the margins had become one at the center and was, perhaps, absorbed by the center, blinded by it. This, unfortunately, likely explains his reputation as sympathetic to slavery. I say "sympathetic" because he was, in fact, explicitly opposed to slavery. The tragedy was that as a leader in Charleston and as one undeniably Jacksonian in his politics, he rationalized the existence of slavery in the Southern states. Confronted with Pope Gregory XVI's Apostolic Letter on the Slave Trade, he parsed the issue of slavery and the Vatican. In the end, he suggested the Vatican opposed only the slave trade and had not condemned slavery itself. In an era when the Abolitionists were plentiful, the bishop's failure to be forthright, indeed, the suggestion that slavery itself was tolerable in any manner leaves a bitter scar on his legacy. How do we explain it? In part it is the center-periphery image we have used throughout this study. There is also, however, the fact that whether we call it adaptation or inculturation, once we identify ourselves with a people, their culture or their customs we, by that very fact, may lose something in our perspective. Does this argue against inculturation or missiological adaptation? I would say not. The presupposition of this study, and I believe of John England, has been that a universalism or Christian exclusivity is not acceptable. The sure consequence is, of course, the risk that immersion in the pluralism of God's creation will necessarily alert us to our finitude, the inability among other things to maintain perspective—that is, to know as God knows. Catholic theology has for the long duration understood the dialectic of sin and grace: We are graced, but not perfect: that is, we our in God's image, but not God. Through human experience we grow in the comprehension of God's revelation. Yet, as Cardinal Meyer noted during the debate at Vatican II on *Dei Verbum*, as noted above, development cannot always be assumed as progressive, though development there is. As we look backwards in history, we know this with certainty; both the bold and the cautious erred. Our best hope is to learn from our histories so as to act more judiciously. If risk is the alternative, then theologically that risk does not rest either on a gamble or an existential leap of faith, but upon a theological esthetics. In this latter case, however, we must be aware that not every product of the artist nor every hypothesis of the scientist proves worthy, but the artist we nonetheless recognize in the whole of their work.

7.) The bishop's apologetics and polemics, and an unconscious bias toward the Irish mixed with an interesting and paradoxical dose of anti-elitism bias led him too frequently to focus on and value too strongly his own community's needs and identity. This pattern often left Catholicism, as many minority groups before and since, so absorbed by their own needs and identity that they failed at the central Christian imperative: "We must die to ourselves if we are to find ourselves." In this sense, John England's effort at the inculturation stood astride both inclusivity and exclusivity. He did not simply accommodate totally and promote Catholic assimilation into the larger Protestant culture. But within Catholic circles, as well as the Protestant milieu of the American South, he did "assimilate" himself readily as an Irishman and Southerner. This appears to be inherent to the question of identity. As the anthropologist, Mary Douglas has observed boundaries are necessary to a community's identity. Yet, the razor's edge of identity is exclusivity. Without falling into cliché, we may be able amply to appreciate here Robert Frost's "Mending Wall." Boundaries can fortify both engagement as well as isolation.

8.) While theologians still struggle to articulate clearly a sound ecclesiology and the proper role of the church to the life in the believer, John England stated extremely well the communal dimension necessary to a person's faith in order to avoid pure subjectivism, if not delusion. Faith's plausibility must rest firmly upon the same type of social-cultural verification given to the non-tangible personal and social experiences of the individual and community. It is such Catholic ecclesiological insights, along with the theological anthropology mentioned above that distinguish the Catholic appreciation for the role of culture and experience to a proper understanding of divine revelation. At the same time, he was adamant to clarify the notion *extra ecclesiam, nulla salus* ("no salvation outside the church") required inclusion, in effect, of membership in the Church to all persons who sought the truth. This latter particularly finds its support in Catholic theology's grasp of God's grace as prevenient. The "world of grace" in which the bishop with such a theology resided also led him to extraordinarily wide contacts and working relationships with, as he called them, the "separated brethren." So amenable was he to learn from them, who were also graced, that the convention structure that he adopted for his diocese was received from the Episcopal Church almost without change. It is true that John England did not articulate theology as I do here, but the influences we saw in his early seminary studies, as well as my suggestion of his awareness of his contemporaries of the Tubingen school offer strong circumstantial evidence for his positions. In any case, whether articulated or not, over against the critics, we can amply note his orthodoxy and catholicity because of these theological principles.

9.) The bishop also espoused explicitly the twin principles of republicanism and constitutional law in response to the trustee question. He argued eloquently the value of both principles in governing his Catholic diocese. The Charleston bishop likewise became an articulate spokesman for the separation of Church and State. Unlike some others, he saw the value of the principle in itself and not just as the issue of expediency. Theologically he appreciated the diverse discourses that existed in the United States. For him these reflected the reality of the ages. He was more than aware of the diverse discourses within the Church over time and alluded to them often when speaking of the republican traditions in religious life and cities such as San Marino, while fully cognizant of Catholic discourses surrounding the "divine right" of kings. The post-liberal assertion of a biblical discourse that must determine the Christian's engagement with the world would have been as alien to John England as it would have been for Justin, Martyr, Francis, Dominic and Ignatius.

10.) In his efforts to distinguish between the spiritual and the temporal authorities, England grappled to the end of his days with the tension of a non-political Church and a prophetic Church that required its opposition to the errors and moral abuses in society. This has been, however, the classic dilemma of Catholicism and Christianity itself. It was not infrequently resolved with the "two swords" principle: the Church holds authority of the spiritual aspects of life and the State holds authority in the secular, but that the spiritual sword held ultimate authority over the secular insofar as it could exercise the right of moral judgment and final determination as regards moral right and wrong, even in the secular realm. [2] England's lack of clarity, either in the application or in the point of the principle itself, was all too obvious in the case of abolition. He backpedaled and passed responsibility to the State. In other instances, such as education, religious liberty and so forth, he was clear.

11.) As we have seen, many of the bishop's writings were polemical. He was a man whose passions could be easily aroused. Concomitantly, on occasions he was known to be contentious. At times this contributed, no doubt, to blurred vision. His anti-French passions, his partisanship in the Duff Green controversy and his exchange with John Forsyth were examples. The exchange with Forsyth on the question of domestic slavery was tragically much more telling in its ramifications than the others. Not only did he acquiesce in the intolerable continuance of the enslavement of people, but also as the nationally recognized spokesman of Catholicism he confirmed Catholicism's identification at the time with the pro-slavery bloc. This was a significant factor, no doubt, in the diminished influence he had among Catholics for the next several generations. It also witnesses, perhaps, to the loss of appreciation and embrace of those contributions that would have more effectively engaged Catholicism with its American milieu rather than the withdrawal into the immigrant Catholic ghetto that came to characterize it from the late 1840s until Vatican II.

12) One of those extremely valuable contributions Bishop England offered to the experience of Catholicism in the United States was and can be easily overlooked. He broadened and alerted the Church to the authority the laity could exercise in the Catholic tradition. His submission as a bishop to the moral authority that arose from a written

commitment, the constitution, to his people demonstrated that real authority is found in morally binding relationships. This principle has found revival in post–Vatican II parochial structures such as parish and finance councils. It has still to find application at the diocesan level with the same canonical effectiveness.

13.) As an early crusader for Irish emancipation and as a Catholic apologist, John England brought a type of interdisciplinary awareness to the Catholic tradition that had not been broadly evident at the time. This is evidenced in his frequent recourse to political analogies to explain Catholic customs and, in turn, Catholic contributions to the secular dimension through the ages. Protestantism had not been bashful in its recognition of Luther and Calvin's contributions to the development of the modern political world of democracy, separation of Church and State and religious liberty. John England justly claimed that such institutions were founded not solely in Reformation or Enlightenment but also in the Catholic tradition and thought developed during the Lay Investiture controversies, the emergence of an early popular sovereignty in the monastic movement as well as the secular polities of San Marino and Venice. To be sure these do not exactly parallel modern institutional expressions, but their claim to stand in the developmental process of modern polity is as great as other early expressions of republicanism outside the Catholic tradition. All too frequently, John England noted the Western tradition was myopically believed to originate at and develop following the Reformation. John England also alerted us to manifold lessons from political theory that enable us to dwell more comfortably with the age-old philosophical conundrum of the "one and the many." There can be no freedom without rights. No society without individuals, no fully human individuals without a social network. There could be no social or individual accountability without a balance of power, a notion arguably more directed by Montesquieu's thought than Locke's.[3] These he brought to ecclesial leadership.

Context and Circumstances

In addition to particular actions and beliefs that shaped the leadership that the bishop brought to his ministry, we must also recognize factors were present that transcended his ability to affect. In the preceding we saw the way in which John England responded to social and cultural issues, crises, and opportunities that were before or within him as an individual. In this part of our summary we want to highlight those factors over which he had no control. They were internal, so to speak, or the unconscious cultural atmosphere of which he was inextricably a part. These were "in charge" of him. Of these, some promoted his progression forward, while others impeded it. We can see these factors in particularly unusual and paradigm-changing events from which leaders emerge but for which they can claim no responsibility. Circumstances call forth leaders to meet a challenge that is addressed to one generation, but had not been to another. In the following we will review the characteristics that had fortuitously arisen and from which John England's actions and activities flowed. Such factors have often been among those historians have opined as significant, even determinant in the emergence of leaders, for example, such as Abraham Lincoln and Franklin D. Roosevelt. The times as much as the person, account for the leadership that emerges. In other words, the "great presidents were lucky enough to have great crises." The Civil War, the Depression of 1929-1940, and the World War scan, therefore, be understood respectively to have called from these presidents talent and dynamism that may never have otherwise been recognized in them. I will call this type of circumstance the immediate context in the case of John England. The reason I highlight this is to note that the individuals, Lincoln, Roosevelt or England, may reflect leadership that emerged from a *social pool* (a select group) in given social circumstances. In other words, genius is too individualistic an understanding of the talents and charisms that exist within a community. God's grace, the Christian believes, is sufficient to the circumstances. If the talents to inculturate seen in John England do not exist in the American Catholic Church today, it may have more to do with factors other than the absence of individuals with such potential.

There is another cluster of circumstances, however, that I believe ought to be recognized as well. I refer to the personal traits, characteristics, chosen social circles, and temperament that shape the individual in that these are givens over which the individual, most usually, is largely unconscious or not conscious. To illustrate the point, I suggest we recall the "brilliant" people we have known who have never been able to make their full contribution because of personality or identity clashes in their work life. In other words, those traits were unrelated to conscious intention or the presence of others whose freedom of action over which they had no control. Such factors set their world and work context. An example would be the decision in Rome to appoint or not someone a bishop and, as pertinently, to where or what the appointment is made. The norms used to decide England's episcopal appointment are quite pertinent to our interest in inculturation.

Irish Socio-Political Context
John England betrayed early in his life the characteristic often seen in those attracted to ministry—a quick and committed response in favor of the poor, the weak or the "underdog." He was educated in Protestant schools in pre-Republican Ireland. For some Catholic students this may have evoked a strong sense of privilege or identity with fellow students and their background. For some others, particularly if they are not socio-economically much different than their peers who are members of the dominant group, they may find identity and pride in being somewhat different. This latter may lead one to choose to identify with the "underdog." In John England's case we saw that he chose the less prestigious seminary to attend, and, as a young priest during the Anti-Vetoist controversy, he confronted some of the Irish bishops and especially the British Crown's claims to prerogatives in the appointment of Catholic bishops in Ireland. He was a man with authority in an institution who witnessed to a rather strong anti-authority streak. The dialectic would not always work itself out in a fully consistent manner, but it is clearly a dynamic of great importance to understand the man. Might we say the man was a bit of a rebel, but it may also be that he was what Gramsci later would label the "organic intellectual."

Education beyond Catholicism
Prior to his seminary training, John England's education as a youngster was not singularly in Catholic institutions. In addition to identification with the "underdog," his education outside the Catholic ghetto as it existed at the time provided him with personal and working experiences that made him more comfortable with pluralism or heterogeneity and the diverse discourses found even in eighteenth century Ireland. It may also have contributed to his irritation with, and prevented him from understanding, some of his fellow Catholics as well as he may have.

Appointment to Small Diocese
The appointment to the Charleston diocese was given him; he did not choose it. We must recognize that his actions, talents and an earlier

request to be sent to America argue that John England was not totally without a voice or effort in the matter. In any case, the result of the specific appointment was significant and fortuitous and he certainly did not have any influence over it. The small, even miniscule, number of Catholics allowed him to deal with both ecclesial and political issues face-to-face. He did not face heavy administrative responsibilities that certainly allowed him to think and focus on larger national ecclesiastical and socio-political issues in the way more busy bishops may or could not. He emerged as the writer of seven national pastoral letters and a public theologian. He wrote in numerous journals, Catholic and otherwise. The appointment also afforded him the opportunity to play a public role in relatively compact Charleston and other South Carolina communities of the time. The latter provide him a platform from which his public presence could be launched. He spoke before the U.S. Congress and a variety of national organizations that were not Catholic.

In addition, Charleston placed him in a heavily Protestant context and this continued to feed his development both intellectually and pastorally in ways Ireland, New York or Philadelphia would not have. His place in history would have likely been quite different had he received the appointment to New York some say he harbored. Finally it is worth noting that had he not been in a diocese so far-flung geographically, he may never have maintained his conscious desire to reach people beyond the confined circles of urban development. In this sense, the few sheep he had, nonetheless, called him to stray far beyond the well-worn paths of the see cities that often captured the imagination and efforts of his episcopal colleagues.

Identity with Irish Immigrants

As a Catholic, a bishop and an intellectual, John England was confined to the hinterland. This factor, no doubt, strengthened the propensity to identify with the "underdog." This, as we saw, had both positive and negative dimensions. He arrived in the United States without a warm welcome from his archbishop, the Frenchman Ambrose Marechal. In England's mind, Baltimore and the Catholic leadership there held the recent uneducated Irish immigrant arrivals as an embarrassment or possible embarrassment in the sophisticated world of the new republic to which Baltimore's Catholics, he believed, had aspirations. In any case, the duration of John England's life reflects a firm commitment to his own people, in his case the Irish Catholic immigrants. In most ways, John England came to be much more the American republican than his French colleagues who saw the Irish as inveterate, subservient followers of the political authority they vested in their priests. England did not shrink from the advantages, on the other hand, of being the Irish priest with a virtually unquestioned authority. Yet, he also proved to be the best apologist for Catholicism, republicanism, and religious and political liberty. Insofar as the bishop identified with the Irish immigrants, he found their cause most in the populist, political vision that Andrew Jackson and his party brought to the scene.

As an apologist, England was strong and passionate in his commitments. While never one to attack another's social, political or religious beliefs in a personal or derogatory manner, he was nevertheless partisan. Identity is singularly important to a leader and so it must be, but the fine line between identity and appreciation for another's values beyond one's circle can be treacherous terrain for any leader. Intellectually, England strode that line well. Emotionally, he was not always clear-sighted. His bias against the French clergy was palpable. We already saw the same issue as regards slavery.

Personal Temperament
The overall consequences of John England's self-understanding, personal identity and temperament may be seen in some significant decisions. The Anti-Vetoist as the editor of *The Cork Mercantile-Chronicle* followed upon choices he had made for not only the Catholic priesthood but also the seminary in which he would pursue his studies. Unlike the sociological aspect that propelled some to the priesthood as upwardly mobile, his motivation appears the opposite. The ferocity of his alignment with the Irish immigrant laborer in the United States, his opposition to the more established ecclesiastical and social style evidenced in the French Sulpicians and their English Catholic patrons in Maryland, and his unabashed sympathies for the rowdy, populist, Western Jacksonian Democrats, each attest to a virtually knee-jerk response to support the "underdog." Nonetheless, as appealing as his instincts may be, we also recall that this temperament was accompanied with a degree of partisanship that frayed his relationships and his vision as regards the French archbishop, Marechal, and French émigré priests but most consequentially of all the African-American slaves and freedmen. Yet on the other hand, he more than any of his contemporaries

appeared to be rooted in his American citizenship and in his Catholic people, who were largely immigrants who struggled to make financial ends meet. To them he offered leadership opportunities, education, and self-pride.

Rome's Criteria in the Selection of Bishops

Perhaps, for those of us who view Bishop England from a perspective of more than one hundred and seventy years, his appointment appears as one that would not have been expected. He was controversial. He apparently "bucked heads" with some of the Irish bishops and clearly took some positions that were, at the least, in tension with those of the Vatican. The process of episcopal appointments today is so honed that the screen through which a candidate must pass is such that someone far less controversial than John England's pointed and venturesome nature could never pass. The ideology, in contrast to England's own pragmatic esthetics (or Von Balthasar's theological dramatics), that drives the vetting process currently is weighted against the emergence of creative or dynamic leadership. A premium is placed upon traits associated with the personality who administers well, may be socially skilled, but most eminently, it would seem, is a reliable organization person.

The early Church apologists appropriated much of Greek thought as evidenced by Justin, Martyr or Origen and others who found precursors in the Greek philosophers. Augustine appropriated neo-platonism and Aquinas, Aristotle. Each represented a risk to the eyes of the institutional leaders of the time. But risks were taken in the effort to present the Gospel to new peoples in a manner consistent with their culture and experience. The tradition's faith found its voice through its belief that the Spirit animated the Body of Christ, the Church, and it need not be afraid. Faith assured the Church's leaders in the eras of great enthusiasm that for all the risk involved, revelation had indicated that God's spirit would never be absent. The body was indefectible. Unfortunately, the process of inculturation has understandably met numerous obstacles through the centuries. It cannot be doubted that often the obstacle is simply us. It is our inability to stretch as we know we ought. This marked the sad relationships between Catholicism, Eastern Orthodoxy and Islam during the course of the first millennium and into the Middle Ages. Culture inhibited the Latins and the Greeks who labored under the burden of cultural identity, pushing dialogue in such a way as to foreclose growth. By the time of the High Middle Ages, the European Church found itself by and large trapped in a glorious isolation. While the eighteenth century placed the Church on the defensive, it would not be until the events of 1848 and Vatican I that an era driven largely by fear that the world in which it found itself would overcome it that the Church tightened the ideological reins. Loosened somewhat by the saintly John XXIII, fear appears to have reemerged within the Church with a newer focus. The focus is no longer solely on the world outside, but is now turned inward with the belief that the institution itself is being undermined by modern secularism, particularly through its theological community.

It is a fear or an obsession to manage or control that did not characterize the conservative leadership prior to 1848, at least insofar as it did not require tight strictures on those areas of the Church deemed less strategic. The United States, we recall, was under the supervision of the Diacastery of the Propagation of the Faith (mission lands) rather than recognized as an established national church. It is a fear to manage or control that, as we have noted, came into a new expression following John XXIII and Vatican II when ideological purity became the firewall against the incursions believed being made by theologies of its own membership that seemed to undermine the Church's sacral identity. The point to be learned from John England and inculturation of American Catholicism is this: Inculturation can occur only when both progressives and conservatives are healthy enough that neither fears the messiness of differences and believe deeply enough in the assurance that "the *Paraclete* will be with us to the end of time." It serves no purpose here to rehearse the Christian appropriation of numerous pagan feasts, architecture, governmental structure and law through the ages since these are already well known. It need only be observed that such appropriation was accomplished by a deep faith that overcame the fear most everyone experiences when we encounter the strange and unexpected. It was possible only when they came to understand that their discourse was not the only one, when they returned to their roots and could unabashedly affirm that the natural order never exists without the presence and assistance of divine grace, when they could focus on human experience as a contributor to theology and that a single discourse can only lead the human family to ideology, then they could evangelize the world effectively.

Yet, "a John England" does not appear a likely appointment in the Catholic Church today because of the failure to appreciate the role of experience and esthetics in the evaluation of candidates for the episcopacy. The "when" referred to above seems so distant. Indeed, the ideological screen through which the process vets candidates casts an unfortunate light on the contradiction in a Church that has so valiantly fought rationalism for generations but comes now with propositional and rationalist criteria in the pursuit of its judgments.

John England and others (John Carroll, John Ryan, John Courtney Murray and John Dearden for example) in the American Catholic tradition provided the Catholic tradition a service that transcended a deductive and rationalist process and incorporated new experiences into the life of the Church. They rooted their reflections on contemporary experience as they recalled and retrieved the pluralist, democratic and populist dimensions found scattered through the centuries in various Catholic expressions. John England's ability to inculturate the Catholic experience to the world of the American Republic indicates that luckily "he was not a man ahead of his times," but was very much a "man of his times" that the Church was able to accept not only into its household, but into its leadership. It is this last feature, being a person of one's times ,that marks an effective leader. In 1820, Rome did not fear a person of his times.

The Reception by Peers in the American Hierarchy
John England was not broadly appreciated by his contemporaries in the American hierarchy. In part this surely was due to his positions, but it cannot be dismissed that his personality and personal relationships may actually have been the more prominent factor. This is not to say he did not have the admiration of some. Yet, the archbishops in Baltimore never warmed to him and the consequence for the American Church is difficult to assess. Certainly one aspect of this alienation from the archbishops was that he was never promoted to New York as some had, at the time, expected. Such a promotion, speculative as it would be, may have furthered or hindered England's leadership. It is arguable whether New York would have provided a better platform from which he could exercise national leadership. Such an appointment may have consumed him more thoroughly in the affairs of the Church and limited his role in the socio-political world Charleston afforded him. On the other hand, New York may have leveraged him within the American Catholic Church and set it more firmly in the direction of those propositions later condemned by Pius IX in the *Syllabus of Errors*, namely popular democracy (government arises from and is accountable to the people),

separation of Church and State, and religious liberty. Whether the failure of an appointment to New York reflected Roman hesitancies, as opposed to the hesitancies and, perhaps, rivalry of his peers in the American hierarchy about precisely these propositions, we cannot say for certain. It can be argued, however, that such a promotion appears to have been thwarted in Baltimore rather than in Rome. Had the appointment been made and had John England shaped more broadly the American hierarchy as a result, the impact on Rome and the Vatican under Pius IX may have been quite different.

Notes

1. We cannot develop this theological anthropology and the centrality it must be given in positive evaluation of the very notion of inculturation. In this study we referred to authors who lay out the long-standing Catholic theological position, e.g. Aquinas, Mohler, Drey, Rahner, Newman, and *Dei Verbum*. The best and most lucid discussion of the issue of Catholic optimism *vis-a-vis* doctrinal development, the role of experience and post-liberal criticism is John E. Thiel, *Imagination and Authority* (Minneapolis: Fortress, 1991), 167-200. See also Joseph Ratzinger's commentary on *"Dei Verbum,"* in Herbert Vorgrimler, et. al. eds. *Commentary on the Documents of Vatican II*, vol. 3 (NY: Herder & Herder, 1968).

2. John Witte, Jr. *God's Joust, God's Justice: Law and Religion in the Western Tradition.* (Grand Rapids: Eerdmans, 2006), 49-62, 263-293.

3. James F. Jones, Jr. "Montesquieu and Jefferson Revisited," *The French Review*, 51(1978) 4, 577-585. Jefferson certainly rejected much of the British and monarchical aspects of Montesquieu's thought, but "the balance of powers" argument (also found in Locke) is more conservative in its basis as given by Montesquieu and it is precisely this that reflects the American Senate's original composition as "more or less peers" who sit separately from the House and assure that the latter does not move too quickly in the passage of legislation. See also Robert Caro. *Lyndon Johnson: Master of the Senate*, 7-24, for a graphic description of this point. Caro cites De Tocqueville, "The Senate contains within a small space a large proportion of the celebrated men of America. Scarcely an individual is to be seen in it who has not had an active and illustrious career: the Senate is composed of eloquent advocates, distinguished generals, wise magistrates, and statesmen of note, whose arguments would do honor to the most remarkable parliamentary debates of Europe" 23.

Appendix

The Constitution of the Diocese of Charleston, 1839 (condensed)

Preface

The portions of our church government are very like to those of the government of this Union. The entire consists of dioceses, the bishop of each of which holds his place, not as the deputy of the Pope, but as a successor to the Apostles; as the governor of each state holds his place not as the deputy of the President, but as vested therewith by the same power which vests the President with his own authority. And as all the states are bound together in one federation, of which the President is the head, so are the dioceses collected into one church, of which the Pope is the head. Each state has power to make its own laws, provided they do not contravene the general Constitution of the United States; so in each diocess there exists the power of legislation, provided the statutes made therein, be not incompatible with the faith or general discipline of the Catholic Church. The legislature of the Union is collected from all the states, and the decisions of the majority bind the individuals and the states which they represent; the general legislative body of the church is a council composed of the representatives of each diocess, and the decision of the majority binds the members and their dioceses. It is the duty of the President to have the laws of the Union executed in every state, as it is the duty of the Pope to have the general laws of the church executed in every diocess. The bishop is also bound to have them carried into execution within his own diocess, and he has power, and it is his duty to make such special regulations and laws as circumstances may render necessary for their more effectual observance, and for the spiritual benefit of his own district. As our states are subdivided, so are our dioceses: and as the laws of Congress and those of the state are binding in each subdivision, so are the general laws of the church and the laws of the dioceses in each parish or district of the same; but in each subdivision, special regulations are made, each corporate city, town, or district, has its own by-laws, which would be invalid if incompatible with the laws of Congress or those of the states, otherwise they are of force; so in each parish or district by-laws which are incompatible with the general law of the church or the law of the diocess, are invalid.

With this general view, the frame of the following Constitution will be more easily understood.

Title I
Doctrine

1. Our principle is that man is bound to believe all those things, and only those things which God hath revealed. Hence we have no right to select some of those doctrines which we will believe, and others which we may reject; for the divine authority and credit is equal as to each; therefore we admit no distinction between the doctrines of revelation, so as to call some fundamental, which should be received in preference to others to be called not fundamental, as if they may be rejected.

2. We are not to reject doctrines revealed by God, because they exhibit to us matters beyond the force of our reason to discover. For the unlimited knowledge of God comprehends many things beyond the discovery of our limited reason,— and he may, if he thinks proper, reveal to us that such things do exist, though he should not manifest to us the manner of that existence.

3. Faith is the belief, upon the authority of God, of all those matters which he hath revealed to us, even though they should be above or beyond the comprehension of our reason.

4. Although we be not obliged by faith to submit our understanding to our fellow-creature, as to God; yet we may have evidence, and of course certainty, that God hath made that creature his infallible witness to us. In receiving the testimony of that witness, we therefore pay our homage, not to our fellow-creature who testifies, but to the Creator, who, by that witness, reveals to us his doctrines, or gives to us his precepts.

5. We have evidence that God hath spoken frequently, in divers ways in times of old, by his prophets to the fathers, and last of all by his beloved Son, who hath on earth established his church as the pillar and the ground of truth; and who hath commanded all persons to hear and obey that church as the infallible witness of his doctrine and precepts.

6. We have evidence that, notwithstanding many persons have in several ages gone out from this church, and formed for themselves new associations, yet that Church of Christ hath subsisted in every age, and still continues to be a visible body of believers, united under one visible head, in the profession of the same faith, using the same sacraments, teaching doctrines of moral and religious observance which are confessedly holy, and which, being reduced to practice, have exhibited, at all times, men and women of eminent sanctity in the bosom of that society spread through the whole civilized world.

7. From this church we receive the testimony of the doctrines and precepts which God hath revealed; to which doctrines no man may add, from which doctrines no man may take away.

8. We therefore believe with a firm faith, and profess all and every one of those things which are contained in that creed which the holy Catholic (Roman) Church maketh use of, to wit: [Here followed the Nicene Creed]. We most steadfastly admit and embrace apostolical and ecclesiastical traditions, and all other observances and constitutions of the church.

We also admit the holy Scriptures according to that sense which our holy mother, the church, hath held and doth hold, to which it belongs to judge of the true sense and interpretation of the Scriptures; neither will we ever take and interpret them otherwise than according to the unanimous consent of the fathers.

We also profess that there are truly and properly *Seven Sacraments* of the new law instituted by our Lord Jesus Christ, and necessary for the salvation of mankind, though not for everyone. . . . We also receive and admit the received and approved ceremonies of the Catholic Church in the solemn administration of the aforesaid Sacraments.

We likewise undoubtedly receive and profess all other things delivered, defined, and declared by the sacred canons and general councils, particularly by the holy Council of Trent. And we condemn, reject, and anathematize all things contrary thereto, and all heresies whatsoever condemned, rejected and anathematized by the church.

This true catholic faith, without which none can be saved,* we do at this present, freely profess and sincerely hold, and we promise most constantly to retain and confess the same entire and unviolate, with God's holy assistance, to the end of our lives.

*[Bishop England inserted the following note.] The following declaration of the bishops of the Irish Church gives the exact meaning of this too often misrepresented tenet of exclusive salvation. +John, Bp. of Ch.

"Catholics hold, that, in order to attain salvation, it is necessary to belong to the church, and that heresy, or a wilful and obstinate opposition to revealed truth, as taught in the Church of Christ, excludes from the kingdom of God. They are not, however, obliged to believe, that all those are wilfully and obstinately attached to error, who, having been seduced into it by others, or who, having imbibed it from their parents, seek the truth with a cautious solicitude, disposed to embrace it when sufficiently proposed to them; but leaving such persons to the righteous judgment of a merciful God, they feel themselves bound to discharge towards them, as well as towards all mankind, the duties of charity and a social life."

Title II
Government
Section I

The Church of Christ on earth, of which we here treat, is the visible body of true believers under its proper government. (See I, 6.)

1. The government of the church is not of human invention, nor established by the agreement of men; but it is the positive institution of God; and is subject only to the administration of those persons whom he hath commissioned to regulate and carry it on.

2. It is not in the power of men by any convention or law, or act of authority, or of force, to change the nature of that government which our Lord Jesus Christ hath established for his church.

3. We do not believe that our Lord Jesus Christ gave to the civil or temporal governments of states, empires, kingdoms, or nations, any authority in or over spiritual or ecclesiastical concerns.

4. We do not believe that our Lord Jesus Christ gave to the rulers of his church, as such, any authority in or over the civil or temporal concerns of states, empires, kingdoms, or nations.

5. We do not believe that our Lord Jesus Christ hath appointed any special or particular mode of civil or temporal government for mankind, so that men

should be bound by the divine law to adopt or to prefer one mode of civil or temporal government to any other.

6. We believe that as Church government and temporal government are not necessarily united the one to the other, nor dependent the one upon the other; the one unchangeable mode of Church government may therefore continue for ever to subsist, as it hath, during all ages of Christianity, subsisted, in the several nations which have had different modes of temporal government; and that the several members of that one Church may still continue in their respective nations, as they have hitherto been, faithful and meritorious citizens of republics, and loyal subjects of limited or of absolute monarchs. Nor does, therefore, the difference of temporal government in their several nations require or make lawful any change in Church government, so as to assimilate the same to the temporal governments of those several nations.

7. We do not believe that our Lord Jesus Christ gave to the faithful at large the government of the Church, nor any power to regulate spiritual or ecclesiastical concerns; neither do we believe that he gave to the laity nor to any part of the laity such government nor such power, nor any portion of such government or of such power.

8. We believe that our Lord Jesus Christ hath appointed his Apostles the governors of his Church; to be witnesses of his doctrine in Jerusalem and all Judea, and Samaria, and to the very ends of the earth; his ministers the dispensers of the mysteries of God, the Sacraments instituted by our blessed Redeemer; and bishops placed by the Holy Ghost to govern the Church of God, by establishing and preserving wholesome discipline therein.

9. We believe that for the purpose of preserving his Church in unity and in that peace which the world could not give, and of making it one as he and his heavenly Father are one, the Saviour Jesus Christ did establish one chief ruler amongst his Apostles, with a primacy of honour and of jurisdiction: to which supreme ruler every member of the Church ought to pay the reverence and the obedience justly due to a person placed by the divine authority in so eminent a station.

10. We believe that this supremacy in and over the universal church was promised by our blessed Redeemer to Simon the son of Jonas, when the Saviour changed the name of that Apostle to Peter, and that it was conferred upon him principally when our blessed Lord told him that he had prayed for him that his faith should not fail, and exhorted him when he should be converted, to confirm his brethren; and again, when after his resurrection the Saviour having required from him a declaration of greater love, gave to him more extensive authority; to feed his lambs and to feed his sheep: we behold in his subsequent acts, evidence of his exercise of this power, and the same doctrine is testified to us by the Church.

11. We are taught, and do believe that this office of supreme ruler was ordained by our Lord Jesus Christ to remain in the Church during its existence: and we find undoubted evidence that St. Peter, the chief Apostle, did finally establish his seat of authority in the city of Rome, near to which he and the Apostle St. Paul were put to death, and that the power with which he was invested by our blessed Redeemer was thus caused to descend to the Bishops of that Holy See.

12. We also find that the Christian Churches from the beginning did re-

ceive and hold this doctrine of the supremacy of one see, and did recognize and acknowledge the fact, that it was vested in the Bishops of Rome, who have at all times by divine appointment exercised the power thereof, and to which power those churches that did continue in the primitive communion have at all times willingly submitted.

13. We therefore acknowledge the primacy of honour and of spiritual jurisdiction throughout the whole world to be, of divine right, in the Pope or Bishop of Rome, duly and properly appointed; and we pay to him the reverence and the obedience justly due to his eminent station, and we feel it necessary to adhere to his communion and to be subject to his spiritual and ecclesiastical authority.

14) We are not required by our faith to believe that the Pope is infallible, nor do we believe that he is impeccable, for it is not a consequence of his being vested with great authority that he should be exempt from the frailties of human nature; but we do not believe that his authority would be diminished, nor the institutions of our blessed Saviour destroyed, even if the Pope were to be guilty of criminal actions.

15) We do not believe that by virtue of this spiritual or ecclesiastical" authority, the Pope hath any power or right to interfere with the allegiance that we owe to our state; nor to interfere in or with the concerns of the civil policy or the temporal government thereof, or of the United States of America.

16. We believe and acknowledge the majority of the bishops of the church, who are the successors of the apostles, in union with their head aforesaid, to be an ecclesiastical tribunal appointed by our Lord Jesus Christ to decide by his authority, with infallible certainty of truth, in all controversies of doctrine, and to testify truly to us those things which have been revealed by God to man. We also recognize and acknowledge in that same tribunal full power and authority, by the same divine institution.

17. We believe and acknowledge that in the several dioceses, bishops are placed by the Holy Ghost to govern the Church of God. And we acknowledge the bishop regularly appointed, according to the usages of the church, and in due time consecrated according to the form of the same, and holding communion with the Pope, to be the ordinary lawful governor and ecclesiastical legislator of the church of this diocess: to whom we are bound to pay reverence and obedience in all spiritual and ecclesiastical concerns.

18. During the absence of the bishop, we acknowledge the power of governing the church of this diocess in conjunction with him, to be in the vicar whom he may appoint. And even when the bishop may be present, we acknowledge the vicar appointed by him to be vested with such spiritual and ecclesiastical authority as the bishop may specify, and that such vicar is to be respected and obeyed accordingly.

19. During the vacancy of the see, we acknowledge the power of governing the church of this diocess to be in the vicar who may be regularly appointed by the proper ecclesiastical authority; and that such vicar is to be respected and obeyed accordingly.

20. We acknowledge the priests of the church to be, in subordination to the bishop, the preachers of the doctrine of Christ, the ministers of the sacraments, and, when duly appointed, the local rulers of ecclesiastical districts, and that they ought to be respected and obeyed accordingly.

21. As in the church there are other orders of clergymen, who may occasionally receive from the bishop authority to perform those duties of which they are capable: we acknowledge the existence of the orders of deacon and sub-deacon and minor clerks.

22. As our religion was not invented by men, but revealed by God, and as the government of the church was not framed by human convention, nor by human authority, but by the institution and by the authority of our Lord Jesus Christ; we acknowledge its source to be divine; we therefore disavow and disclaim any right or power, under any pretext, in the laity to subject the ministry of the church to their control.

Title III
Property

The maintenance of our church requires that we should have clergymen to perform the ministerial duties, and churches in which they could officiate: for the support of which clergymen, and for the erection and preservation of which churches, temporal means are required. Prudence and charity also demand that in the church there should be, when practicable, funds for other purposes connected with religion.

Section II

Mode of raising, securing, and managing Funds

1. The majority of the lay-members, together with the clergymen of each district, shall from time to time determine upon some mode which, being approved by the bishop, shall be adopted for raising money to meet the exigencies of that district.

2. The churches, cemeteries, lands, houses, funds or other property belonging to any particular district, shall be made the property of the vestry of that district, in trust for the same.

3. The vestry shall not have power to impose or to levy any tax or price upon persons attending religious duties at the church, nor to assess or fix a price for interments in the cemetery, without the consent of the bishop in writing, under his hand and seal, first had and obtained. Nor shall they have power to increase the rate of payment beyond what may be specified in the said instrument.

Section IV

Creation and regulation of property for general purposes.

1. Every member of this church shall pay towards the general fund of the church of this diocess, the sum of fifty cents quarter on the first days of February, of May, of August, and of November in every year; and they whom God hath blessed with means are exhorted to give more abundantly.

2. The purposes to which the general fund is applicable, at the discretion of the convention of the church of this diocess, are:—

1. The erection or improvement of the cathedral, as being the great church of the whole dioceses.
2. The aid of students in theology.
3. Giving aid to missionaries to preach the Gospel.
And after the accomplishment of those objects,
4. Giving aid to small or poor congregations.

Title IV
Membership
Section I

Qualifications, &c.

1. No person shall be considered a member of the Roman Catholic Church of the diocese of Charleston, nor of any Roman Catholic Church within the same, except he have the following qualifications, viz,
1. That he be a man of at least twenty-one years of age.
2. That he be baptized.
3. That he be free from church censures.
4. That he have subscribed his assent to this constitution. And
5. That he be a resident within the diocese, or a clergyman having spiritual jurisdiction therein.

Section II

How Membership may be lost, or regained

1. A member of this church shall lose his rights and privileges in the same, by his own voluntary resignation, or in either of the following modes, viz.:
1. By his defection from the doctrine of the church, or by his wilful and deliberate opposition to its discipline.
2. By knowingly encouraging or tending, in the discharge of any religious duty, any unauthorized clergyman of church.
5 By refusing, during twelve months, to pay the regular and accustomed contributions which are established by this constitution.

Title V.
District Churches
Section I.

How created and regulated.

1. The power of creating a separate church, by the formation of a parochial or other district, belongs to the bishop.
2. When the bishop shall create a separate church, he will give due public notice for a meeting of the members thereof, to be held at some convenient time and place, for the

necessary purposes consequent upon such creation, at which meeting he or his deputy will preside.

3. At this meeting the members will, by a majority of votes, determine what are to be the special qualifications, if any, in addition to membership for voters in that district, and for vestrymen therein; also how many lay members shall serve in the vestry. They shall then proceed to elect by ballot so many discreet, well-conducted men, having a regard for religion, and if possible, persons who are in the habit of receiving the sacrament of the holy Eucharist; and those laymen, together with the clergyman or clergymen of that district, shall be the vestry of the same, and shall continue in office during one year.

4. Those special qualifications for voters and for vestrymen in any district, and also the number of laymen to serve in the vestry thereof, may be altered by the majority of voters, at a general meeting of the members of that district, specially convened for that purpose after at least ten days' public notice; but such alteration shall not be of force until it shall have been approved of by the bishop or vicar.

5. The members qualified to vote in each district shall . . . assemble in the church. . . and there by ballot elect the proper number of qualified laymen—who, together with the clergy, shall be the vestry thereof . . . until their successors shall be elected and admitted into office. But should the election, by any cause, not have been held on the first Sunday in January, it shall be held as soon as possible thereafter, upon public notice of at least one week, which the clergyman shall give.

6. The laymen elected to serve upon the vestry shall, before entering into office, subscribe in presence of the clergyman, if he be in the district, and of the congregation, the proper declaration and promise.

7. No person elected to serve upon the vestry can, during the year of his office, be removed therefrom, except by 1. His voluntary resignation. 2. His refusal or neglect during one month to qualify; or 3. His loss of membership.

8. Should there be a vacancy in the vestry by reason of death, removal the district, or either of the causes in the foregoing clause, the same as soon as possible be filled up by an election to be held for that special purpose after a public notice of at least one week from the clergyman.

9. When the clergyman is present, the elections shall be conducted under his regulations; in his absence, they will be conducted by the secretary and the wardens then in office.

Each separate church thus formed shall have power to make by-laws for its own special regulation in the following manner, provided they be not inconsistent with this constitution: 1. Such by-law must be an act of vestry 2. It must be confirmed by a majority of the members of that church who be present at a public meeting . . . and 3. It must be approved of by bishop or vicar.

Section II.

Mode of proceeding, power and duty of the vestry.

1. In the meetings of the vestry, the principal clergyman who may be gent is to be president; and in order to proceed to business, the presence of one clergyman and of three laymen shall be necessary. But if there be no clergyman resident in the district, the lay-

men may proceed to business, and procure the subsequent confirmation of their acts by the proper clergyman.

2. For the validity of an act of vestry there will be required the assent majority of the lay-members who may be present, and of the proper clergyman—or in case of the refusal of the clergyman, the assent of the bishop or of the vicar.

3. But in making contracts or agreements for the performance of any work or duty which shall have been directed by an act of vestry, and in all elections and appointments to be made by the vestry, no clergyman shall have a negative power, but shall only possess his right of precedence and right of vote.

4. At all meetings of the vestry, the president, or, in his absence from district, the layman who may take the chair, shall, in case of an equality rotes, have a second or casting vote, so as to enable the meeting to decide.

5. When the vestry assembles without the clergyman, the chair shall be taken by one of the wardens, according to the precedence of the name upon the entry of their appointment; and if the wardens be absent, by that vestryman whose name stands first upon the list of their appointment.

6. It shall be the duty of the vestry to exert themselves to procure for the bishop and the clergymen of their own district decent and comfortable support; to have the church and other buildings kept in good order and repair, and to provide all the necessaries therefor, according to the means which they shall be able to procure; to provide and to keep in order a burial ground for the interment of members . . . and to see that the church property intrusted to their care be well preserved and improved, and faithfully administered.

7. The vestry have the right of electing the organist, the clerk, the sexton, and the other lay-officers or servants of the church; also they have the appointment of their own secretary and treasurer, and of the church wardens of their district, and of the collector of the general fund within the same. The church wardens shall be chosen from amongst the lay-members of the vestry. The treasurer, the secretary, and the collector for the general fund may be chosen by the vestry either from amongst their own body, or from the other members of the church.

8. The bishop or the clergyman of the district has a right and power, whenever he may see a cause to suspend the organist, the clerk, the sexton, or any other lay-officer or servant of the church. But the church warden, the secretary, or treasurer of the vestry, or the collector for the general fund, are only removable by an act of vestry.

9. The vestry shall every year lay a fair and correct statement of their accounts and of the situation of the church before the congregation, and another such statement before the bishop previous to the first Sunday in January. And they shall also furnish and exhibit their accounts at any other time to the bishop, and to the congregation when called upon by either of them to do so.

10. Should the vestry of the district be displeased with the conduct or the proceedings of the clergyman of the same, they shall have power, upon sufficient notice from the secretary, who must issue such notice upon the requisition in writing of two vestrymen, signed by them, to assemble without the clergyman, for the sole purpose of conferring together upon their cause of complaint and of embodying the same in writing; to be immediately transmitted to the bishop or vicar for his judgment thereupon; but which complaint they shall not publish in any other way without the leave, in writing, of the bishop or vicar first had and obtained therefor.

11. Should the vestry of any district lodge a regular complaint in the manner prescribed against the clergyman of the same, the bishop or vicar will, as soon as possible,

diligently inquire into the same; and as soon as may be, give his judgment and decision to the best of his ability for the benefit of religion and according to the canons and usages of the church: and the vestry will support and accede to such decision, unless they shall see cause for making their appeal to a superior ecclesiastical tribunal; in which case they shall abide by the said decision, until it shall have been set aside by such competent superior ecclesiastical tribunal; and in case such tribunal shall not set aside such decision, it shall be considered final and conclusive.

Section III

Duties and Powers of Officers.

1. The duty of the secretary shall be to summon and to attend at all meetings of the vestry; to keep a fair record of their acts and appointments and resolutions, and when necessary to publish or to furnish extracts of the same; to sign their orders upon the treasurer when duly passed; to inform the bishop or vicar, when by him duly required, of their proceedings; to make out such report of their proceedings as may be required by the convention of the church of the diocess, or by the delegates of the district; and to notify to the vestry or to the church of the district such directions or information as may be conveyed to him for that purpose by the general trustees, or by the convention of the church, or by the bishop or vicar, or by the See of Rome.

2. The duty of the treasurer shall be, to keep fair and plain accounts of the income, and expenditure, and of the property of the church of that district; to collect the money payable to its use or due thereto; when necessary, to sue for the same; to have charge of the money and other valuable property of the church; except the sacred vessels and vestments, of which the clergyman shall have charge, and for which he shall be accountable to the proper ecclesiastical persons; to pay, as far as the funds in his hands will allow, all orders of the vestry signed by the secretary and approved by the proper clergyman; to render an exact and fair statement of all his accounts on the first day of January in each year to the bishop, and another to the vestry at the same time, and also to the bishop and to the vestry when so required by either of them.

3. The duty of the church wardens shall be, to superintend the execution of any work ordered or contracted for by the vestry; to preserve in decency and repair the buildings and other property of the church; to aid the clergyman in preserving order and decency in the church, to remove therefrom all disturbers or nuisances.

Title VI
The Convention
Section I

Composition, and mode of assembling.

1. There shall be held yearly in some convenient part of the diocess, to be designated by the bishop or vicar, and at the time by him appointed, a convention of this church, which shall consist of the following portions, which shall hold their sessions separately, viz.:

    1. The bishop, or in his absence the vicar.

… Appendix content …

2. The clergy having spiritual jurisdiction in the diocess and not claiming any exemption from the bishop's ordinary jurisdiction, nor any special privileges except such as may arise from the special act of the bishop, or from statutes of the diocess.

3. The lay-delegates from the districts of the diocess.

2. The bishop, or in his absence, the vicar, will give at least two months' public notice of the time and place of holding the convention, as well by one or more public advertisements in the newspapers, as also by special letter to each clergyman who is entitled to a seat; the clergymen shall also publish the same to their respective flocks.

3. Upon the creation of a new district the bishop will specify how many lay delegates shall be elected therefrom to the next convention, which number shall be elected and admitted accordingly.

4. The delegates of the laity to the convention from each district shall be men having the qualifications which, in that district, are required for members of the vestry, and they shall be chosen by the voters of that district, upon due notice to be given by the vestry of the time and place for holding the election, within six weeks preceding the day for holding the convention, the election to be conducted in the same manner as that for electing the vestry.

5. The districts of the diocess shall be ranked from time to time by the house of lay delegates according to the Catholic population, as of the first, second, and third rank; districts of the first rank shall, during their being so classed, send four delegates to the convention; districts of the second rank, two delegates; and districts of the third rank, one delegate; and each district will contribute its proportion to defray the expense of the Convention.

The bishop or vicar will judge of the qualifications of the clergy; the house of lay delegates will judge of the qualifications of its own members.

Section II

Order of proceeding

1. The clergyman highest in dignity, and if there be no precedence in dignity, the clergyman senior in ordination shall be president of the house of the clergy.

2. The house of the laity will choose its own president.

3. Each house shall appoint its own officers and servants, and regulate the internal order of its own proceedings.

4. When a majority of both houses shall have met, and the presidents have been ascertained, they will inform the bishop of the same, and he will appoint the time when the convention will be opened.

5. The convention will be opened with a solemn mass.

6. After mass each house shall meet apart for business, and the bishop will cause to be laid before them the treasurer's account, the report of the general trustees, and any other documents and communications which may be necessary.

7. Neither house shall adjourn, except from one period to another of the same day, or from day to day, before the third day of business, unless with the consent of the bishop. And after the dissolution of the convention, neither house shall meet, except it be specially convened for some particular purpose by the bishop or vicar.

Section III

Powers

1. The convention has no power or authority to interfere respecting any of the following subjects, viz.:
    1. The doctrine of the church.
    2. The discipline of the church.
    3. The administration of sacraments.
    4. The ceremonies of the church.
    5. Spiritual jurisdiction.
    6. Ecclesiastical appointments.
    7. Ordinations.
    8. The superintendence of the clergy.

2. The convention is not to be considered as a portion of the ecclesiastical government of the church; but the two houses are to be considered rather as a body of sage, prudent, and religious counsellors to aid the proper ecclesiastical governor of the church in the discharge of his duty, by their advice and exertions in obtaining and applying the necessary pecuniary means to those purposes which will be most beneficial, and in superintending the several persons who have charge thereof; to see that the money be honestly and beneficially expended; wherefore the convention has the following powers, viz.:
    1. To dispose of the general fund of the church in the way that it may deem most advantageous.
    2. To examine into, and to control the expenditures made by its own order or by that of a former convention.
    3. To examine into, regulate and control, with the exception of their spiritual concerns, all establishments of its own creation; or which being otherwise created may be regularly subjected to its control.
    4. To appoint the lay-officers and servants of such establishments.
    5. The house of the clergy has power to examine into the ecclesiastical concerns of such establishments, and to make its private report thereon to the bishop or vicar, together with its opinion and advice, but such report of advice shall not be published in any other way, without the consent of the bishop or vicar first had and obtained in writing under his hand and seal.

3. In those cases where the convention has no authority to act, should her house feel itself called upon by any peculiar circumstances to submit advice, or to present a request to the bishop, he will bestow upon the same the best consideration at the earliest opportunity; and as far as his conscientious obligations will permit, and the welfare of the church will allow, and the honour and glory of Almighty God, in his judgment require, he will endeavour to follow such advice or to agree to such request.

4. No act shall be considered a valid act of the convention except it all have been passed by a majority of the clergy and by a majority of the use of the laity, and been assented to by the bishop or vicar.

5. In all elections to trust, or places or offices, the decision will be made by a majority of the clergy and laity voting conjointly, and their choice assented to by the bishop, except when in any instance a different ode of election shall have been specially provided for.

Title VII
Amendment of Constitution
Section I

What parts may not be altered.

1. There are parts of this Constitution which are of the doctrine of the Holy Roman Catholic and Apostolic Church—of course they are part of the revelation of God; they are unchangeable, for we have no power to add the revelation of God, nor to take from it. Those parts may be known by e decision of the bishop, or in case of an appeal from his decision, by the testimony and decision of the See of Rome; which decision shall be final id conclusive.
2. There are parts of this Constitution which are matter of divine institution, they are unchangeable; for no human power has authority to change the institutions of God. Those parts which are of divine institution may be known in the same manner as those parts which are of doctrine.
3. There are parts of this Constitution which are of the general discipline of the Holy Roman Catholic and Apostolic Church: those parts, so far as regards our power are unchangeable; because the Church of the diocess of Charleston, being only a very small portion of the Universal Church, is bound by the general laws of the same, and bath not authority alter the enactments of the supreme legislature of that body, of which it so small a particle: neither hath it power to withdraw itself from the observance of the general discipline of the Universal Church, without thereby separating from its communion, and thus incurring the guilt of schism. Those parts which are of such general discipline may be known in the same manner as those which are of doctrine, or those parts which are of divine institution.

Section II

What part the Bishop may change

1. There are parts of this Constitution which are part of the special ecclesiastical discipline of the diocess of Charleston, and which are enacted by the bishop, who by divine institution is the proper and competent ecclesiastical legislator thereof: those parts are distinguished from the former as they relate only to this diocess, and from the parts recited in Section III, and may be known by the bishop's testimony and decision, which in that case is final and conclusive.
2. Those parts of this Constitution which are of the special ecclesiastical discipline of the diocess of Charleston, may by the bishop of the diocess, be altered and amended as he may see cause; especially after he shall have advised with the diocesan synod thereupon, according to the canons and usages of the church; but such consultation, though useful, is not essential.
3. But the said special discipline of the diocess of Charleston, and its alterations and amendments, must be not in opposition to, but in conformity with the doctrine and general discipline of the church, and the divine institutions; upon all which matters, in case of doubt, or of appeal, the supreme See of Rome is to judge and determine; and such judgment and determination shall be final and conclusive.

Section III

What parts many be amended by the Convention, and how

1. The parts of this Constitution, which regard the collection and regulation of property, the appointment of trustees, and lay-officers, and servants; the qualifications for lay-delegates, and vestrymen, and voters, and generally all the parts thereof which are not of, or belonging to the divine institution, or the doctrine or general discipline of the church, or the special diocess of Charleston, may be altered and amended in the following manner only, viz.:

    1. A copy of the proposed alteration, addition, or amendment shall be laid before the bishop with a request to know whether the same is compatible with the doctrine and the general discipline of the church, and with the special discipline of this diocess, and with the divine institutions.

    2. Should the bishop answer that he judges such alteration, and so forth, to be so compatible, the said propositions, in the same words in which they shall have been returned by the bishop, shall be submitted to the two houses of the convention, and if a majority of each house should concur in their support, they shall be submitted to the bishop for his approbation.

    3. Should the bishop approve the alterations so concurred in, he will send copies thereof to the several vestries of the diocess, who will, as soon as may be, signify their assent or dissent to the bishop.

    4. Should two-thirds in number of the vestries approve of the propositions so sent to them, and the bishop continue of the same judgment as before, he will at the next convention signify the same to both houses, and the said proposed alterations, or additions, or amendments shall then be finally submitted to the decision of those houses, and should a majority in each house be in favour of the same, they shall then be part of this Constitution.

2. But should a majority of both houses differ from the bishop respecting the nature of the said proposed alterations, as to their compatibility with the doctrine and general discipline of the church, or the divine institution, they may of course appeal from his judgment to the See of Rome, but pending the appeal they must conform to his judgment.

3. And should the judgment of the bishop be set aside upon such appeal, he shall not thereby lose his power of assent or dissent which he possesses as one branch of the convention.

Digested from: Ignatius A. Reynolds (ed.), *The Works of the Right Reverend John England*, V, 91-108.

Selected Bibliography

Primary Works:

England, John, Rt. Rev. *The Works of the Rt. Rev. John England.* Sebastian G. Messmer, ed. 7 vols. Cleveland: Clark, 1908.

──────. *The Works: Bishop John England (1786-1842).* Edited by Ignatius A. Reynolds. 5 vols. Baltimore: Murphy, 1849.

──────. *Letters on the Subject of Domestic Slavery.* New York: Negro Universities Press, 1969.

──────. *Letters Concerning the Roman Chancery.* Baltimore: Fielding Lucas, 1840.

──────. "Diurnal of the Rt. Rev. John England, 1820-1823." Records, A.C.H.S. 6 (1895): 29-55; 184-224.

──────. "Papers Relating to the Church in America" 2nd series. *Records, A.C.H.S.* 7 (1896): 454-492.

──────. "Papers Relating to the Church in America" 3rd series *Records, A.C.H.S.* 8 (1897): 294-329.

──────. "Papers Relating to the Church in America" 4th series. *Records, A.C.H.S.* 8 (1897): 454-463; 468-475; 195-240.

──────. "Letters from the Rt. Rev. John England, D.D., to the Honorable William Gaston" (1821-1840). *Records, A.C.H.S.* 18 (1907): 367-388.

──────. "Letters from the Rt. Rev. John England, D.D., to the Honorable William Gaston". *Records, A.S.H.S.* 19 (1908): 98-121; 140-184.

Secondary Sources on Bishop John England:

Carey, Patrick Wayne. "John England and Irish American Catholicism, 1815-1842: A Study of Conflict." (Ph.D. dissertation, Fordham, 1975).

──────. *An Immigrant Bishop: John England's Adaptation of Irish*

Catholicism to American Republicanism. New York: United States Catholic Historical Society, 1982.

———. *People, Priests, and Prelates: Ecclesiastical Democracy and the Tensions of Trusteeism.* Notre Dame: University of Notre Dame, 1987.

Clarke, Peter. *A Free Church in a Free Society: The Ecclesiology of John England, Bishop of Charleston, 1820-1842, a 19th Century Missionary Bishop in the Southern United States.* Greenwood, SC: Center for John England Studies, 1982.

Guilday, Peter K. "Church Reconstruction Under Bishop England: 1822-1842." *American Ecclesiastical Review* 68 (1923): 135-147.

———. "John England: Catholic Champion." *Historical Records and Studies, U.S.C.H.S.* 18 (1928) 172-173.

———. *The Life and Times of John England.* 2 vols. New York: America Press, 1927.

Kaib, Sr. Virginia Lee. "The Ecclesiology of John England, the First Bishop of Charleston, South Carolina. (Ph.D. dissertation, Marquette University, 1968).

Kearns, Daniel F. "Bishop John England and the Possibilities of Catholic Republicanism." *South Carolina Historical Magazine.* 102 (2001): 47-67.

Kelly, Joseph. "Charleston's Bishop John England and American Slavery." *New Hibernia Review* 5(2001): 48-56.

Kenrick, Francis Patrick. (unsigned) "The Works of John England." *Brownson's Quarterly Review* 7 (1850): 137-159.

LeBuffe, Leon A. "Tension in American Catholicism, 1820-1870: An Intellectual History." (PH.D dissertation, Catholic University of America, 1973).

Rousseau, Richard W. "Bishop John England and American Church-State Theory." (Ph.D. dissertation, St. Paul's University, Ottawa, 1969).

Saunders, R. Frank, and George Rogers. "Bishop John England of Charleston: Catholic Spokesman and Southern Intellectual." *Journal of the Early Republic.* 13(Fall, 1993): 301-322.

Theological Studies:

Baxter, Michael J. "Catholicism and Liberalism: Kudos and Questions for *Communio* Ecclesiology," *Review of Politics*, 60(1998) 4, 743-764.

Congar, Yves. *Lay People in the Church.* Westminster, MD: Newman, 1957.

DeLubac, Henri. *The Mystery of the Supernatural.* NY: Crossroad/ Herder, 1998.
Denzinger, Heirnrich and Adolf Schonmetzer. *Enchiridion Symbolorum.* NY: Herder, 1967.
Gaillardetz, Richard R. *Teaching With Authority: A Theology of the Magisterium in the Church.* Collegeville: Michael Glazier, 1997.
Hauerwas, Stanley, and Charles Pinches. *Christian Among the Virtues: Theological Conversations with Ancient and Modern Ethics.* Notre Dame: ND Univ. Press, 1997.
McCool, Gerald. *Catholic Theology in the Nineteenth century: The Quest for a Unitary Method.* New York: Seabury, 1977.
MacIntyre, Alasdair. *After Virtue*, Notre Dame, IN: University of Notre Dame Press, 1981.
———. *Whose Justice? Whose Rationality?* Notre Dame, 1988.
Murray, John Courtney. "Contemporary Orientations of Catholic Thought on Church and State in the Light of History." *Theological Studies* 10 (1949): 177-234.
———. "The Problem of State Religion." *Theological Studies* 12 (1951): 155-178.
Noonan, John T. *A Church That Can and Cannot Change.* Notre Dame: University of Notre Dame, 2005.
Plantinga, Alvin, and Jonathan Kvanvig, *Warrant in Comteporary Epistemology: Essays in Honor of Alvin Plantinga's Theory of Knowledge.* Lanham, MD, Rowman & Littlefield, 1996.
Schindler, David. *Heart of the World, Center of the Church: Communio Ecclesiology.* Grand Rapids: Eerdmans, 1996.
———. "Introduction." Henri De Lubac. *The Mystery of the Supernatural.* NY: Crossroad/Herder, 1998, xi-xxxi.
Schoof, T.M. *A Survey of Catholic Theology, 1800-1970.* Paramus, NJ: Paulist-Newman, 1970.
Thiel, John E. *Imagination and Authority: Theological Authorship in the Modern Tradition.* Minneapolis: Fortress, 1991.

General Studies:

Appleby, Joyce. *Liberalism and Republicanism in the Historical Imagination.* Cambridge, MA: Harvard, 1992.
Billington, Ray Allen. *The Protestant Crusade.* New York: Rinehart, 1952.

Burstein, Andrew. *The Passions of Andrew Jackson.* NY: Knopf, 2003.
Cornelius, Janet Duitsman. *When I Can Read My Title Clear: Literacy, Slavery and Religion in the Antebellum South.* Columbia, SC: Univ. of South Carolina Press, 1991.
Dunn, Stephen. *The Highland Settler.* Toronto, Univ. of Toronto, 1953.
Foner, Eric. *Free Soil, Free Labor, and Free Men: The Ideology of the Republican Party Before the Civil War.* London: Oxford, 1970.
Gaustad, Edwin S. *Neither King Nor Prelate: Religion and the New Nation, 1776-1826.* Grand Rapids: Eerdmanns, 1993.
Gay, Peter. *The Enlightenment.* 2 vols. New York: Random House, 1966. (reprint Norton, 1995, 1996.)
Hofstadter, Richard, William Miller, and Daniel Aaron. *The American Republic.* Vol. 1. Englewood Cliffs: Prentice-Hall, 1959.
Holifield, E. Brooks. *Theology in America: Christian Thought from the Age of the Puritans to the Civil War.* New Haven: Yale, 2003.
Honohan, Iseult. *Civic Republicanism.* NY: Routledge, 2002.
Jones, James, Jr. "Montesquieu and Jefferson Revisited," *The French Review.* 51(1978) 4:577-585.
Locke, John. *The Selected Political Writings of John Locke.* Paul Sigmund, ed. NY: Norton, 2005.
McWilliams, Wilson Carey. The *Idea of Fraternity in America.* Berkeley: California, 1973.
Miller, Perry. *The Life of the Mind in America: From the Revolution to the Civil War.* NY: Harcourt, Brace and World, 1965.
O'Brien, David and David Moltke., eds. *Intellectual Life in Ante-Bellum Charleston.* Knoxville: University of Tennessee, 1986.
Pettit, Philip. *Republicanism: a Theory of Freedom and Government.* NY: Oxford, 1997.
Peirce, Charles S. *The Essential Peirce,* 2 vols. The Peirce Edition Project. (Indianapolis: Univ. of Indiana, 1991, 1998.
Porter, Roy. *The Enlightenment.* 2nd ed., NY: Palgrave/ MacMillan, 2001.
Remini, Robert V. *Andrew Jackson: The Course of American Empire, 1767-1821.* Baltimore: Johns Hopkins, reprint 1998.
Rogers, Daniel. "Republicanism: The Career of a Concept." *Journal of American History* 12 (June, 1992): 11-38.
Schlesinger, Arthur M., Jr. *The Age of Jackson.* London: Eyre and Spottswoods, 1946.
De Tocqueville, Alexis. *Democracy in America.* New York: Mentor, 1956.

Watson, Harry. *Liberty and Power: The Politics of Jacksonian America.* NY: Noonday Press, 1990.
Watts, Stephen. *The Republic Reborn: War and the Making of Liberal America, 1790-1820.* Baltimore: Johns Hopkins, 1987.
Wilentz, Sean. *The Rise of American Democracy: Jefferson to Lincoln.* NY: W.W. Norton, 2005.

Church History Studies:

Baisnee, Jules A. *France and the Establishment of the American Catholic Hierarchy.* Baltimore: Johns Hopkins, 1934.
Baltimore, Provincial Council 1829. *Concilia Provincialia Baltimori, Habita ab Anno, 1849.* Baltimore, Joannem Murphy, 1851.
Baxter, Michael J. "Notes on Catholic Americanism and Catholic Radicalism: Toward a Counter-Tradition of Catholic Social Ethics. In Sandra Slocum Mize and William Portier, eds. *American Catholic Traditions: Resources for Renewal.* Maryknoll: Orbis, 1997.
―――――. "Writing History in a World Without Ends: An Evangelical Catholic Critique of Three Histories of Catholicism in the United States." *Pro Ecclesia.* Fall, 1996.
―――――. "The Unsettling of Americanism: A Response to William Portier," *Communio* 27(2000) 161-170.
Capizzi, Joseph. "For What Shall We Repent? Reflections on the American Bishops, Their Teaching and Slavery in the United States, 1839-1861." *Theological Studies,* 65(2004) 767-791.
Caravaglios, Maria Genoino. *The American Catholic Church and the Negro Problem in the Eighteenth and Nineteenth Centuries.* Rome: Gregorianum, 1974.
Carey, Patrick W. ed. *American Catholic Religious Thought.* Mahwah, NJ: Paulist, 1987.
Carthy, Sr. Mary Peter. *English Influence on Early American Catholicism.* Washington: Catholic University, 1959.
Casey, Thomas F. *The Sacred Congregation de Propaganda Fide and the Revision of the First Provincial Council of Baltimore, in the United States.* New York: Kenedy, 1879.
Ellis, John Tracy. "Church and State: An American Tradition." *Catholic Mind* 52 (1954): 209-216.
―――――. *Documents of American Church History.* Chicago: Regnery,

1967.

Guilday, Peter K. "Arthur O'Leary." *Catholic Historical Review* 9 (1923-24): 530-545.

―――――. *The History of the Councils of Baltimore.* New York: MacMillan, 1932.

―――――. *The Life and Times of John Carroll.* New York: 1922. Reprinted ed. Westminster: Newman, 1954.

―――――. *The National Pastorals:1790-1919.* Westminster: Newman, 1954.

―――――. "Trusteeism." *Historical Records and Studies* 18 (1928): 7-73.

Hennessey, James. "Papacy and Episcopacy in Eighteenth and Nineteenth Century American Catholic Thought." *Records*, A.C.H.S. 77 (1966): 175-189.

Kauffman, Christopher. *Tradition and Transformation in Catholic Culture: The History of the Priests of St. Sulpice, 1791 to the Present.* NY: MacMillan, 1988.

―――――. gen. ed. "*Dignitatis Humanae*: The Declaration of Religious Liberty, on its 40th Anniversary," *U. S. Catholic Historian* 24(2006)1: (entire issue).

Kenneally, Finbar. *United States Documents on the Propaganda Fide Archives: A Calendar.* 6 vols. Washington: Academy of American Franciscan History, 1966.

Kenrick, Francis Patrick. "Papers Relating to the Church in America." 1st series. *Records* A.C.H.S. 7 (1896): 283-388.

Larkin, Emmet. "Church and State in Ireland in the Nineteenth Century." *Church History* 31 (1962): 295-306.

Lynch, Patrick. "Reports of Bishop Lynch of Charleston, South Carolina, Commissioner of the Confederate States to the Holy See." *American Catholic Historical Researches* 22 (1905): 248-259.

McGreevy, John T. *Catholicism and American Freedom.* NY: Norton, 2003.

MacSuibhne, Patrick. "The Early History of Carlow College." *Irish Ecclesiastical Record,* 5th series. 62 (1943): 230-248.

McAvoy, Thomas. "The Catholic Minority on the United States, 1789-1821." *Historical Records and Studies* 39-40 (1952): 33-50.

―――――. "The Formation of the American Catholic Minority, 1820-1860." *The Review of Politics* 10 (1948): 13-34.

MacKenzie, Archibald J. "Christmas Island Parish," in *Mosgladh*, n.s. 8, n. 5, 1931.

McNamara, Robert F. "Trusteeism in the Atlantic States: 1785-1863."

Catholic Historical Review 30 (1944): 135-154.
McNeil, Lou. ed. *Moving Beyond Confined Circles: The Home Mission Writings of William Howard Bishop.* Atlanta: Glenmary, 1990.
———. "Catholic Mission," in Bill Leonard, ed. *Christianity in Appalachia.* Knoxville: University of Tennessee, 1998.
Miller, Randall, and Jon Wakelyn. *Catholics in the Old South: Essays on Church and Culture.* Macon, GA: Mercer University Press, 1983.
Moody, Joseph N. "American Catholicism's Influence on Europe." *Historical Records and Studies.* U.S.C.H.S. 38 (1950): 1-21.
Murphy, Miriam. "Catholic Missionary Work Among the Coloured People of the United States, 1776-1866." *Records,* A.C.H.S. 35 (1924): 101-135.
O'Brien, David. *Public Catholicism.* NY: MacMillan, 1989.
O'Connell, Jeremiah J. *Catholicity in the Carolinas and Georgia.* New York: Sadlier, 1879.
Panzer, Joel S. "The Popes and Slavery: Setting the Record Straight," http://www.cfpeople.org/Apologetics/pages51a003.hmtl (accessed March 28, 2005).
Portier, William L. "Americanism and Inculturation," *Communio* 27 (2000) 139-160.
Rice, Madeleine Hook. *American Catholic Opinion in the Slavery Controversy.* New York: Columbia Press, 1944.
Theobald, Stephen L. "Catholic Missionary Work Among the Coloured People of the United States, 1776-1866." *Records,* A.C.H.S. 35 (1924): 325-344.
Willging, Eugene, and Herta Hatzfield. *Catholic Serials of the Nineteenth Century in the United States of America:Part II.* Wash., DC: CUA Press, 1968.
Witte, John Jr. *God's Joust, God's Justice: Law and Religion in the Western Tradition.* Grand Rapids: Eerdmans, 2006.

Index

Adams, John, 184
Appleby, Joyce, 154
Arupe, Pedro 5, 6, 50, 99
Aquinas, 90, 153, 188, 191, 233
Aristotle, 119
Augustine 90, 126, 185, 191

Bachman, Rev. 119
Bailly, G, 28, 53, 190
Ball, Terence, 154
Bancroft, George, 58
Baum, Gregory, 1
Baxter, Michael, 17, 96-97, 100-101, 103, 150, 154, 175, 211, 214
Beecher, Lyman, 55
Bellah, Robert, 185, 212-213
Bellarimine, Robert, 123, 152, 207
Bilbo, Theodore, 201
Billington, Ray, 61-62, 66, 83-84
Blondell, Maurice, 5, 16
Bokenkotter, Thomas, 84-85, 150, 213
Bolivar, Simon, 119
Bowen, Dr., 129
Brennan, James, 30, 53
Browne, Robert, Fr., 67, 75
Brownson, Orestes, 58
Bryan, William Jennings, 201
Brunini, Joseph, Bp., 82
Brutte, Bp., 79

Calhoun, John C., 59
Calvert, Cecil (Lord Baltimore), 177
Calvin, John, 107, 127, 152, 186, 225

Capizzi, Joseph, 199, 214
Caravaglios, Maria, 214
Carey, Patrick, 9, 17, 30-31, 38, 53, 54. 65, 76, 85, 87, 151, 153, 173, 176-177, 182-183, 209, 211-212
Caro, Robert, 56, 83, 233
Carroll, Charles, 61
Carroll, John, Abp., 1, 3, 7, 13, 49, 64, 67, 232
Casey, Thomas F. 84, 87
Chateaubriand, Francois, 212
Churchill, Winston, 113
Cicero, 119
Clarke, Peter, 86
Cloriviere, Fr., 67
Collins, Mary, 154
Connolly, John, 25, 44
Consalvi, Cardinal, 63, 110
Conwell, Henry, 25, 44, 65, 79
Congar, Yves, 5, 16
Copleston, Frederick, 151
Coppinger, Bp., 33
Cornelius, Janet Duitsman, 214
Crisp, Roger, 154
Cullen, Paul Cardinal, 79, 147, 162

Daugherty, Mary Lee, 165, 210
David, Bishop, 111, 144
Day, Dorothy, 18
Dearden, John Card. 95, 232
DelaHogue, Louis 28-29, 53, 190
Delaruelle, Emile, 213
DeLugo, Juan, 123, 125, 152
DeLubac, Henri, 5, 17, 99, 102, 150, 175, 218
DeMastre, Comte Joseph, 63

257

Index of Names

DeToqueville, A., 36, 147, 188, 191, 213, 233
Douglas, Mary, 222
Doyle, Bp., 28, 35
Drey, J.S., 31-32, 42, 125-126, 217, 233
Dubois, Bp., 78-79
Dulles, Avery, 17, 101, 204, 215
Dunn, Stephen, 210
Dworetz, Steven, 213

Ellis, John Tracey, 85
England, Thomas, 27
Eagan, Bp., 44
Eccleston, Arbp., 208
Emerson, H.W., 188
Evans, Jeanne, 57

Fackenheim, Emil, 2
Fenwick, Benedict, 20, 67, 70, 74
Fontana, Cardinal, 19-20
Forsyth, John, 198, 224
Ford, John T., 154
Francis of Assisi, 224
Franklin, Benjamin, 21
Freemantle, Anne, 85
Frost, Robert, 38, 222
Frye, Northrop, 2

Gabriels, Bp., 183
Gaillardetz, Richard, 74, 86, 152
Gallagher, Felix, 67, 75
Gaston, John, 76, 168, 204
Gibbons, James Cardinal, 49, 95
Goodwyn, Lawrence, 215
Gramsci, Antonio, 113, 202
Greeley, Andrew, 86
Green, Duff, 194, 224
Gregory XVI, 49, 64, 84, 86, 91-93, 100, 108, 149, 181, 187, 198, 207, 221
Guilday, Peter K., 21, 51-54, 80, 83, 85-86, 111, 151, 153, 209, 211-215

Habermas, Jurgen, 127, 153
Haight, Roger, 54
Hamilton, Alexander, 41, 157
Hanley, Thomas, 84
Harrison, William H., 119, 194, 198-199
Hart, Ray L., 153
Hartz, Louis, 15, 17
Hartzfield, Herta, 150
Hauerwas, Stanley, 38, 90, 103, 151, 154, 209
Hayes, Richard, 68
Hebermann, Charles G., 20, 51
Hegel, Georg, 112, 151
Hennessey, James, 52
Hermes, 125
Herr, Dan, 154
Hill, Harvey, 83-84
Hofstader, Richard, 83
Hogan, William, 65
Holifield, E. Brooks, 161, 209, 211
Hooke, J., 29, 190
Hutchinson, Christopher, 33
Hughes, John, Arbp., 44
Hughes, Thomas, 85, 151

Ignatius of Loyola, 224
Ireland, John, Abp., 49

Jackson, Andrew, 56-57
Jefferson, Thomas, 2, 42, 57, 154, 182, 233
John XXIII, 231
Jones, James F., 233
Justin, Martyr, 224, 230

Kaib, Virginia, 52
Kauffman, Christopher, 54, 86, 152, 183, 209-210, 212
Kearns, Daniel F., 22, 36, 50, 53-54, 69, 86, 106, 150
Kelly, Patrick, Bp. 20, 44, 48
Kenneally, Finbar, 54, 87, 151

Index of Names

Kenrick, P. F. Bp., 28, 52, 65, 79, 86, 132, 147, 154, 158, 183, 209
Kirvan, John J., 153
Kohlman, Anthony, 79
Komonchak, Joseph, 154, 209

LaGrange, P., 5, 16.
Lambruschini, Card., 64
Lamenais, Felicite, 63, 84, 93, 149
Lane, Dermot, 154
LaRochefoucald, 217
Latourette, Kenneth Scott, 84, 150
Law, Bernard Cardinal, 83
LeBuffe, Leon, 34, 52, 215
Leo XII, 61, 63-64
Leo XIII, 17, 95, 179
Lincoln, Abraham, 226
Lindbeck, George, 128, 153
Lonergan, Bernard, 2, 96, 99
Long, Huey, 201
Longenecker, Richard, 2
Locke, John, 35, 53, 148-149, 154, 182, 184, 186-187, 213, 225, 233
Lukes, Steven, 206, 215
Luther, Martin, 90, 107, 127, 185-186, 191, 225
Luzbetak, Louis, 5, 17

Madison, James, 41, 182
MacKenzie, Archibald, 210
MacIntyre, Alasdair, 103-104, 150, 154, 209
Marechal, Ambrose, Abp. 19-22, 25, 67-68, 77-78, 117, 151, 162, 208, 228-229
Marechal, Joseph, 5, 16
Maritain, Jacques, 5
Marx, Karl, 3
Mast, Dolorita, Sr. 86
McAvoy, Thomas, 61, 66, 84-85
McCarthy, Mary P. 84
McCarthy, Thomas, 153
McCool, Gerald, 31, 53, 125, 152

McGreevy, John T., 24, 52, 84n.
McLuhan, Marshall, 2
Meyer, Albert Cardinal, 222
McNamara, Robert 85
McNeil, Lou, 57, 211
McNeill, John T., 91, 149
McNichols, Abp., 95
McSorley, Harry, 1, 153
Millar, Francis X., 212
Montesquieu, Charles, 35, 148-149, 154, 182, 184, 190, 225, 233
Morse, Samuel, 177
Moylan, Bp., 32, 42
Murphy, Bp., 33, 47
Murray, John Courtney, 95, 100, 103-104, 150, 161, 209, 213, 232

Napoleon, 63, 112
Neale, Leonard, Abp., 67
Newman, John H. Cardinal, 5, 43, 233
Niebuhr, H. Reinhold, 172, 185-186, 213
Noonan, John T., 84, 200, 214
Nussbaum, Marhta, 154

O'Brien, David, 45, 54
O'Brien, Joseph L. 153-154
O'Connell, Daniel, 131, 174, 180, 183, 198
O'Donovan, Oliver, 2
O'Leary, Arthur, Fr. 34-35
Origen, 230
Osborne, Kenan, 150

Pattison, Stephen, 155
Paul, 90, 185, 191
Peirce, Charles S., 2-3, 14-16, 51, 57, 99, 101-102, 109, 151 122, 127, 152
Pettit, Philip, 40, 54, 102, 161, 174, 185, 213
Pinches, Charles, 38, 151, 209

Pius VII, 63-64, 110
Pius VIII, 64
Pius IX, 3, 232-233
Pius X, 3
Pius XII, 4, 206
Plantinga, Alvin, 127, 153
Plato, 119
Portier, William, 154, 209, 212-212, 214
Principe, Walter, 2
Purcell, Arbp., 133

Quinn, John, 84

Rahner, Karl, 99, 102, 150, 153, 175, 188, 204, 212, 215, 233
Rand, Ayn, 97-98
Ratzinger, Joseph Card., 233
Read, William, 48, 52, 54, 168
Reynolds, Ignatius, Bp., 82
Rice, Madeliene, 198, 214
Richard, Gabriel, SS, 7, 68, 210
Ricoeur, Paul, 2, 51, 57, 103
Rogers, Daniel, 83
Romero, Oscar, Abp., 101
Roosevelt, Frnaklin, 113, 226
Rousseau, J.J., 188
Rousseau, Richard, 30, 52, 153
Ryan, John A., 178-179, 212, 232

Saenz, Arb. 101
Schlesinger, Arthur, 58, 83
Schindler, David, 100-102, 150, 211, 214
Schmidlin, Joseph, 5, 17
Schniller, Peter, 5, 17
Schoof, T.M., 152
Schreiter, Robert, 5, 17, 215
Seumois, A., 5, 17
Sigmund, Paul, 213
Slote, Michael, 154
Smith, Elwyn, 84, 114, 151
Sullivan, Francis, 74, 86, 122, 152, 211

Stone, Brian, 17, 103, 150
Suarez, 123, 152

Tell, William, 119
Theobald, Stephen, 198, 214
Thoreau, Henry D., 188
Tillman, Ben, 201
Tolstoi, Leo, 19
Thiel, John, 53, 233

Van Buren, Martin, 193, 198
VonBalthasar, H.U., 101-102, 230
Vorgrimler, Herbert, 233

Wallace, George, 201
Wallace, Fr., 68, 70
Watson, Tom, 201, 215
White, Blanco, 129
Whitehead, A.N., 2
Whitfield, Abp., 68, 79, 162
Willging, Eugene, 150
Witte, John, Jr., 17, 87, 150, 233
Woodward, C. Vann, 215
Woodward, James, 155
Woltersdorff, Nicolas, 127, 153

Yoder, John H., 103

About the Author

Lou F. McNeil, raised in Detroit, received his Ph.D. in theology from the University of St. Michael's College, in the University of Toronto (1982). Prior to his graduate studies, he had spent a number of years in Mississippi and Georgia. He served as Director of the Glenmary Research Center in Atlanta, 1986-1994, and served a stint as associate and, then, director of the United States Catholic Mission Association in Washington, DC. He is currently Associate Professor of Religious Studies-Theology at Georgian Court University. He is married to Dr. Jeanne Evans and they share delightful and endless exchanges on the merits and relationships in the philosophies of C.S. Peirce (Lou) and Paul Ricoeur (Jeanne) about whom they respectively did their dissertations. He has published numerous articles and reviews centered on his interests in American Catholicism and ecumenism. He was a member of the research team with Martin Bradley, Norman Green, Dale Jones, and Mac Lynn that produced *Churches and Church Membership in the United States, 1990,* with a major grant from the Lilly Endowment. Finally, I thank the graduate ministerial students who have taught me so much during the past ten years in the classroom and in their papers.